AMEN, AMEN, AMEN

* * *

Memoir of a Girl
Who Couldn't Stop Praying
(Among Other Things)

ABBY SHER

SCRIBNER

New York London Toronto Sydney

SCRIBNER
A Division of Simon & Schuster, Inc.
1230 Avenue of the Americas
New York, NY 10020

for Jay and Sonya Joan

I have been driven many times to my knees by the overwhelming conviction that I had nowhere else to go.

—Abraham Lincoln

contents

AMEN, AMEN, AMEN

author's note

. . . .

I have changed the names of many people and places in the following pages to protect their privacy. Or because I can't remember their real names. Still, I know others will have different versions of these same events. This is just the way I see it. A few times I've asked friends and family to help draw together some of the disconnected moments, but just as often I've chosen not to. I remember it this way for a reason. I tell this story with all the honesty and clarity I possess today. I hope no animals or feelings were hurt in the making of this book.

I hope you get there in time. I hope you get there in time. I hope you get there in time. I hope you get there in time. I hope you get there in time.

I hope you get there in time. I hope you get there in time. I hope you get there in time. I hope you get there in time. I hope you get there in time.

I hope you get there in time. I hope you get there in time. I hope you get there in time. I hope you get there in time. I hope you get there in time.

I hope you get there in time. I hope you get there in time. I hope you get there in time. I hope you get there in time. I hope you get there in time.

I hope you get there in time. I hope you get there in time. I hope you get there in time. I hope you get there in time. I hope you get there in time.

I hope you get there in time. I hope you get there in time. I hope you get there in time. I hope you get there in time. I hope you get there in time.

I hope you get there in time. I hope you get there in time. I hope you get there in time. I hope you get there in time. I hope you get there in time.

I hope you get there in time. I hope you get there in time. I hope you get there in time. I hope you get there in time. I hope you get there in time.

I hope you get there in time. I hope you get there in time. I hope you get there in time. I hope you get there in time. I hope you get there in time.

I hope you get there in time. I hope you get there in time. I hope you get there in time. I hope you get there in time. I hope you get there in time.

I hope you get there in time. I hope you get there in time. I hope you get there in time. I hope you get there in time. I hope you get there in time.

the night that kinny's gone

Rebecca's backyard always smelled like it had just rained. The grass sank in under our feet and the air felt swampy, especially in the summer. We were up on her screened-in porch watching the gnats swarm like tornadoes. Rebecca was my best friend and it was usually fun to go to her house after school and melt crayons on her radiator or put on talent shows, but we'd already run out of things to do. It was still the first week of fifth grade; we didn't have homework yet and we'd even finished covering our books with brown paper bags and decorating them with stickers. We'd eaten our grilled cheese sandwiches hours ago and when we asked for a snack Rebecca's mom said it was too close to dinner.

My mother was always late to pick me up. Even when it was her turn to drive for dance car pool, she swung into the parking lot ten minutes after everyone else, her feathered hair flying in all directions like she'd been shot out of a cannon. Most days something had tied her up at work or she'd started cutting carrots and forgotten about the time. Tonight she was particularly late. The clock in Rebecca's den said ten after seven. I started thinking about how to draw my mother's profile for the police if she'd gone missing.

"Mom! I'm hungry!" yelled Danny, Rebecca's big brother. He was three years older than us and never came out of his room during the daytime except when he wanted to tackle Rebecca or fart at us.

"When are we going to eat?!!!!"

I heard Mrs. Mills answer him in a half-whisper, something about *waiting for Mrs. Sher* and *maybe traffic, but that's not the point.* Why did adults have to whisper so much, especially when it wasn't about something magical or fantastic like hidden candy or a water slide? It made my mother's absence even more embarrassing.

By the time Mom did tap on the Millses' screen door, it was pitch black out—or as close as it got to pitch black in the summer. More like an inky purple. It was still too sweltering to feel like the sun had completely vanished. Mom and Mrs. Mills whispered some more while I packed up my knapsack, and Rebecca told me, "I wish you didn't have to go home."

"Me too," I said, though it wasn't true. I was starving and annoyed at my mother for forgetting about me and not even apologizing.

On the drive home, Mom and I didn't say much, but there was no space to hear anyway because the cicadas were clinging to the trees, screaming in waves. My older brother, Jon, had read all of our *World Book* encyclopedias and he said that only male cicadas could make noise and they did it with a special membrane near their stomach. They were supposed to visit our part of the country once every thirteen or seventeen years, but they must've loved my town because they seemed to descend upon us every summer. They nested in clumps, crouched under beach chairs, and scuttled beneath ice cream trucks. At night they were so close I could feel them pulse in my skin.

When we got to our house, the lights were on and I could hear the voices and punches of laugh track from my older sister, Betsy, watching TV. Mom said it was too late to start cooking so we'd be having leftover spaghetti and whatever was in the vegetable drawer. Dad came downstairs and poured himself and Mom a scotch and soda, kissed me on the head, and disappeared in his chair behind the newspaper. By the time we all sat down to eat, the noodles were hard on the ends like dried rubber cement, and the salad was more brown than green, sloshing in a small pond of Italian dressing. I tried to cover my whole plate with a flurry of Parmesan cheese and not say anything.

Nobody said anything. Which made the whole night seem even heavier and sweatier and I wanted to tell those cicadas to shut up so I could figure out what was going on.

Finally, Betsy started talking. She'd been reading this *totally amazing book about Jim Morrison, who was much more than just, like, a song-*

writer, you know? He was a poet and he fought, like, a ton of demons. And she had learned so much about life and art and it would really help if she could get her allowance raised so she could buy more art supplies and experience life more. *Seriously.*

Betsy was only four years older than me, but those four years had given her boobs, her own blow dryer, and a fearlessness that made me squirm in my seat. She wasn't afraid to let anyone know what she was thinking.

"We'll see," Mom said slowly.

"What does that even mean? *We'll see?*"

"We'll see."

"So stupid." Betsy put down her fork and crossed her arms.

Jon would typically jump in at this point. He didn't talk much, but when he did, he liked to point out the facts we were overlooking, like what percentage of the earth's population had never heard of an allowance. But Jon had left for college three weeks earlier. We drove him down to Virginia, stopping at Dad's best friend Marty's house and playing with their dog Penny and eating Chinese food on a giant lazy Susan. It was a spectacular trip until we came home and the dinner table seemed too long and too quiet. Like it did this late and airless night, when only Betsy seemed unaware.

"I just have to say, it's really unfair because if you're gonna say no then just say no now." She sighed indignantly.

"I didn't say no. I said we'll see," Mom responded, her voice low and deliberate, like she was giving an important speech at our synagogue or helping with math homework. She sounded too careful, and somehow a little creepy. Dad still wasn't saying anything, not even his daily routine: *What'd you learn in school today? Does two plus two still equal four?*

After we finished clearing our plates, Mom told us to sit down, and I thought maybe there would be a momentous announcement like we were getting a new TV or she'd picked up a fancy dessert to make up for the crummy dinner. We hadn't had dessert in a while. The freezer was stuffed with frozen chicken necks and rye bread. Dad wasn't allowed sweets because of his weight and blood pressure.

But when Mom sat down again, there was nothing in her hands

except a waterlogged dish towel. Not even some canned fruit cocktail. She smiled briefly, nodded at Dad, and then submerged into that peculiar silence again, picking fretfully at a spaghetti sauce stain on her blouse. Maybe we were about to get in big trouble. I hadn't been making my bed in the mornings; I'd tried, but it seemed so pointless. And I hadn't cleaned up after the dog when I walked her the day before, but I didn't think anyone had seen. Who saw? I looked at Dad, but he sat there with his chair pushed back so his potbelly could have some room, folding and refolding his paper napkin.

I didn't know why this night felt so shadowy and wrong, but I did know my napkin was almost gone. I'd ripped it into a hill of pulpy snow on the floor below me. I'd been shredding my dinner napkins for as long as I could remember. I didn't even think about it; just when I wasn't holding my fork, my fingers were working apart the soft skin into smaller and smaller strips. The first time it happened, it was mildly amusing:

Look what Abby's doing!

Abby's making a mess. What are you making, a flake fortress?

Then it wasn't so funny.

Clean that up.

Ab, come on.

After dinner I usually spent a good ten minutes under the table, pulling the wisps of paper out of the Oriental rug, but it seemed I could never get it all. Maybe that was what this hulking silence was about. I stared at my last bits of napkin and noiselessly promised I'd work extra hard plucking the rug clean if this stillness would please end.

My father put both hands on the table and puffed his cheeks out, like he was steeling himself for a steep incline.

"So. Your mom and I went to visit Aunt Simone today. You remember that we got the call last night, she had to come home early from vacation?" I was pretty sure he was talking to Betsy and me, but his eyes shifted every which way around the room. His lips kept twitching after he was done talking, and he drew circles distractedly in the condensation on his water glass. Even his nose couldn't seem to settle on his face.

I wanted to tell him that I remembered now; that I was sorry if

8

I'd been cranky before, that it was okay if Aunt Simone, my dad's sister, also my all-time hero, needed them, and I took back my ugly thoughts about Mom being a bad mom because she picked me up late and fed us rubbery pasta.

"And . . ." He started, then stopped, his face going so still now, that even when he began again it was as if the words were coming from somewhere else.

Nothing he said after that fit into a story or even a sentence. I tried to fill in the details while he stalled into long, solemn pauses between phrases:

Aunt Simone was on vacation in Nantucket with Uncle Murray.

They had dinner at a small restaurant near the beach—I'd like to think they had something fancy like a seafood buffet with lots of dinner rolls and cocktail sauce and tall glasses of white wine. Her eyelids would have been dusted with her favorite shimmery violet powder. His hair slicked back straight with a comb.

They returned to the inn where they were staying and washed their faces and brushed their teeth. They read in bed for a little while and then kissed each other good night before turning out the light.

Sometime during the night—Dad couldn't explain when or why or how—Aunt Simone had an aneurysm. Dad tried to draw it on our green- and blue-striped tablecloth like he was piecing together a map. An artery in Aunt Simone's brain grew too big, swelling until it burst, flooding her cranium. It didn't hurt, he assured us, but there wasn't enough room in her head for all that blood. Her body slowly shut down, just like a house turning off all its lights at night. When they went to see her that afternoon, she was already in a coma and all they could do was kiss her and say good-bye.

My father never said the word *dead.* Just that Aunt Simone was gone. Done. *Poof*—no more.

My father also didn't say this but he didn't have to: The cicadas were out in full force that night. I knew they were. They threw themselves against every window screen in Nantucket, beating their crazy stomach membranes. Throbbing. Making it too loud to think or sleep. I'd never liked cicadas and now I knew why—they were carrying the worst kind of night with them. In her brain, behind her dusted eyelids, Aunt Simone had throbbed too. Her blood splashed wildly, like a water slide gone mad. All of her ideas and music and jokes and dreams crashing against the back of her skull. Until she exploded.

Dad was still talking. Something about a service in New York City with Aunt Simone's friends and Dad was going to say something about how much we loved her and he would play a tape of her at the piano.

"Does that sound okay?" he asked.

He waited for us to answer, only I wasn't sure exactly what the question was. Betsy said, "Okay," and I nodded too. But no matter how slowly Dad spoke, what he said still didn't make sense. We had seen Aunt Simone the weekend before at their cabin in Connecticut. She had been so delighted because she'd gone for a bicycle ride and found a black kitten on the side of the road. When she brought her home Uncle Murray had said, "Aw, whad'ya go and do that for, 'Mone?"

The kitten was sick but Aunt Simone named it Yofi, which is Hebrew for *All right!* My cousin Aviva and I sat in the field in back of the cabin and played with Yofi while she wriggled and mewed. Then Aunt Simone brought us out matching bowls of crackers and a dish of water for Yofi. She picked up the mangy kitten, lifting her toward the sky. The sun leaked through Yofi's tiny hairs and we took turns kissing her tiny white belly.

Dad stood up from the dining room table, his whole body looking fidgety and sore. I pretended not to watch him as he walked the length of the living room rug and back again. His body tipped forward and his slippers scuffed along the rug as he looped in the most lopsided circles I'd ever seen.

"Do you have any questions?" Mom asked. She smiled hesitantly, tapping her fingers on the table and picking up crumbs that were invisible to the naked eye.

Yes, I had questions. Had Aunt Simone's head made a popping sound? Did she fall off the bed and cry? Did she flap like a fish on the floor or go straight into a coma? Are aneurysms common? Contagious? Hereditary? Was she unconscious on the plane ride back to New York? Why couldn't they fix her in Nantucket? How long did it take to fly and did she lie down or did they prop her up in a seat like a mannequin and did Uncle Murray get to sit next to her and who was flying and if the pilot was faster would she have lived?

And then there was the question that I could never ask, but that I knew each of us had to be thinking:

What did Aunt Simone do that was so bad she deserved to die?

I looked at Betsy to see if she had questions because I didn't want to be the only one talking. Betsy was crying and asked if she could take the phone into her room and call her best friend. Mom agreed and then turned to me.

"Don't worry about the napkins tonight. You want to go to your room too?"

"Yeah," I said. Going to my room sounded lonely and dismal, but it seemed like the only respectful thing to do. I had to step around Dad to get to the stairs. He didn't even acknowledge me as he continued his sloppy laps around the living room. He was whistling, too, some song that was muffled and meandering and made no sense either.

Fourteen steps to my bedroom. I closed the door partway and lay down on my bed with all my clothes on. I didn't know what else I was supposed to do. The moon leached through my window screen, casting a gauzy gray over everything. My bedroom was built into the roof and the walls sloped down so I could only stand up straight in the middle. By daylight the carpet was light blue except for the brown spot by my bed where I threw up after eating bad chicken kebobs on a trip to Boston. I had a white dresser with rusting metal handles that looked like whales yawning. A white radiator that clucked and burped in the winter. I could tell when it was getting cold before everyone else because my radiator clucked so fast it sounded like it would blast off into outer space.

In one corner was a white bookshelf with my ribbon collection, my sticker album, my blue plastic box for buttons and pins, and my favorite books. And over my bed were two spotlights with yellow plastic hoods for reading in bed. Dad had taken me to pick them out because he said I was a good reader and it was important to take care of my eyes, they were the only ones I was going to get. Sometimes I stared straight up into the filaments until it hurt, then switched off the lights quickly so the night came out in floating spots. Or else

I ducked under my yellow bedspread and rubbed my toes on the sheets until I saw sparks. Mom said that was static electricity.

The best part of my room was my wallpaper. It looked like a giant patchwork of stripes, flowers, polka dots, dashes, dots, squiggles, and leaves in all my favorite colors—minty green, lemon yellow, sky blue, bubblegum pink, and the orange of creamy sherbet. I loved to run my finger up through the white alleys that separated each square. Also lying sideways on my bed and walking my feet up the wall into the fields of blue flowers and puddles of pink curlicues.

But that night I tried to lie perfectly still. And think.

Aunt Simone was my favorite aunt. I knew I wasn't supposed to have a favorite, but it was true. She was a concert pianist and she thought I could be one too. I'd only played for her once but she had said she could tell that I was *feeling* the music. A few years ago she'd asked me to be her pen pal. For three years she wrote to me about the woods, the weather, the soft buzz of cocktail receptions after her concerts, and the downy touch of the lake by the cabin when she dove in for that first summer swim. Her letters were thick, each word vivid and elegant and written just for me on paper trimmed with black and white piano keys. She was only a few inches taller than me, at five-one, so she had to ride kids' bikes. She loved to practice yoga and meditation and she wore giant sunglasses and leotards. She was the only grown-up who ever sat Indian-style in my room with me to talk about music. One time after we swam we took a shower together and I tried not to stare but I couldn't help it. She had small, perfect nipples and wide, milky colored ribs and she lifted her arms up under the spray of water and sang, "Mmmmm. Delicious!" so I did it too.

Best of all was Aunt Simone's marble eye. An eddy of blue, gray, brown, emerald—plus colors that hadn't even been invented yet. When she was a baby, the nurse in the delivery room had put in the incorrect eye drops and erased Aunt Simone's iris. So the doctor tried to give her a new one, but Aunt Simone could never see out of it again and it never truly looked like an eyeball. It was dappled and swirling and infinitely beautiful.

My dad adored Aunt Simone—his kid sister. Kinny he called her, a pet name from when they were young. He took us to her piano performances and taped them with a recorder hidden in his lap. Afterward he labeled each tape with her name and the date in neat, rounded letters. When he hugged her, she fit exactly into his shoulder.

I knew Aunt Simone as leotards and Chopin études and floppy hats and fingers so small they disappeared when she swooned over the piano keys. All of her friends were either musicians or painters or sculptors. One time I had stayed at the cabin with her and Uncle Murray all by myself, and they took me to a smoky party with long-necked ladies and vases. Aunt Simone introduced me as *her important niece, the pianist.* A man with a puffy moustache gave me a book of music he'd composed and told me Aunt Simone was his all-time hero too.

This was what I knew about her. Or what I wanted to be true. But this night, lying on my bed listening to the roar of the cicadas in the densest dark, I began to wonder what I didn't know about her. There must have been something else, something that no one was telling me. There were a lot of hours between the times that I saw Aunt Simone and the days that she wrote me letters and maybe, probably definitely, she had done something awful to die this way, so suddenly. She had done something so bad that no one could even speak of it, some gruesome and ghastly crime. Maybe she stole from a bank. Or had a lover—and then stabbed him. Had she brought home that kitten so she could eat it? Had she worn a ski mask and robbed people, slicing off their ears with a hatchet? You just didn't go on vacation in Nantucket and eat clams and mussels and then have your brain explode.

I lay in bed making a trail through the wallpaper with my finger. Tracing its quilted pattern was like shredding napkins. I did it unconsciously, my finger skating from green to pink to orange to blue. Most nights, the paper was cool and boundless and the last thing I'd remember before falling asleep was sliding past a pink leaf.

This night was different. Everything was different, even those familiar walls. Bumpier. Rougher. As if the colors were mismatched and all the squiggles were springing in opposite directions. As if there was something churning underneath them. Something secret and dangerous. A wave of death coming toward us.

Mom had once described dying as a well-needed rest, just like going into a profound sleep. There was a girl in my grade who said no one ever really died, we just started over as another person or even an elephant or a tree. Maybe these theories held up if you'd lived a full life, but if you were young and vibrant and playing with a kitten in the field one day and a week later gone forever, there had to be a better answer.

My finger moved faster, pressing hard. Swerving through dots, dashes, hearts. Mashing mounds of leaves and digging through junkyards of polka dots. Up and down and around in diagonals and diamond shapes, trying to find the smooth spots. Trying to find a logical path from here to there, from life to death to whatever lay beyond. I don't know who had told me, but I knew there was a G-d above us all. He was further than the farthest star but also inside every blade of grass. And I couldn't explain why, but I believed He was the Creator who could unlock any hidden code. As I traveled through the cluttered squares, this was what I now decided about the world. You couldn't look it up in an encyclopedia because it was so true that no one tried to write it down. It wasn't a discovery; it was just the only thing that made any sense.

There is a reason for everything.

An order to life and death.

When you do something bad, something bad will happen to you. If you do something really bad, then you will die. And death is bottomless and murky, a flood in your brain with no way out of it and no one to save you. G-d is the only one who knows when or why someone dies, and you can only hope that you did enough good things to visit Him up in heaven while you float in your forever slumber.

I kept tracing through the walls, trying to steer Aunt Simone up to the clearest part of the sky. Trying to close this gulch of death and destruction. The cicadas were screeching louder and madder and my skin grew hot and prickly, but I had to keep going. It felt like the only way to keep all of us from drowning too.

CEMENT MIXER SONG*

Cement mixer, put-ty put-ty
Cement mixer, put-ty put-ty
Cement mixer, dooby dooby
Cement mixer, dooby dooby
Da bi da daaaa

Cement mixer, put-ty put-ty
Cement mixer, put-ty put-ty
Cement mixer, dooby dooby
Cement mixer, dooby dooby
Doo doo doo deeee!

*Must be repeated at least once for each cement mixer in the road.
**Add dance moves if alone or walking the dog.
***Good to finish with an air kiss or a wink.

the party's over

. . . .

New Jersey Turnpike
Ugh Ugh
New Jersey Turnpike
Pee-yu Pee-yu

This was one of my father's favorite songs. There is music in every-thing, he told me. Even in things that stink. In the morning when he walked me to school, Dad made up songs about how many fish were in the ocean, why it rained, the price of gasoline. Many of his songs ended with *bippety scap bap bap badabada.* On Sundays after our big omelet breakfasts, he would dance around the house while he sang, swinging one of us (usually Mom) into his slippery two-step. He also had a lot of songs that were instrumental, played with a knee-slap drum and a keen whistle. He was a master whistler, trilling and twittering like the smallest sparrow, then rolling languidly into saxophone-land, or vibrating like the drum-bellied opera stars he loved to watch on public television. He could whistle anything from classical to jazz to Ethel Merman to the Beatles. He had an actual violin too and a guitar, but they both sat in the corner of the living room obscured by the drapes, collecting colonies of dust mites.

My father taught my brother, sister, and me music every day, from the moment he woke us up, singing, *It's time to get up it's time to get up it's time to get up in the mooooorning!* until his finale of *The party's over, it's time to call it a day! The party's over, ya dada dida doobi da!* as we kissed him good night. One of Dad's best friends had made him a compilation of every song ever recorded by Cole Porter, and Jon, Betsy, and I learned these lyrics not long after *mama* and *dada*. On road trips, we shouted out our requests: *Tape eight, side A, please! I want the song where the lady sleeps with a horse!* In the hour before dinner each night, Dad's wooden stereo speakers crackled with majestic fleets of cellos and trumpets. On weekends the radio was tuned to jazz standards and show tunes all day, with Count Basie, Kaye Ballard, Gene Kelly, and Dad's favorite host, Jonathan Schwartz. If there was ever a dance break in the middle of the song, Dad would be up on his feet, one hand on his wide ribs, the other outstretched, as he tried on Fred Astaire's toe-tingling routines.

As soon as I could reach the keys of our piano, I began taking lessons from a man who lived around the corner, Mr. Diamond, just as Jon and Betsy had. Only by the time I went to him, Mr. Diamond was so old his fingers were bound together in arthritic knots and he was going blind from diabetes, so I had to describe for him the notes on my music. Often when I arrived for my lesson he was asleep next to the window and I just sat in the hallway by his door, too scared to wake him. His house smelled like cat pee and sometimes when I was playing, his wife flitted between teetering columns of sheet music like a frizzy-haired ghost.

In spite of it all, I kept going back. I never felt more important than when I sat down in front of the keys that looked skinny and bare and pressed into them a new sound. I came home each week and lifted up my music for both of my parents to inspect. Mom had played the piano too—not professionally like Aunt Simone, but she did know a lot of pieces by heart and remembered each chord I tried. Dad accompanied my clunky waltzes with *yada dada*'s and sometimes a lilting promenade around the house as he called, "Louder!" Both of my parents loved to hear us play. Dad made recordings of Jon, Betsy, and me practicing in the living room, and I felt sure I was only steps away from being on a real radio station. His voice was velvety and resonant as he announced our full names for the imaginary audience and he asked us important questions about the pieces we were playing.

"So today we are very privileged to have Miss Abigail Judith Sher performing. Abigail, what are you going to present to us today?"

"This is called *Run Doggy Run*."

"Wonderful. And I notice this uses two hands. How long have you been playing with two hands at once?"

"This is my first time!"

"Fantastic! We're in for a real treat then. Okay, again, this is Abigail Judith Sher, and the date is July 22, 1979, and we are recording this concert live from 114 North Chatsworth Avenue on this beautiful sunny day. Take it away, Abigail."

Sometimes we had to start the concerts over because our dog, Sandy, got frisky and barked near the microphone. More often Mom forgot we were making live recordings and she yelled for Jon to bring down his laundry or for someone to please clean off the table so we could eat on it. Or the tape caught her humming along to our songs in the kitchen and throwing out the occasional "Try B-*flat*!"

I begged both of my parents to join us in a family jamboree. Jon soon graduated to the trombone and Betsy to the flute and I was sure with Dad on his violin and Mom next to me on the piano we could make a Jewish Trapp Family ensemble. But Mom said her days at the keyboard were long gone and Dad didn't seem interested in dusting off his violin—he said it was out of shape and so was he. I continued to study *The Sound of Music* and the Osmond siblings, eager for the day when our parents would announce we were ditching the house, painting a van in rainbow colors, and taking our act on the road.

Music was the most intimate language spoken in our home. Both of my parents were loving but not overly affectionate. They never kissed us on the lips—Mom said that a lot of germs were spread that way and cheek-kissing was just as pleasant. She also said "I love you" shouldn't be overused or it lost its meaning. Instead, Mom and Dad had a special code that was more romantic than anything possible in the English language. It usually happened in the car while Dad was driving and skedap-bopping. He'd have one hand on the wheel and with the other he'd give Mom's knee two quick squeezes.

"You're okay. You know that?" he said, his voice so low I could feel it more than hear it over the trumpets and timpanis. Mom never said anything back, she just put her hand on top of his and hummed louder.

When I was old enough to read music I felt that I really started to earn my parents' respect, and I wanted to be fluent in every arpeggio and astound them with each crescendo. I belted out my lyrics in the car so my father could hear me first.

Cement mixer, put-ty put-ty
Cement mixer, put-ty put-ty
Cement mixer, dooby dooby
Cement mixer, dooby dooby
Da bi da daaaa

Dad sang this song every time we made family trips into New York City and passed the polka-dotted cement mixers that lived in a lot on the Harlem River Drive. We went into the city for special treats. Our house was in the suburbs of Westchester, so it only took a half hour to get to Shea Stadium for a baseball game or to Chinatown for dim sum, and a few times I got to go on dates with just Dad to Lincoln Center. Afterward we slowly strolled arm in arm around the fountain in the middle and then we went to Tower Records and listened to the big headphones plugged into the walls. Whatever our city excursions were for, whenever we got close to the cement mixer lot, I made sure I was the loudest one singing in the car. Once, I mixed up the verses and I was mortified, but Dad said the words weren't what was important. It was more about the syncopated rhythm between *put* and *ty*. I held the last note as long as possible. Sometimes we had contests. My dad could sing the same note for a full minute or even more. That's what it is about music, he told us. It's bigger than time.

The night Aunt Simone drowned in her head, my father taught me that music was the one thing that survived death. I had trouble looking at him as he wandered around and around the living room. He was hunched over like a melting candle, stooped almost into a C. But he was still whistling. The tune was up in the sparrow ranges, and as he trudged it grew fainter than a whisper. But it was definitely a song and it was all he had left. It didn't matter what he was whistling exactly, he was holding up our world with whatever notes he could find. It was his only way of carrying on now that Kinny had disappeared.

Simone and Roger. They had been inseparable as children. Both small, with dark wavy hair and olive skin. They made up secret code names, dirty limericks, and of course songs, and put on talent shows with their friends. They loved to perform, especially for each other. When they were old enough to get a dog, they smushed their names together and named the pup SiRo.

19

He had his own theme song: *SiRo my doooog! My dog SiRooooooo!*

My grandparents Bill and Elizabeth never learned the SiRo song. They were gone before I was born, but I've been told that they were both wild and passionate and completely miserable in a marriage pieced together with thunderclouds. They threw themselves into their careers—hers as a therapist and his as a tax lawyer—and lived decadently, with a second home in the countryside of New York and weekend parties on Long Island. Elizabeth was the daughter of a celebrated Hungarian opera singer. She dressed extravagantly in gold lamé capes and grapefruit-size brooches. She delighted in taking the children to the Beaux Arts Ball, where they saw naked models, and she taught them how to play poker and pinochle with her. Her bursts of laughter and tears rushed through the home in squalls.

Bill was steely and fierce in his silent disapproval. He only spoke when ordering the children to do chores or berating his wife. Aunt Simone escaped by immersing herself in the piano while my dad spent rainy Saturdays playing supernumeraries at the old Metropolitan Opera House. In their painfully mismatched household, music became the only thing they could all agree upon. As Simone's talent emerged, it became the tether binding them together. Whenever she sat at the piano bench, Elizabeth pleaded with Bill to dance with her. He would most often refuse, preferring to listen with stern concentration. At which point Elizabeth swept her son into her arms instead. My grandmother taught my dad the fox-trot, the waltz, the box step, and the rumba, while my aunt played tirelessly.

As they danced, Elizabeth serenaded her beloved dance partner. Her favorite song was "Cheek to Cheek," in which she inserted my dad's name:

Heaven,
With Roger Evan
And my heart beats so, that I can hardly speeeeeak
And I seem to find the happiness I seek
When we're out together dancing cheek to cheek

Dad dreamed of opening up a cabaret with his friend Marty called the Club Marro (Marty and Roger smushed together). They would host artists and exhibits and begin each night with tap dancing and the occasional violin-piano duet. But while my grandfather was willing to send his daughter to Juilliard, he insisted that my father was not as talented and needed to become "a real grown-up," which meant pursuing a degree in law like him. I never learned why my father complied, even working for Grandpa Bill for a wretched three years before setting out on his own. When my parents met, they connected over a mutual ardor for Irving Berlin and Itzhak Perlman. They vowed to create a home together that was always infused with a sunny refrain.

We lived in Westchester, in a white stone Tudor with a red door and black shutters, a comfortable life for which my father worked diligently. We had a backyard with a rock big enough to slide down in the rain, neighbors who threw barbecues and served marshmallow-fruit salad, and a housekeeper named Nancy Maloney, who made us egg salad sandwiches and picked me up by my tights so I could touch the ceiling. My mother stayed home to raise all three of us until I was in third grade, then she took a part-time job as public relations director for a nursing home.

The best part of every weekday was when we piled into our station wagon and Mom drove us to pick Dad out of the wave of suit jackets rolling up the hill from the train station. When he got home he turned on the radio, changed into his dungarees and Syracuse sweatshirt, and made scotch and sodas for him and Mom, followed by a chaser of Tums. Sometimes he slapped his knees and I climbed into his lap. At dinner, Dad always began the meal with *So, what'd I miss? Who has a good story about today?*

On the weekends, Aunt Simone and Uncle Murray usually stopped for supper on the way from Manhattan to their cabin in Connecticut. It always felt like a party when they came, though it was only our two families. My cousins Aviva and Rachel were a few years older than me and they let me play beauty parlor with their long glossy hair. Often the neighbors would stop over for a cocktail too and I could perch by the cheese platter and eat crackers for hours before Mom remembered it was past my bedtime.

Some weekends we went to the cabin with them. It was in a town called Woodbury, Connecticut, where there were dirt roads with houses that were built in the 1700s and only one general store for groceries. The cabin had a plaque on it that said *1789 Built by Ichabod Stoddard*. My cousins and siblings and I were never happier than when we were all together, chasing stray dogs, doing our crazy hat parade through the woods, trying on Aunt Simone's giant sunglasses, and making up songs of our own. In Woodbury I learned my best dirty words, how to start a compost pile, serve a volleyball, and howl like a hyena. The parties there were legendary, especially on the Fourth of July when Uncle Murray dressed up in red-, white-, and blue-striped suspenders, saddle shoes, socks, and boxer shorts. He put watermelons in the creek to keep them cold and made a gigantic bonfire in the field. Everyone skipped and traipsed around the flames like drunken fairies in a sparkler dance.

On nonparty days, Aunt Simone and Dad led us in mountain hikes, pond races, and choruses about the importance of the New York subway system. They taught us to clap for the sun when it set in golds and fuchsias behind the trees. Mom tucked us all in and made sure we said *P.D.,* which stood for *pleasant dreams,* before we went to bed. My cousins had comforters that were the same pattern as my wallpaper, so I could trace my way through the creaks and shadows of those cabin nights.

Simone and Roger. I don't want to remember them without each other because it feels like life was fullest and brightest when they were both here.

After Aunt Simone died, I pulled out the untouched journals she'd given me and started writing in them. *Dear SiRo,* I wrote, pretending I still had my special pen pal. I also began singing "Cheek to Cheek" (or as I called it, the Heaven song), every time I walked the dog and the Cement Mixer song every time a mixer went by on the street. If they were paving a road or there was a pack of them at a building site, I sang two choruses for each truck. Even though I was alone, even when my dad was at work, I thought maybe he could hear me, or at least feel me. I wanted him to know that I *got* it.

Music was everlasting and indestructible and stretched across all worlds.

And I was pretty sure that as long as I kept singing and writing to SiRo, nobody else would disappear.

WAYS THAT PEOPLE DIE
EVERY DAY LIST

1. An aneurysm
2. Whatever was wrong with the man at the corner store who had a golf ball bump in his neck
3. Heart attack (like Jim Tripper's dad)
4. AIDS (a lot of people in Africa and California)
5. Cancer (lots of people, especially if they have too many freckles or smoke)
6. Starvation (Ethiopia)
7. Car accident (every day)
8. Drunk driving accident (Helena's mom)
9. Really bad diabetes (this happened in a movie I watched)
10. House fires (we did a special unit in school on this)
11. Just die in your sleep and nobody knows why or how unless they cut you open (I saw this on TV, but it's true, I asked)

woody's children

Sunday night was usually the best night of the week in my house. Our neighbors, Estherann and Arthur, came over for vodka tonics and crackers and to talk politics. Estherann was always knitting fuzzy sweaters and scarves and she let me sit by her feet and dig through her canvas bag of yarns. Then Mom pulled out the Chinese take-out menu and we each got to choose a dish to order.

"You know what that means, kiddo," Dad would say with a wink my way. I was his special helper.

As soon as Dad and I climbed into the station wagon, he would turn on *Woody's Children,* Woody Guthrie's radio show where he sang folk songs with a team of banjos and little kids whom I imagined living on a prairie and frolicking through enchanted forests. Dad usually had one palm on the steering wheel and with the other he'd tap out Woody's rhythmic rhapsodies on my thigh. We'd sing "This Land Is Your Land" and "If I Had a Hammer" and scores of songs about love and dandelion wine, rolling into new melodies as effortlessly as the hills themselves. Sometimes Dad went extra slow and switched the headlights to bright so we could search for raccoons. There was never anybody out except for us. In the car, on the road, in the whole world.

It was two months after Aunt Simone died and the cicadas had finally gone; the first snow of the season had just fallen, but it was too clumpy and uneven to warrant a school closing the next day. The grass poked through in little hairy patches and the air was the sharpest kind of cold in my nostrils. The station wagon took a long time to warm up and the vents could muster only small splutters of luke-

warm mist that smelled burnt. There was no time to look for raccoons on the way to the restaurant. *The food'll get cold,* Dad explained.
He also didn't sing along with Woody, so I decided I shouldn't either.

When we got to the China Lion parking lot, Dad gave me a fold of
money that I squeezed in my fist. I walked past the two stone lions
guarding the tall wooden doors, my back stiff and straight, and told
the lady at the desk who looked like a China doll our last name. She
knew me because this was my job every week. She put the greasy
brown paper bag in my hands and made me promise to walk carefully to the car so nothing tipped.

"That's some hot chopsticks. You okay?" Dad said when I got back
to the car.

"No prob, slob," I said, nodding proudly.

We were quiet as snow again the whole way home. I held the bag
on my lap and opened just one corner so I could sniff the moo goo
gai pan dripping into the vegetable lo mein and then into the General
Tso's, seeping into a salty puddle on the bottom. My thighs got red
and tight from the heat, but I didn't budge an inch. Not even when
we got home and Dad turned off the engine and we just sat there
in the driveway. The Japanese maple tree that Dad had planted was
sighing and swaying above us and the car was ticking and farting out
leftover exhaust and I wasn't sure why we were still in the car while
Mom and Betsy were inside waiting for the food. I snuck a peek over
at Dad but he was looking out at the snow so I looked there too.

Then he said, "Hey kiddo, you know what? You go on ahead. I'll
meet you inside."

"Huh?"

"Food's getting cold. I'll be right there."

I didn't want to go, but it felt as though he was waiting for me to
leave, setting his face toward the windshield so I couldn't even guess
what his eyes were saying. By the time I slid out and walked to his
side of the car, he was standing next to it with the door open, letting
out a long, heavy breath.

"I'll wait for you if . . ."

"Just go!" he said, and there was something coarse and ragged in
his voice that I'd never heard before, icier even than the night sky.

I started up the walk, hugging the bag close. I could hear the wax paper from the egg rolls crinkling and my corduroys rubbing together. I could hear everything. Especially something rumbling behind me. A horrible noise somewhere between a groan and a growl. When I turned around my father was crouched on the lawn. I ducked among the hedges so he couldn't see me and through the tangle of frozen branches I watched his body roll forward, the muscles in the back of his neck clenched together. He vomited into the snow. It made a small, steaming hole in the ground. He stayed there on his hands and knees, staring into it, this place where his insides had gone. I stayed staring too. At the moon falling on his head just where his crown of hair curled up at the ends. At his shoulders rising up like looming hilltops under his jacket and his jaw drooping open like a dog's. At how small he was all of a sudden.

Then he leaned back on his heels, took a scoop of fresh snow, and covered the hole so it looked like this moment had never happened.

I crept into the house through the side door and delivered my leaky parcel to Mom, then went to wash my hands. When I got to the dinner table, Dad was already there, licking his lips.

"Mmm, I'm hungry," he said, and gave me a quick smile. I didn't look at him for the rest of the meal.

After I'd helped with the dishes, when I was supposed to be getting ready for bed, I slinked into my parents' room. It was completely dark except for the light from the street, and the blue spotted wallpaper looked like a sky turned inside out. I went to the window to find the hole my father had covered up. It was under the snow somewhere, I knew it, and I had to find it and see if it had grown bigger or deeper. I needed to know where it led. I had this queasy feeling it could be tunneling down all the way through the ground like sour molten lava. Only, when I got to the window, I couldn't see anything on the ground except white. In school they had made us cut out paper snowflakes and then write about how each one was unique and delicate. That was a lie. This snow was not delicate at all. It was monotonous and hard and it made the entire universe slowly sink into its unyielding hush. And I knew something ugly and sinister was lurking just below it.

"What are you doing?" Betsy was standing in the doorway in only her underwear and bra. She had a line of cream bleach on her upper lip.

"Nothing. What are *you* doing?"

"Nothing. You shouldn't be in Mom and Dad's room, you know."

"You shouldn't either." I wanted to sound tough, but my voice came out thin and whiny.

"I'm just getting the nail scissors. What are *you* doing?"

"I'm just . . . looking."

"At what?" said Betsy, putting her hand on her hip.

"Never mind," I snarled as I stomped past her. I wasn't about to tell her that I was looking for a pile of hidden puke.

"Freak," I heard her grumble as she closed her bedroom door.

I checked every night from different windows in the house. The snow turned gray and splotchy and then it broke into warped continents across the lawn, but there was still no sign of the hole. Not even a speck. I tried to measure where the car was parked and where Dad's knees could've sunk in the ground, but any mark he had made was gone. I didn't even know what I was looking for after a while; I just knew I had to look for it. It was as if the dirty snow had swallowed this fermenting secret and every time I stepped over it, or worse, on top of it, I was driving it farther into the earth's core. I hated that I was the only one who knew it was there and that I had become its sentinel, watching to see where it would surface. One night when Mom was tucking me into bed, I tried to tell her that I had seen something that maybe I shouldn't have. Just in case Dad hadn't told her; I didn't want him to get in trouble.

"I think I might've seen Dad maybe get sick."

"What do you mean, sick?"

"I think maybe throw-up sick. Maybe."

"I don't think so, sweetie. But even if he did, you know sometimes his gas gets bad. Don't worry. I'll make sure he eats more Tums."

Then it snowed again and this time it fell in thick, imposing flakes. I knew I'd never find the hole after that, no matter how hard I looked, but I couldn't stop. I also decided that for the rest of the winter I would enter the house only through the side door and I would step on the stone wall to get there. I didn't trust the frozen front lawn at all.

Inside our house wasn't much better. The radio was still on continually, but it had subsided to a muted chatter and I knew without asking that we were not to raise our voices above it. Dad began staying home from work a lot and going to doctors' appointments. Mom said that something was going on with his kidneys, a genetic disease. The doctors were working on it, but in the meantime, we had to leave all the cranberry juice for him and not make too much noise.

Often when I came home from school, Dad was already in his drippy dungarees and cream-colored fisherman's sweater, shuffling around the living room in his moccasin slippers with his hands in his back pockets as if he was holding his kidneys into his sagging frame. Sometimes he was asleep in the big armchair, his head listing backward, the skin of his neck collecting limply like a plucked chicken's.

I'd clear my throat and he would jolt forward to declare groggily, "Well, hello there, madam!" scrambling to rearrange his face into a genteel grin as if he hadn't been asleep and I was a Southern belle sidling up for lemonade.

"Hi, Dad. What are you doing here?" I'd ask. I didn't intend to sound mean, but I didn't like it when he was home before me. I'd think about all those other dads coming up the hill from the train with their blue suits and briefcases and get impatient with him for being so droopy and pale.

"Oh, you know," he'd say.

I didn't know. I didn't know anything. I never learned the whole story. I didn't know how that hole had dragged us all down into its evil silence. I didn't know why Dad's sweater had grown so long and loose that he was lost in it and I was too scared to ask where he had gone. I didn't know when the diagnosis had changed because first Mom would say it was a fever and then Dad would say it's nothing and then Betsy and I were in the bathroom one night and in between spits of toothpaste she whispered, "It's really bad. Like, this is *serious*."

"Serious how?" I asked with an annoyed shrug.

"*Serious* serious."

"Shut up. You don't know that." I turned on both faucets as far as they would go, hoping to drive her away in a puff of steam.

I don't know how much my parents shared with either of my siblings. I don't know what they knew themselves. I just knew it was my obligation to trust them when they said it was a nothing fever. Each night as I gripped the windowsill and bore my eyes into the matted ground, I was convincing myself it was something out *there* that was rotten and not right here—this close and this real.

Dad had dealt with bouts of pain caused by his polycystic kidneys, but never like this. Now there were overnights at various hospitals where they tested my father for all kinds of diseases and pumped him with antibiotics. When Mom brought us to visit, he pulled his arm quickly under the covers so I couldn't see the IV needle pricking his cloudy skin. I hated when he did this, especially when I caught him in the act, the small tubing snapping lightly on the starched sheets, dribbling some radioactive-looking elixir into his veins. I wanted to tell him he wasn't being sneaky enough; I could see he was trying to hide something, I just couldn't figure out what it meant.

"The doctors are working hard on it," Mom kept saying as she kissed me good night. "They're really good, too."

Months later when the ground thawed and the first crocuses shot up, my father took off his grimy sweater and he'd shrunken in half. Still, nobody said anything. I decided I wasn't talking either. At my sixth-grade graduation, even though it was almost ninety degrees out on the playground, Dad showed up in his blue corduroys and winter oxford, his Nikon hanging around his neck, pulling him toward the blacktop. He kept asking me to gather my friends together for more pictures but I politely explained that we were very busy signing year-books and making summer plans and then I ran away from him and hung out by the bleachers for the rest of the afternoon.

That night, even with my bedroom door barricaded shut, I couldn't tell my diary the real reason I took off. I was too hot and twisted up inside. I was mad at Dad for being so rickety looking, huddled over in a sorry crescent, like he was making a game plan but there was no team beside him. I was mad at Mom for her outdated haircut and flimsy-looking smile. And I was mad most of all at the doctors for being fine and good and working so hard.

My father's decline was swift, though of course I'll never know how much he suffered. I don't remember much about that summer, except that the cicadas swooped in again in their screeching gales and Dad's hospital refrigerator was only big enough to hold cans of vanilla drink that he said tasted like glue.

I still hold on to the slivers of sunlight that we shared.

My mom rented a cabin in Massachusetts with a dock that bobbed absently while we dipped our feet in the lake. When I looked down at our legs in the water, I thought Dad had seaweed climbing up his until I realized those were his veins. The lake was cool and still and looked like a big bowl of muddy soup to me, but Dad said it was the best lake he'd ever seen and I said, "Me too," because I just wanted us to be the same.

The glass cups of orange sherbet that he ate meditatively, longingly, his lips slick and stained as he smiled with humble relief.

The strings hanging like cobwebs from the bottom of his dungaree shorts.

I remember Betsy coming home from summer camp prattling incessantly about her new boyfriend, showing me his clumsy sonnets of adoration and saying that one day they would run away together and it would be better that way because things at home were only going to get worse.

I remember Jon coming home from his summer job teaching tennis and retreating to his room without a word. I only knew he was there because I could smell the salami sandwiches he loved to microwave or hear him socking tennis balls against the wall.

I remember the night Mom made sure Betsy and Jon were both out of the house. She cooked my favorite meal—crispy chicken, peas, and onion rye bread, which tasted extra delicious and salty until Dad said that he had something to tell me. The doctors had decided it wasn't the kidney thing after all, it was actually cancer and they're working on it but they're not sure what kind or where it all is and it could be spreading through his lymph nodes but there isn't really any way to treat it because his kidneys can't process chemo and whatever they tell him he promises to tell me and he'll make me a deal that if he gets impatient or crabby just know that he still loves me and it's just that he's not feeling well and if I have any questions or I feel worried I can always ask him and he will promise to tell me everything except we don't know everything yet but he's still my dad and he always will be and does that sound fair?

I wagged my head loosely, which passed for a yes. Then we ate for a little while longer until Mom asked why I hadn't touched my peas. She said she thought they were the kind I liked.

"C'mon, Ab. Just a couple," she coaxed.

"Leave her alone, Joan. She's got a lot to digest right now."

"I know, but she needs her greens."

Usually I liked when they were both talking about me and not my siblings, but not that night.

"Hey, Ab, you want to be excused early?" asked Dad.

I nodded to that too. Dad gave me a big smile and a wink as if we were business partners and I'd just made a smart decision.

Then I went up to my room and lay on my bed and squeezed my hands into fists in my pockets so I couldn't be tempted into touching the wallpaper. I just stared at it with my cruelest glare instead. Those flowers and polka dots had known about this all along. They had their own secret language they spoke with the squiggles and stripes and they recognized when someone was going to explode and someone was going to get cancer and they had been laughing at me this whole time while I thought it was the kidney thing. The flowers had hideously wide toothy smiles and the curlicues were bouncing up and down, soaring gleefully off some invisible trampoline, and I hated them all. They were phony and babyish and liars. As I was scowling, even though I didn't want to or mean to, my hands came unleashed. I traced vigorously, stormily, plowing through the pastel brush, trying to make it all better somehow.

The rest of the summer was trips to the hospital and then to the pool. Mom worked half-days and went straight to visit Dad. Sometimes she stayed the night with him while Betsy, Jon, and I ordered Chinese takeout. But it wasn't Sunday night so it tasted off and all the fortune cookies had messages I'd heard before.

One day in early August, Mom told me that instead of going to the pool, she was taking me to work with her and then we were going on a date to Pizza Hut. We each ordered personal pan pizzas and the all-you-can-eat salad bar buffet, which included croutons and black olives, so I was particularly pleased. Mom tucked my hair behind my ears and said, "Remember Dad promised to tell you what was going on, even if it was bad?"

"Yeah."

Twenty-two minutes and eleven seconds.

I had one eye on my watch to time our pan pizzas because if they didn't come out in exactly a half hour, the whole meal would be free.

"Well . . . so . . . things are not so good."

"Okay."

Twenty-three minutes and three seconds. I couldn't let the waitress see me timing her because I wanted it to be a surprise.

"So . . . yeah. It's not so good and the doctors want Daddy to stay in the hospital but he has decided to come home and we'll make the New Room like his bedroom with a special bed and a nurse." The New Room, where we watched TV and played board games, wasn't really new—we had been calling it that since Mr. Finneman built it for us nine years earlier.

Twenty-four. It wasn't even that busy in the Hut. This waitress was really cutting it close.

"Did you hear me?"

"Yeah, sure. That's good, right?"

"Well, good that Dad'll be home again. But . . . it'll be different. First of all, there won't be much TV watching going on."

That wasn't big news, since we didn't watch that much TV to begin with, but Mom was acting very serious, so I scrunched my eyebrows to let her know I was hearing every word she said.

Twenty-five and forty-four seconds. I smiled into my napkin. I loved the number four and took two in a row as a very auspicious sign.

"So, I just thought I'd tell you. And also, I thought maybe it'd be fun if Betsy and you went to visit the Massachusetts cousins for a week or so. That way, Dad can get settled back at home, and you two can get a few days at the beach."

Twenty-seven . . . and fifteen seconds. This meal was definitely going to be free.

"Does that sound good? Hey, Chicken? C'mon, sit up straight."

"Sure. Sure." Should I stand up and yell *Time's up!* I wondered, or should I just let them—

"And here we are. Sorry for the delay, there. We have one personal pan with green peppers and onions, and one with extra cheese and black olives."

Damn it!

The waitress's name tag said Kiki. She had silky hair and a pert ski-jump nose, which only made me feel more gangly and defeated. *Twenty-eight minutes and forty-three seconds.* I wanted to tell her that she almost didn't make it.

"Be careful not to touch the pan 'cause it's super hot!" Kiki sang as she galloped away. Mom folded her napkin into her collar because she didn't want to get her plum work suit dirty.

"Do you have any questions for me, Chicken?" she asked. Everyone was always asking if there were more questions but I felt like she hadn't given me any information except that we were rearranging the house and I was going on a forced vacation and meanwhile I'd lost the free pizza race.

"Nope!" I declared loudly, shoving a slice into my mouth. It was delicious and crowded with olives, but I felt gypped. Big-time. I knew my mother was still talking but I couldn't hear what she was saying because I was trying to chew in time to the second hand of my watch. Its rhythm was logical, predictable, much more definitive and comforting than the open-ended question-sentences Mom was spewing.

Two days later, Betsy and I packed up our duffels and boarded a train to stay with the Massachusetts cousins, who were on Mom's side of the family. Any other time, I would have liked hanging out with my cousins, but all they wanted to do now was talk about boys with Betsy. I pretended to be absorbed in the biography of Anne Frank that I was supposed to read for school. But from behind the jacket cover, I glowered at them bitterly, thinking, *You'll be sorry when my dad dies and I'm the most important, even more important than boys.*

The one place I found calm was underwater, where the world was nothing more than a muffled blur. I felt the deep cradling me, protecting me from my cousins and my anger and all the questions that led to more questions. Betsy was a great swimmer and I loved it when we held contests to see how long we could hold our breath and pick up treasures from the mushy bottom. I lasted to nineteen and got sand dollars, mussel shells, snails, and the entire backside of a hermit crab. At night we laid the ocean's floor on the wooden porch railing so it could dry out in the sun. My cousin Eddie boiled up big pots of clams and afterward we dumped out jigsaw puzzles on the floor so we could look for the corner pieces first like Dad taught us. There were no cicadas up here, only a night so clinging and close it lay on top of us like tar. With no patterns to track in the walls, I often tossed and turned, and one night I even wet the bed. When I told Mom about it she said it was okay, there was a lot going on, and I should try enjoying the beach.

So I plugged my nose and plunged under the horizon, trying to blot out everything on land, everything in the sky, everything unknown.

MOURNER'S KADDISH*

Yit-ga-dal ve-yit-ka-dash she-mei ra-ba be-al-ma di-
ve-ra chi-re-u-tei, ve-yam-lich mal-chu-tei be-cha-
yei-chon u-ve-yo-mei-chon u-ve-cha-yei de-chol beit
Yis-ra-eil, ba-a-ga-la u-vi-ze-man ka-riv, ve-i-me-ru:
a-mein.
Ye-hei she-mei ra-ba me-va-rach le-a-lam u-le-al-mei
al-ma-ya.
Yit-ba-rach ve-yish-ta-bach, ve-yit-pa-ar ve-yit-ro-
mam ve-yit-na-sei, ve-yit-ha-dar ve-yit-ha-leh ve-yit-
ha-lal she-mei de-ku-de-sha, be-rich hu, le-ei-la min
kol bi-re-cha-ta ve-shi-ra-ta, tush-be-cha-ta ve-ne-che-
ma-ta, da-a-mi-ran be-al-ma, ve-i-me-ru: a-mein.
Ye-hei she-la-ma ra-ba min she-ma-ya ve-cha-yim
a-lei-nu ve-al kol Yis-ra-eil, ve-i-me-ru: a-mein.
O-seh sha-lom bi-me-ro-mav, hu ya-a-seh sha-lom
a-lei-nu ve-al kol Yis-ra-eil, ve-i-me-ru: a-mein.

Let the glory of God be extolled, let His great name be
hallowed, in the world whose creation He willed. May
His kingdom soon prevail, in our own day, our own
lives, and the life of all Israel, and let us say: Amen.
Let His great name be blessed for ever and ever.
Let the name of the Holy One, blessed is He, be
glorified, exalted, and honored, though He is beyond
all the praises, songs, and adorations that we can utter,
and let us say: Amen.

For us and for all Israel, may the blessing of peace and
the promise of life come true, and let us say: Amen.
May He who causes peace to reign in the high heavens,
let peace descend on us, on all Israel, and all the world,
and let us say: Amen.

May the Source of peace send peace to all who mourn, and comfort to all who are bereaved, here and wheresoever they may be, and let us say: Amen.

*Must be repeated daily (in English and in Hebrew).
**If you are saying Kaddish in synagogue and your aunt just died, you get to stand up and the rabbi says your aunt's name and everybody tries not to look at you but they are looking at you so be sure to brush your hair and wear blush.

jews like lists

· ·

That summer, besides following my second hand, holding my breath, and collecting shells, I sang. I especially liked to sing when I was out walking our dog, Sandy. I had dance moves that went with most of the songs too.

Some of the things I liked to sing were:

1. The Cement Mixer song
2. The Heaven song
3. The Nabisco theme song, but really just the part at the very end where they sang *Na-bis-co!* and then a bell dinged. I loved this part so much that after Aunt Simone's memorial service I told my mother that when I died I wanted them to play it at my service after all the speeches were over.

Often I tried to do one dance move for each square of cement in the sidewalk, *without* touching the cracks. The nursery rhyme about touching cracks and breaking your mother's back made me nervous and it just felt safer to stay inside the lines. Every time I got all the words to time out exactly with the dance moves, I felt a bit taller, like I'd just made it through an obstacle course in one graceful leap. As the summer thickened and my father faded, I added more songs to my repertoire—usually ones from Dad's Cole Porter tapes. Sandy didn't seem to mind and I sang them under my breath with my mouth almost completely closed so no one would think I was crazy or belonged in special ed class.

I wasn't crazy. I just liked to sing.

Or rather, I *had* to sing. I couldn't name who or what was compelling me to memorize these lyrics and polish my sashays, but once I introduced a new tune or pirouette into the routine, I had to duplicate it exactly the next time. Though I would never admit it, I began to fear my walks. With each new verse there was greater potential to mess up and if I went inside without singing it correctly or reworking any missteps, I would be disappointing or hurting someone—mostly Dad or even Cole Porter. And there were so many cracks to step over.

I also started repeating things. I had certain rhymes or sayings that I thought were clever and important, so I said them a lot. But they could get tricky, too, because sometimes they got caught in my throat and I had to reiterate them more carefully just in case they came out wrong the first time. Some of the things I liked/had to repeat were:

1. The words to my favorite Shel Silverstein poem, "Sarah Cynthia Sylvia Stout Would Not Take the Garbage Out!"

2. Everything is off, off, off. I said this out loud every night while I checked the toaster, stove, and electrical outlets to make sure nothing had been left on that might cause a deadly fire while we were asleep. Our neighbor Frank had had a fire in his TV set when I was five and his windows were still boarded up six years later. Also, I saw a TV special with Sandy Duncan in which the whole house erupted in flames from a faulty light switch. So saying this was not only important but essential.

3. P.D. (pleasant dreams).

4. The Shema. I'd probably been repeating this longer than anything else. The Shema is a universal Jewish prayer. I repeated it every night when Mom tucked me in for bed. Betsy and Jon had repeated it for many years too but I guess Jon got too old for it and Betsy said she didn't believe in G-d anymore. The Shema goes like this:

Ayl me-lech ne-men She-ma Yis-ra-eil: A-do-nai E-lo-hei-nu, A-do-nai E-chad! Ba-ruch sheim ke-vod mal-chu-to le-o-lam va-ed!

Which means:

Hear, O Israel: the Lord is our God, the Lord is One! Blessed is His glorious kingdom forever and ever!

There was a longer version too but we only said that in synagogue. I loved saying the Shema with Mom because it was the quietest part of the day. She would close the door so it was just the two of us whispering in the night together and no matter what had happened in school or if I had had a fight with Betsy or if I couldn't make friends or Dad hadn't finished dinner because he was too busy pacing with his hands on his kidneys, the world became as small and complete as those two sentences. And we ended with *Amen,* which meant, *So be it.*

Some nights Mom would stay longer and we'd make lists together. She was an expert list maker. She said lists helped put things in perspective and I agreed. She had lists for everything: groceries to buy, recipes to cook, books to read, movies to rent, thank-you notes to send, people to phone. To do. To buy. To return. To look for. To check. To do NOW!!!—taped to the refrigerator, stuffed in the bread box, crammed between seat cushions, and sometimes in a trail from the front door to the bottom of the stairs. She wrote them on pieces of cardboard from the cleaners, old receipts, and decapitated tea boxes in big, loopy letters that swirled off the page like a typhoon. I was usually in charge of copying them for her because her letters were too chaotic to read.

My favorite of the lists we made together wasn't written down, though, because we didn't want anyone else to see it. *It's not exactly kosher,* Mom said. But she also said it was okay as long as we kept it to ourselves, so I memorized it and we added to it whenever I was feeling especially sorry for myself. It was called *The people in the neighborhood who are having trouble list.*

We had started it the winter before; just about the time Dad started running fevers. One night after the Shema, I had crumbled into a heap of self-pity about how life was viciously unfair. Sixth grade was about as much fun as getting hangnails all over my body, and every lunchtime I had to decide if I was cool enough to chew gum and be bored with the bleacher girls or if I should pretend to have a social studies project so I could stay inside and eat my sandwich alone. I wasn't popular and I'd told Rebecca Mills that she was less popular than me, so we weren't hanging out anymore. Plus, I had too much arm hair and not enough matching outfits and I couldn't even try to bring home new friends after school because Dad was always sleeping and being sick. I couldn't stop crying and they were the kind of tears that dripped into my ears and made me feel useless and soggy.

Mom stroked my cheek slowly and said, "You know, Chicken, you're not the only one going through a rough time."

"Yeah, but Lindsey Bussey gets to buy clothes out of a catalog and she's the fastest runner in gym," I sobbed.

"Okay," said Mom. "I'm telling you this, but you can't tell anyone else, not even your sister. I happen to know that Mr. Bussey lost his job last year, and they're living on just Mrs. Bussey's salary, which isn't much because she works at a nonprofit."

"Really?" Maybe it wasn't kind or kosher, but I had to smile a little because Lindsey had it so easy and she had blond ringlets and always came in to school with homemade cinnamon cookies, too. Maybe her dad made them while he was stuck at home calling people and asking for a new job.

Mom smoothed back my hair. "You see? Everybody has some-thing."

"What about Mindy Sullivan?" I sniffed. "She gets to have sleepovers all the time."

"Yeah, but there's alcoholism in that family. I think the brother has it too now."

"The Wolcotts."

"This isn't very nice, but I heard they're having their . . . issues. You know, marital."

"The Melmans."

"Are outspending their means."

"Miss Spinner?"

"Someone told me clinical depression, but don't quote me on that. And you do know that Mrs. Schlamm is her sister and they don't talk to each other anymore?"

"The Lunnicks!"

"Cra-zeeeee!"

Mom also said in a hushed tone that *several people from the temple who shall remain nameless* were having affairs, including one couple who was in the middle of a vicious divorce. I wanted to ask who, but I knew she'd never tell.

Mom finished the list by wiping my cheeks, kissing my forehead, and saying, "Okay, Chicken. That's enough, huh?" I could feel her low, soulful humming filling the room. "I promise," she soothed, "it's not going to be this hard always." I didn't know if she was talking about the bleacher girls or whatever was going on with Dad or the list of things I needed to turn off in case of fire, but her voice was so calm and her lips were so warm that I had no choice but to believe her. She tamed even the scattered leaves and zigzags in the wallpaper and if I held on to her breath we could float away on a raft of stillness and safety.

Then we said the Shema again. After all, we had just said a bunch of insulting things about the neighbors. It seemed right to offer up one last prayer.

Ayl me-lech ne-men She-ma Yis-ra-eil: A-do-nai E-lo-hei-nu, A-do-nai E-chad! Ba-ruch sheim ke-vod mal-chu-to le-o-lam va-ed!

I'd come to realize that making lists and repeating things were a large part of being Jewish, too. There were lists of things we could and couldn't eat; lists of prayers to say over and over and commandments to follow, the ten plagues that G-d sent down on the pharaoh so the Jews could get out of Egypt, the twelve tribes of Israel, and my favorite, the list of Dearly Departed. Rabbi Poller read this list out loud every week at synagogue before we said the Kaddish—the prayer for people who'd died. Each week there were new names on the DD list and new people to feel sorry for.

After Aunt Simone died, we began going to synagogue more often on Friday nights and the rabbi added her, too. I loved hearing him stammer and stumble through the long tongue-twistery names like Kabelevski and Melkowitz. The list was never perfectly alphabetical and he often became sweaty and confused while he was reading. Since Dad got sick, Mom and I were the only members of our family who went to services regularly, and we stood up through the whole recitation of the DD list. When the rabbi said *Simone Belsky* I squeezed Mom's hand and she patted me on the head and I relished the sorrowful gazes and meek smiles we received. When the list was done, everyone said the Kaddish in subdued, respectful voices and I learned the Hebrew words by heart from having it wash all over me.

I challenged myself to memorize more and more of the passages in my prayer book, and each week I tried out new harmonies on the songs. We had an organist at my synagogue who played behind a copper-colored screen, and when he hit the full minor chords, the whole room quivered. Some Fridays I was convinced that everyone on the planet was praying at the same time, and I trembled as Rabbi Poller intoned *Here and wheresoever they may be, and let us say: Amen.*

I'd also discovered that Judaism was a lot about suffering. Jews respected suffering, and the more you'd endured the more they paid attention to you at synagogue, carrying you on their Kaddish shoulders and coming up to Mom and me after services to say how sorry they were to learn of our loss. Whenever someone approached us, Mom thumped my back, which meant *Stand up straight, Chicken,* but also *See? I'm so proud of you.* I loved going to temple, particularly for these moments. I got to wear Mom's blush and a little bit of lipstick and have as much Manischewitz and as many butter cookies as I wanted. But more important, I was part of a uniquely fragile circle of sufferers and survivors. I scooped punch next to old men with concentration camp numbers etched into their arms. I nodded knowingly to Inma, whose skin was so thin you could see all of her veins crisscrossing under her eyes, and Beverly, who smiled in slow motion even when no one was talking to her.

The whole point of synagogue, as far as I could tell, was that it was a place where anybody could come to sing or listen or cry. It didn't matter whether you were popular or stuck in slow motion or irrevocably scarred. Once you walked through the big oak doors you *belonged.*

There were many elements of Judaism that I didn't quite understand—the rules about food, for example. I also wondered why all the Jews I knew had the same smell of bad breath and talked so fast it sounded like a typewriter out of control. But my biggest question was too portentous and too sacrilegious to breathe into words.

It was about Him.

I had learned in Hebrew school that He was all-powerful and all-knowing and all-seeing. And I'd learned that outside of prayer books we were supposed to write G-d's name with a dash, which seemed an important rule to me. I couldn't recall exactly why we were supposed to replace the *o,* but it had something to do with using His name in vain and people throwing out papers that had His name on it, and it being very disrespectful. I thought about this a lot. I pictured piles of loose-leaf paper, ballpoint ink soaking in the rain, and G-d's name puddling into watery blue stains. I didn't dare ask what would happen if you forgot to use the dash. I wasn't sure what He did with bad people; I didn't think He killed anyone with angry lightning bolts, only that it was most important to speak of Him carefully and to consecrate His name. He, and only He, knew where Aunt Simone was now and who would be next to leave earth.

He was watching with His all-seeing eyes. Listening with His all-hearing ears. Tallying all of our sins on His jumbo-size legal pad in the sky. He blessed us with matzoh ball soup and lilac sunsets and a synagogue sanctuary where anyone could be a hero. I put that dash in His name and always used capital *H*'s to show Him that I was good and appreciated everything He gave us. For good measure, I also made sure never to utter His name out loud except during prayers, and I tried to avoid writing words that ended in *g-o* next to words that started with *d,* just in case they were smushed together and then thrown out by accident. Mom told me not to go nuts about the name stuff—she was president of the synagogue Sisterhood for two years and hence my expert on Judaism. But whenever I thought about Him up there surveying everyone and all of our reckless depravity, my skin got goose bumps and my head felt staticky.

The truth is, I couldn't figure out exactly who or what He was.

I thought I could *feel* Him most when we were in synagogue singing those slow, achy songs with full minor chords. I thought He probably looked a lot like the wizard in *The Wizard of Oz*—the vapory formless face, before they discovered that he was just a man playing with levers behind a curtain. But I didn't know what else to think. How close was He? How could He be here and also in Ethiopia at the same time? Did He see us lighting candles on Friday nights? Or fighting over the heel of the challah? Or rubbing myself when I had sexy dreams? Did that make Him mad? I also hoped that babies who died and people like Beverly and anyone with lifelong illnesses got to try life over again. Maybe there was a cutoff, like anyone who died before they turned forty got another go-around?

Sometimes I was convinced that I'd inadvertently said His name in vain or held my curse finger up toward the sky and I didn't know how to say sorry to Someone who could rearrange the solar system if He wanted to. I tried to blow kisses at the synagogue when we went by in the car, to let Him know He was and is and always will be the Supreme Leader and I promised to kiss His name wherever it appeared in the prayer books.

That summer, as my father prepared to die, I held my breath underwater so I could feel Him and linger in His infinite refuge. I squeezed my eyes shut and counted as the sea pulsed around me, wordlessly begging Him to protect us all. Hoping He could see how devout I was being and would reverse whatever was coursing through my dad's veins.

A few nights after Betsy and I were settled in Massachusetts, Mom called us just as we were getting ready for bed.

"Dad's home. He says he loves the Welcome Home sign you made."

"Did he laugh? Is his new bed fancy? What did you have for dinner?"

"Here, you can talk to him."

"Hi, Abidab."

"Dad!"

"You go to the beach?"

I told him about the sea, the driftwood; I counted up my mosquito bites for him and reported that I saw two ferries and six jellyfishes.

"Don't touch them. They can bite you."

"I know."

We talked about *The Muppets Take Manhattan,* which Dad had seen that night on TV. He thought it was better than the first Muppets movie. He promised me we would watch it together when I got home. And that we would dip our toes in the water again and eat tons more orange sherbet before the end of the summer.

"Is that a deal?" he asked.

"Deal."

We shook on it to make it official. We shook and I swore and he promised and it *would* happen.

Only, we shook over the phone. Which I guess didn't count.

WHAT I BELIEVE NOW
THAT I'M TEN YEARS OLD LIST

1. When you do something bad, something bad will happen to you. Aunt Simone seemed perfect, but she must have done something bad, something really bad like cheating and stealing and lying, but nobody is saying what it was. G-d knows what it is and that is why Aunt Simone is dead.
2. Lying is bad. Cheating on tests is bad. Stealing is a crime even if it's just candy.
3. McDonald's French fries and Mom's matzoh ball soup and Dad's Sunday omelets are the best foods on earth.
4. Anne Frank is a really good role model because she's skinny and Jewish and dead and she didn't complain a lot.
5. Daddy is my best boyfriend and Mommy is my best girlfriend forever and ever.*
6. Forever and ever! (because repeating's fun and it's not just for special ed people).
7. Six is a bad number to stop on because it's the devil's number so from now on I'm going to try not to use six at all or even nine because that's six upside down but this is seven so I'm going to end it here.

Amen.

*This should be written in diary every night. Also, kiss their names ten times each.
**If I don't kiss their names they might not know that I love them the most and then they could be upset or something bad could happen to them.

something's burning

. . . .

The next morning my cousin Sheila woke us up before it was even light out. I had just found the cool part of the pillowcase after a muddled dream about being followed by a swarm of bees and I wanted to go back to sleep but Sheila said it was important. She walked me into the living room and I saw Betsy holding the telephone and sobbing.

She handed me the receiver and I heard what was left of my mother's voice. It was synagogue serious and it came out in gulps more than words.

"Oh, honey your . . . father didn't . . . make it . . . he was . . . in his sleep . . . but it's . . . all right are you . . . all right?"

Then she was crying and Betsy and Sheila were crying and Eddie came in with their baby and they were all crying in a circle. But I wasn't. I bowed my head so they couldn't see my bone-dry eyes. I don't know why I wasn't. I just couldn't feel anything except the sand stuck between my toes and I wanted to be a part of their sadness but all I could think of was *The Muppets Take Manhattan* and I wondered if it really was better than the first Muppets movie or if Dad had just said that because he knew he was going to die and he wanted to give me something nice to look forward to. He had also promised me mountains of sherbet and I had saved those sand dollars for him and now I felt myself fuming, realizing it was all a pack of lies.

My cousin Steve drove us home, and when we pulled into the driveway, Mom came out and stood on the front steps, by the hedge. She was wearing the ugliest dress in the history of thread. It was striped in brown, maroon, orange, and turquoise with triangles and flowers caught between the bars of color. It was supposed to wrap around with a tie, but she had done it wrong so the dress was all bunched up and her cream slip was slithering slowly down her calf. Her face was brownmaroonorangeturquoisetriangled too, and I felt embarrassed by and for her.

Mom's arms weren't working. She pulled Betsy and me into her at the same time like she was going to hug us, and then we all sort of leaned at one another, none of us latching on. Mom even smelled brown. She took us inside and I went straight to the New Room to see where Dad's hospital bed was. I thought maybe there would be a sign like a note to say good-bye and maybe sorry about not getting another swim in like we talked about, or at least a shadow in his sheets. But the bed had already been carted away and Jon was sitting on the couch, watching TV. I asked him what the bed looked like. Was there a little toilet too? Where did the coffee table go? Was the dog allowed in the room? Jon didn't say much more than "Bed over there. Table in the corner. Dog's at the kennel till tomorrow."

It was hard to get answers out of anyone. The house was full of people I didn't know and everybody was wearing the same pinched face. Terry Jaffey was in the dining room pulling out our tablecloths and counting silverware. Terry was the newest president of the Sisterhood at our synagogue and she had two ladies with her to tidy up for shiva—the Jewish custom where people come by and bring cakes and cookies and talk about whoever just died. The kitchen counter was already stacked with deli platters, tubs of whitefish salad, kugels, and big urns of coffee. The Sisterhood had filled our bathroom with vases of dried flowers and paper napkins so it looked like a hotel.

Nothing and nobody in our house felt real. It was as if everyone had disguised themselves as humans but underneath their skin they were hollow. Aunt Doris and Uncle Morris were there too. Aunt Doris was Mom's oldest sister and usually a lot of fun—she let me parade around in her espadrilles or we drank iced tea out of her wineglasses—but now she was busy dusting our bookshelves and sighing. They had been there when Dad died, and Uncle Morris, who was a doctor, pronounced Dad dead. I was so hungry to know what those last moments were like, whether we had shared that same tarry black of night, whether my father simply withdrew from the human race or perhaps let out a telltale death rattle, but all Uncle Morris revealed was, "Very peaceful. Yup. In his sleep, don't you know." Then Aunt Doris announced that Mom needed to rest and brought her upstairs for a nap and they shut the door.

It was one huge and deceitful disappearing trick. The kind of magic that washed-up clowns tried at birthday parties when you could see the cards sticking out of their baggy sleeves. Maybe Dad thought it would be better if he just slipped away, but it wasn't. The house had been upended into this forced inertia and it was too quiet to even think. I couldn't taste or smell either. Everything was infected with this unshakable emptiness. With the couch pushed back into place and the dried flowers in the bathroom, it looked like we were living in a solid well-groomed house, but I knew the first whisper of a breeze could knock us down.

The next day for the funeral I blew my hair dry like Betsy, even though it was so humid my eyeballs were sweating. The limos came to pick us up, and I had to cover my mouth so nobody would see me smile at them idling outside our house. They were long stretch limos like the ones our neighbors had rented for prom, and I felt glamorous climbing into the slippery backseat in my sundress and patent leather shoes. I was pretty sure Betsy thought so too, but she still had her sad face on, so I didn't say a word.

Before the service, Rabbi Poller took us into a study that smelled of old pipe smoke, and said a blessing over us. Then he pinned a piece of torn black ribbon on each of us like a medal of honor for suffering. I'd seen this ritual before. It was in my favorite movie, *The Jazz Singer,* with Neil Diamond, only this time it was happening to me and the ribbon meant I was a primary mourner and everybody had to feel sorry for me.

Mom, Betsy, Jon, and I filed into the sanctuary and the whole congregation stood up like we were celebrities. We had the choicest seats in the front row too, which would've been great, except for the coffin. It was light wood and it was sitting on some sort of stool. I tried to look around it or over it or even through it because it was no more than an overgrown shoe box in the middle of the room. That's all it could be. A plain, stupid, boring box taking up space. It was *not* my father. It did not make any music or smell like Tums. It couldn't tap-dance or host a radio hour. It had no business being in the spotlight, being so compact and finite. Every time a picture of my father lying unmoving inside came into my head I shook it away. He was too vast to be contained in this lifeless crate.

One by one, cousins and friends stood up to talk about Dad. How smart and great and funny and alive he was. They all looked at the front row and gave us bleak smiles and I made sure to keep tissues near my face to look mournful. Dad's best friend, Marty, gave the best speech. He spoke for nearly twenty minutes about how rapt Dad was with each one of his children. He said that "Abigail" meant *father's joy*. I was smiling up at Marty and all ready to clap for him until I realized he wasn't looking at me. He was looking at that horrible box that *had* to have nothing inside of it.

At the graveyard the rabbi said another prayer and he shook with silent sobs as they lowered the coffin into the ground. When he nodded, everybody formed a line to shovel a little bit of dirt on top. Mom went first and she barely got a teaspoonful on the blade before letting it fall off. When it was my turn I tried not to look in but I couldn't help it. The hole seemed ten miles deep and a thousand miles wide and there was no way we'd have enough dirt to fill it up. Maybe this was where that hole in the snow led, because it was the darkest, vilest hole imaginable, rooting into the earth's bowels. There were pebbles mixed with the dirt, clumped into barbed pucks that battered the coffin's lid as each scoop descended. I was furious at everyone, but especially at whoever dug this crater and whoever thought up this cruel tradition, and I wanted to scream, *Just stop it! All of you! Stop knocking on my father's head! Why can't you let him be?!*

If I were a good daughter, I would have jumped into that abyss after him, covered him with my body, and shrieked until everyone went home. I wasn't a good daughter, though. I was weak and pathetic and I just watched while the line filed past and buried my father, pummeling him with the knotted earth.

"I got ya. Come here."

Our neighbor Estherann pulled me away from the grave and took me in her arms. I tried to hide in her woolly perfume, her frizzy helmet of hair sheltering me from the procession of shovelers, but the rocks kept on banging banging banging on that wooden lid. *Leave my dad alone!* He was too small and too gone and he hadn't made the forty-year-old cutoff so there was no chance of his coming back for another go at life. And then everything smelled like soil and rocks, even Estherann's neck as I thrust my face into it. I squeezed her as tightly as I could. I wanted to squeeze the whole world out of that moment. Hugging her was the first and only time I hiccuped and even emitted a tear or two. I wanted more to come out but nothing happened.

When we got back to the house, Terry and the Sisterhood ladies had put a pitcher of water outside on the steps so we could wash our hands. It was supposed to rinse the death off, I think. It didn't work. Now there was a ton more food. Heaps of bagels and olives, macaroons and fruit salads. We pawed at cold cuts and spinach dip with the same fingers that had pitched dirt on my father's head. The house was so crowded there was a line to get into the two bathrooms. People kept walking in with food and plants and dismal faces. One of Mom's coworkers brought me a beaded bracelet even though I hadn't done anything except let my dad die. Nobody rang the doorbell, they just walked in—it was part of the shiva rules. Long-lost relatives, teachers, Dad's tennis friends, and too many people I'd never met before who wanted to hold me in their clammy embrace. They dropped off their goodies and then swarmed around Mom like she was a movie star. When they got to me they sighed and said Dad was an exceptional man and that this was too unfair. The only person I was glad to see was Dad's law school buddy, Stanley. Stanley was so tall his head scraped our ceiling. He drew me into his arms and waltzed me into the New Room, his long nose twitching while he hummed.

Only, when he put me down he looked at me with big bloodshot eyes and said, "You know, it wasn't supposed to be like this." I turned away so I wouldn't have to see his eyes filling up.

That night the rabbi came to our house and lit a candle in front of Dad's picture and led everyone in the Kaddish. There was no DD list this time. We were the whole list. The beginning, middle, and end. Everyone in the house was sniffling. The worst part was watching Mom cry. Her lips buckled and her nostrils widened and turned splotchy. Then she took out one of the five million dirty tissues that she had stuffed up her brown sleeve and dabbed at her nose. I stood next to her and stared hard at the candle so I could at least force my eyes to water a little bit.

I'd often been constipated, but not being able to cry felt bound up and nauseous in a whole new way. I was certain everyone was watching me, wondering what was wrong with me. Maybe I was a monster with no feelings. Or maybe I couldn't cry because deep inside I had *wanted* my dad to die.

You'll be sorry when my dad dies and I'm the most important.

I'd never said these words out loud, but it didn't matter. Someone had heard them and now they had come true. Maybe I had ESP or maybe I had willed my father to die just so I could be a primary mourner and everyone would admire me for my suffering. Staring into that flame, while the room was sobbing around me, I was shaking for a different reason. My thoughts were dangerous and possibly lethal. Maybe my Massachusetts cousins would say *Yeah, Abby was acting all weird and she had an evil look in her eye.* Or maybe they would ask me where I was the night Dad died the way they did in a murder mystery. I pressed my eyes shut with my fingers so all I could see were fierce yellow blobs. I gritted my teeth, desperate to dredge up even a whine. But I couldn't, and now I knew why.

I couldn't cry because I had killed my father with my wicked thoughts.

I wanted everyone to leave because now it was clear to me and I knew somebody else would figure it out soon enough. The whole week of shiva I ducked behind bookshelves and coffee cakes, hiding my parched eyes and the foul truth that I was sure would tumble out of me at any moment. The screen door wheezed open and shut every ten minutes, admitting flocks of sagging shoulders and damp faces. *Ugh. I'm so sorry is there anything I can do what can I do how are you holding up?* I was hugged and petted so often I felt bruised. But the unending stares were even worse. My blank-faced shrugs were bound to give me away and I had no means to prove I wasn't a heartless killer.

One day Mom cornered me by the stairs. I was sure she would confront me, the jig was up. But instead she said I had to call my friend Rebecca (who was barely even a friend anymore) and tell her Dad had died. When I did, Rebecca dropped the phone and I heard her wailing, *Mommy! Mommy!* She came over that night and gave me a peach-colored box with a unicorn on it. She was sogging up a pile of tissues and she said she couldn't stop thinking about my father.

I said, "Thanks, me too," and I waited for her to ask me why I looked so unaffected and suspicious. When she didn't, I told her I had a lot to do and I'd see her later. Then I hid in the bathroom until she left.

After that I invited Ellyn Farber over to keep me company. Ellyn was way more popular than Rebecca and, more important, she didn't know my dad well, so she didn't cry or ask me anything about how I felt. When Ellyn came over we stole grapefruits from one of the big gift baskets and a sugar bowl too. We ran up to my room, peeled off the rinds and dipped the fruit in the sugar, slurping it over the garbage can, which I knew would make a sticky mess, but there was nobody to stop us. We also made magic potions with baby powder, bubble bath, and the end of the toothpaste.

"Can we come in?" asked my Massachusetts cousins, but I hollered, "No!" and Ellyn and I slammed the door and shoved our butts up against it so they couldn't ram their way in.

"Please?" they whined, shoving back in a pushing tug-of-war.

"Nobody's home!" we cackled.

I could do that, I told Ellyn, because I was in mourning. Ellyn high-fived me.

After the week of shiva, I thought things would get easier. I'd made it through seven days and a million miserable *I'm sorry*'s without leaking my secret. Terry and her ladies packed up their coffee urns and Aunt Doris plastic-wrapped all the leftovers and wiped down the counters. Mom actually washed her hair. Jon went back to the University of Virginia, which I didn't think was such a big deal, but Mom acted like he was going off to battle. She stood outside on the top step in her brown dress again, piecing together her bits of tissue, ironing them between her trembling palms. Jon took hours to load up his car, then said *Bye* and *Don't worry, I'll call you a lot.* I almost laughed out loud because I knew he wouldn't. Jon never used the phone except to order Chinese food.

I tried to stay busy and made plans with Ellyn every day. She was the only one with whom I felt safe. I loved going to her house because nobody looked at me with sad eyes and we could do whatever we wanted. Her parents were young and healthy, wore matching leather jackets, and insisted I call them Bibi and Doug. They took us to a Benihana restaurant and we cheered for the flying shrimp and ate pineapple boats for dessert. We watched *The Big Chill,* which was Bibi's favorite movie and now it was mine, too, though I wasn't sure what was going on in it all the time.

Ellyn and I got matching haircuts and also started our own line of beauty products called AbYn. We went through the bathrooms in Ellyn's house and emptied the different shampoos into a big bottle. Then we added cologne, perfume, and liquid soap and shook it crazily while we blasted Motown. It smelled divine, like bubble gum, peppermint, and the first spring flowers, and we passed the bottle back and forth, gulping in its syrupy scent until our throats ached. I made labels that said AbYn in long script, redrawing each letter and holding it up for Ellyn's approval. When I told her that she was not only my business partner but also my best friend in the whole world forever and ever, she smiled shyly and said I was her best friend too.

I wanted to stay at Ellyn's for the rest of my life, or at least until junior high started, in two weeks. But her family went on vacation, which meant I had to go to the pool with Betsy, who was still finalizing her plot to run away with her boyfriend. Mom took off her brown dress so she could go back to work at the nursing home. She painted on big streaks of blush and donned fluffy blouses with chiffon bows around the neck that made her look like a forgotten birthday present. She said if I put on something nice I could come and help her with paperwork, but I said no thanks. Sometimes when it was too rainy for the pool, I snuck into Jon's room to see if he left anything good behind like dirty magazines or forgotten allowance. But there was nothing except a thousand copies of *Sports Illustrated,* empty cassette cases, and the stink of his salami sandwiches and gym socks. He'd even taken down his poster of Bo Derek and all that was left was his old wallpaper of big ships. In between the schooners and steamboats were thick half-moons of dirt where he'd smacked his tennis ball every night, practicing his ace serve. Mom said the plan was to pull down that wallpaper and recarpet so we could have a home office upstairs. I wondered if that meant Jon was never going to live in our house again either.

Nighttime was particularly friendless and haunting. It was only a matter of time before Mom or Betsy asked me why I hadn't cried yet and I couldn't hide in my room because the patchwork walls were closing in tighter each night and I was sure they could see right through me.

Each day, Mom came home around six and changed back into her brown dress. She put on Dad's stereo, with its crackly speakers, and made herself a scotch and sat in the living room on the couch across from his empty chair. Betsy and I were in charge of pulling out the leftover noodle salads and platters of cold cuts Aunt Doris had stuffed in the basement fridge. Instead of five of us at the dinner table it was just three, but Mom told us to take out all the food or it would go bad and then she piled leaning towers of cold cuts on our plates. I felt like I was turning into a piece of turkey-pastrami. There were also four different kinds of coleslaw, two trays of lox and cream cheese, and eight and a half boxes of coffee cake to get through. Mom was determined we'd finish it all. Everything started tasting like salty cardboard, and the lunch meats began to turn a sepia orange.

One night I said, "Maybe when you make the new home office, I can take down my wallpaper too."

"I thought you liked that wall-*pugh-pah*!" Mom was constantly putting too much food in her mouth at once and then trying to talk at the same time so she wound up gagging. Betsy and I yelped, *Are you all right?* and *Take some water!* Sometimes we had to pound her on the back, but this time she coughed it up on her own. Then she picked up exactly where she left off, in case we hadn't heard her.

"I thought you liked that wallpaper. You got to pick it out yourself," she said.

"I know, but that was five years ago. It's a little . . . juvenile." I wasn't going to try to explain how the squiggles and stars snagged me in their unending lanes and loops. How I feared they held cosmic knowledge.

"Well, we'll see," said Mom.

"What does that *mean*? *We'll see*?"

I could see Betsy laughing into her plate even as I said it. Mom didn't answer, of course, but I knew it meant *No* and *I'm so tired* and *It wasn't supposed to be like this* and most of all it meant,

Do you girls smell something burning?

My mother asked us this every night for as long as I could remember, especially after my father died. It didn't matter if we were talking about the new library downtown or the upcoming Olympics or Jim Morrison or if it emerged from those heavy fogs of silence in between. Mom put down her fork, stuck her nose forward, and sniffed for emphasis.

"Do you?" she insisted. Everything was off. We hadn't cooked anything in weeks. I'd already checked the knobs on the stove and smelled inside the oven. *Everything is off, off, off.* The coffeepot was *off.* The toaster was *off.* The radio, TV, tape player, hair dryer—all *off.* I checked the car to see if it was running, because down the street the McWrights had had a fire that way when they left theirs on in the garage.

I wanted to scream *Everything is off, off, off! It's probably your brown dress that's making the burning smell!* I wanted to tell her that her out-fit looked like a volcano throwing up and to get her act together and turn on some Motown and stop acting so old and sad. But I didn't say that. I didn't say anything.

"I do. Something's definitely burning," Mom pronounced, fitting another piece of wilting lunch meat into her mouth. She was so sure she smelled it that she made little *yup yup*'s under her breath. I just shredded my napkin and pretended to be deaf. I didn't detect anything burning but I knew after dinner I'd have to check all the knobs again three times each to make sure I'd done it right. I waited until Betsy was in her room and Mom was settled on the couch with the newspaper. *Everything is off off off,* I spat angrily under my breath as I circled between appliances.

After Mom tucked me in and we said the Shema, I found a seam in that smug and cloying wallpaper and tried to peel it off. I didn't care what the wall looked like underneath, I didn't care if I ripped all the way to the wooden skeleton of the roof; I just needed these patches of pastel gone. I needed to start over. To find a place where nobody knew me and nobody knew my father and nobody could smell these repulsive parts of me smoldering underneath. The ones that had imagined and possibly-maybe-but-I-really-hoped-not invoked my father's death.

Maybe this was what Mom smelled but couldn't put her finger on. Maybe I was the something burning.

a hundred kisses

· ·

The only thing more impossible than filling up a ten-mile-deep grave was digging it up again. Less than a month had passed since my dad died and I couldn't remember what his face looked like. School had just begun and I would sit dazedly in class, trying to excavate his features. I couldn't conjure up even the slant of his nose or the arch of his eyebrows. Did he wear glasses all the time or just when he read the newspaper? Was his chin pointy or rounded? He'd once split open his top lip, but was there a scar?

At home, while Mom was in the kitchen or upstairs changing her clothes, I would casually stroll into the living room to sneak a peek at the bookcase of family photographs. I tried to be subtle about my mission, hesitating by the pictures of Betsy and me grinning on a sun-soaked porch in Martha's Vineyard. The crazy hat parade in Connecticut. Then warily stepping toward the print of my father. He was on a sailboat in a skipper's cap, standing in front of a nest of soaked rigging.

One day, Mom surprised me. She didn't hum as much lately and I hadn't heard her come up next to me.

"You okay, Chicken?" she asked.

I didn't want her to know I was trying to cram my father's face back into my brain.

"Oh yeah. I was just wondering, is that *Puff*?" I gestured toward the photo.

Puff the Magic Sailboat was the name of the 19-footer that my parents had bought with Estherann and Arthur for jaunts in Long Island Sound. When I was onboard, the smell of old beer and seaweed turned me green and queasy, but I stomached it for those charmed moments when Dad let me steer and called me Captain.

"I think so," said Mom.

"Could I maybe put that picture in my room for a little bit?"

"Sure."

I propped the frame up on my windowsill so I could see Dad from any angle when I lay in bed. That night, I waited until after the Shema before tiptoeing over to look at him more carefully. Dad's eyes were hidden behind rust-colored sunglasses and the skipper's cap covered his forehead and ears, but I could make out the rounded chin, the slope of his potbelly.

I studied him greedily, trying to ingrain the curve of his smile. Then I gave the picture a kiss and whispered,

"I love you, Daddy."

I knew it was a picture and that he probably couldn't hear me, but I felt I finally had a way to reach him.

The next night after Mom said good night I crept over again.

"I love you, Daddy."

I kissed the picture and gave it a hug, too. The wooden frame pressed lightly into my skin and tickled my rib. I drew it in closer, until one of the corners dug into my breast and I winced. I took a deep breath and clasped it even tighter. It nipped at my skin, startling me with its sting, but I loved it. I heard myself gulp as I pressed the frame harder still. My eyes started to water and I felt as if the sky were opening up through this compassionate crack in my chest. It didn't matter that I couldn't cry regular tears. If I could hurt like this, if he could hurt me, maybe it would prove that I missed him and loved him too. Maybe I could forget what I'd done to him.

It was around this same time that Mom announced she'd gotten a call from the White Plains Medical Center, the hospital where my father had been treated. They had offered us twenty free sessions in bereavement counseling. Mom thought it would be good if the three of us went to talk about some of our feelings. We could each have our private time with the counselor and afterward go to the gift shop together for egg creams. Betsy said she was too busy studying for the SATs and Mom couldn't make her talk to some stranger about her innermost thoughts. I said no thanks and that I was busy with rehearsals for the school play. Mom looked crushed.

"C'mon, girls. It'll be nice. Plus it's just off Central Avenue, so we can go to Filene's Basement on the way back if you want," she added weakly.

I agreed to go only if Betsy and Mom swore to secrecy. Betsy mouthed,, "Whatever." Mom clapped appreciatively, saying this would be so therapeutic and good for both of us.

Dr. M.'s office was pretty small. It was painted a cool gray and had room only for her desk and two chairs, a filing cabinet, and a pile of jigsaw puzzles. She said we could do one if I wanted, but they looked too easy. On her wall hung a poster of a house with a maze of windows and driveways. I figured it was some sort of metaphor for everybody going along a different path in life. Or maybe it was a form of hypnosis and if you looked at it long enough you'd remember what made you crazy enough to come here. There was a window next to Dr. M.'s desk, but it had bars on it and no latch. It was probably just for show.

Dr. M. asked me if I wanted to tell her anything.

"Not really," I said. "My mom really wanted me to come here so . . ." I trailed off into nothing.

We sat in silence for a while. I'd thought she would have a list of topics to cover—she was the doctor, after all—but she seemed to be content waiting for me to start, which annoyed me. There were tissue boxes on top of the filing cabinet, the desk, the windowsill, and perched next to the puzzle pile. She'd be waiting forever if she wanted me to cry. I could feel her smooth auburn hair and delicate string of pearls follow me as I scanned the room. After an infernal stretch of empty time, she switched the cross of her legs and said she'd heard I'd just started junior high and what was that like? So I told her about seventh grade and all my new classes and getting to be a Munchkin in *The Wiz* and how much fun I had whenever I was at my friend Ellyn's house. I told her Ellyn was my best friend in the whole world and that her parents took us to R-rated movies and fed us coconut-covered marshmallows.

Dr. M. listened and nodded.

"She sounds like a really great friend."

"She is! She is!" Maybe this was why people talked to counselors. So they had someone who agreed with them.

Then she said, "Do you have any thoughts about your father that you'd like to share?"

I knew she'd get to it eventually, so I'd rehearsed a few lines about how he taught me to ride a bike and about the time we dug through the sand in Cape Ann and collected a whole bucket of clams. It had taken me hours to scrape together these dim memories. Even with my nightly examination of his face and my ardent clutching of his photograph, he continued to recede further into the murk of forever gone.

"You really miss him, don't you?" She smiled and looked sad at the same time.

"Yeah," I said. I felt I should cut to the chase. "I'm not that big a crier, though."

"That's okay."

"I know."

"Does that bother you?"

"No. I mean, not really."

"Do you feel like you need to cry or that you should cry?"

This was how crazy people got crazier. She seemed kindhearted enough, but I knew she was trying to lure me in with her words. The whole office was booby-trapped. Each tissue box and every swatch of sunlit carpet was a ruse to break me down and I wasn't about to tell her that I couldn't cry because I maybe, sort of definitely, killed my father or at least played a big part in his death.

"I don't know. It's okay," I told her, and picked up a tissue anyway, to throw her off track. Then we waited for a hundred more hours of silence to pass and finally she said we were out of time and maybe I'd like to come again next week?

I said, "Sure," mostly because I wanted to get out of there as quickly as possible and head to Filene's. Just before she opened the door, Dr. M. asked if maybe I could remember a little bit more about my father for next time and I told her I'd try. My plan was to convince Mom to call during the week and tell her that I was feeling a lot better and we wouldn't be back but thanks anyway.

We went to Filene's and I got a new turtleneck with anchors on it and then we went next door to the bakery and split an entire loaf of onion rye bread that had just been pulled from the oven. But on the way home, I still felt edgy. I was mad at Dr. M. for asking all those questions and looking so serene and especially for giving me homework on our first visit. It was a hard assignment, too—making myself remember things. It was like clamming, except instead of sand I had to use my bare hands to scrape through some mountain of time that was denser and harder than even dried cement. I told Mom that I didn't want to go back and she said how come and I said it wasn't that helpful and she said to give it a few more weeks and then it was the night before my next appointment and I still couldn't come up with a single memory and I was brushing my teeth over and over again, growing guiltier and angrier.

I tried to write out a story in my journal, but all I got out was *Dear SiRo,* and then *Daddy is my best boyfriend and Mommy is my best girlfriend forever and ever.* That's what I wrote at the end of every entry. *Forever and ever* was how all the important prayers ended in synagogue, so I thought it was the best way to show that I loved and missed him even though I couldn't name his favorite food or the city where he was born and the more I tried to reassemble him the further he scattered. Maybe I could tell the story about his lip splitting open. But I couldn't even imagine his teeth anymore. His face had utterly vanished again.

Mom was putting me to bed when she spotted the photograph.

"How did this . . . what happened, Chicken?" She took off her glasses and lifted the picture to just under her nose. I cringed.

"Yeah. I meant to tell you. I think the heat's on too strong or something. The radiator did that." The heat wasn't on yet—it was barely cold enough outside for a jacket, but I needed a cover-up.

"The radiator?" Mom repeated glumly.

"Yeah, I'm pretty sure."

I hated lying to Mom, but I had no choice. I didn't know how to explain what had actually happened.

The first night one kiss had been enough. The next night it was a kiss and a hug. The night after, I thought if I really wanted to show that I loved Dad most of all and that I truly hadn't wanted him to die, I should make it five kisses and five hugs. Then I made it ten because five was too close to six and six was the devil's number. I didn't really believe in a devil, but still it felt better to do ten kisses, then twenty, then fifty. A few weeks later, I was up to a hundred in the morning and a hundred at night, with pauses for strong hugs at every interval of ten. If I was walking by to pick up a hairbrush or something, I kept it to twenty-five. The skin around my armpits was raw and tender from where the picture frame rubbed and I hoped it would turn pink or purple soon. Visual proof that I was entirely devoted to him and that there was no way I could want or wish him dead.

The only problem was that the frame had no glass in it and the photo paper started turning a strange shade of bronze; pieces of Dad's jacket flaked off. Then his face. And bits of the sky surrounding him. I tried to kiss him more gingerly and give him softer hugs, but then I worried that they wouldn't count. I didn't know how to put the picture back together and every time I stopped to look at it my teeth clamped shut and my neck got tight until I kissed him again. Pretty soon, most of Dad's face and stomach chipped off completely, along with a large chunk of sky. Within two months of his death, all that was left of my father was a jaundiced image of his sunglasses, an arm, and the broken sea behind him.

Mom and I said the Shema, and afterward she picked up the picture again.

"I'm just so . . . ugh. I loved that picture," she moaned, putting it on the bookcase across the room.

"Sorry," I mumbled. "P.D.," I added, thinking maybe she'd get the hint that it was time to go.

"P.D., Chicken."

I listened for Mom's footfalls on the stairs and made sure she was in the kitchen before I snuck over to the bookshelf to plant my kisses. I wanted to be gentle, I really did, but I needed to *feel* that frame through my pj's, in my skin, in my bones. It was the only way I knew how to drive away my racing thoughts about killing him. That night, even a hundred kisses wasn't enough. My breath was jagged and my stomach roiled. I had to find another opening, another way through the clutter of fear churning up from my gut to the back of my throat. Mom had also let me keep a few of Dad's shirts in my closet. I found them now and kissed the sleeves a hundred times each. Then I dug through my dollhouse and found the plastic Charlie Brown figurine that Dad had given me two summers ago. I kissed the figurine and seized Charlie's face to my chest as hard as I could until I could picture him boring into my skin, my rib cage, my lungs, mining through the thicket of worry and guilt all the way to my spine. When I pulled us apart, my arms were stiff and shaking. There was a small divot in my skin from Charlie's plastic nose. A marking. An outlet. I smiled into the night. Tomorrow I would try two hundred.

But two hundred kisses wouldn't solve anything by the time the next day was done.

It was dreadful. Ellyn came to school with a plastic bag holding the Snoopy T-shirt and blue eyeliner I'd given her and told me before fifth period that she needed a break. Our friendship was stifling her and I was needy and possessive and it was all "too much."

"What do you mean, *too much*?"

"Everything. The pinky swears and the notes and the *forever and ever* all the time. And did you tell Tina Fischer that I didn't want to be her friend?"

"No! I mean, not really."

What I'd told Tina (and all the other Munchkins in *The Wiz*) was that they shouldn't try to come between me and Ellyn because we didn't need anyone else besides each other. We were best friends forever and ever and we didn't have time for any other relationships. Ellyn said I had no right dictating how she should live her life and that she needed some space. I begged her to reconsider. I told her I was under a lot of stress and I reminded her of the potential of our magic AbYn potions and burgeoning cosmetics career. I had the only bottle of our product line and what was I supposed to do now, just throw it out?

By the time Mom dropped me off at Dr. M.'s after school I was a mess, dripping snot and tears and trying to explain how unjust Ellyn was. I only wanted someone to stay forever and ever and why was that so much to ask? I would stop copying her handwriting and her walk and I'd grow out my matching haircut if she'd just give me another chance. I told Dr. M. all of this, and she was patient and still, letting me disintegrate in front of her. I thought maybe she would offer to call Ellyn and tell her to take it back because I was a really good friend just going through a rough patch, but she didn't and it just grew sadder and sadder in her office. Even my skin felt worn out from being so hopeless.

Dr. M. waited until I was at the hiccuppy part of the cry and then she said, "What kind of shampoo is it?"

"AbYn? It's just a bunch of different shampoos that we poured into a bottle together. Prell and Finesse mostly. With some cologne too. It smells so good."

"You must really like that shampoo."

"I do. And I made labels for it and a wooden sign in shop class and sometimes I write AbYn on the window next to the shower. You know, in the steam."

"Yeah? That sounds like fun."

"And . . . it sounds stupid, but I kiss it."

I hadn't meant to say it. I didn't know what happened. The words just leaked out of me like drool. At first, I thought maybe admitting it didn't matter. Dr. M. simply nodded and said, "That's nice."

But at my appointment the following week she asked about AbYn some more. I told her the ingredients and measurements. Then she gave me a special smile that she must've reserved for the craziest of her clients as she leaned in and asked coolly, "And do you still enjoy kissing it?"

"I guess."

"Is that something you do every time you take a shower?"

"I don't know."

"How many times would you say you kiss it?"

That's when all the air escaped under her door and my mouth filled with saliva like I was going to throw up. I knew I had committed the most heinous betrayal in telling her about the kisses. All of the rooms in her house poster were looking at me too. The driveways twisting together in intricate snarls. Ellyn was miles away but I was sure that she could hear me and that she'd be disgusted with me—first because I had perverted our product with my slobbery kisses, and also that I was blubbering about it in the crazy wing of a hospital. I wanted to shout at her that she was a selfish princess with too many clothes and no appreciation for show tunes, but my inner rage was even scarier. Maybe I could incur her death too. Even though Dr M.'s clock said 3:42, her office plummeted into a dusky chill.

"Abby? Do you kiss it a lot?"

"No."

"How many times?"

"I don't know. Maybe one or two."

Which had been true at first, but of course now I kissed each clouded windowpane up to twenty-five times and then I had to put my finger in the shampoo bottle and kiss the syrupy mixture too. There was no way I was revealing that to Dr. M. She was probably about to call in the doctors with the restraints any minute. I had to get out to the car and make sure that Mom was okay. This was the biggest secret I'd ever divulged, and I felt like I was deceiving more than just Ellyn. Something awful was going to happen to someone I loved and it would be all my fault. There was no amount of kisses that could wipe away my disgrace. Dr. M. kept smiling patiently, oblivious to it all.

"Do you like to kiss anything else?" she asked softly.

"No!" I squeaked. *Nice try, Doc. I'm not showing you my journal or the picture of my dad's face either.*

"Or say things a certain amount of times?"

I shook my head so fast I got a little seasick.

"It's okay if you do," she said. "It really is."

"Okay. But I don't."

"What are you thinking about?"

"I don't know. Just, I have a lot of math homework tonight."

She nodded again. I nodded back at her. I didn't care that I was lying. I didn't care what she thought. She had no idea what I was capable of. That no one was safe from the power of my deadly thoughts and at that moment I was imagining her in a hospital bed with dripping IVs and colorless lips. I needed to get out of her office fast. I needed to break out of that room and formulate a plan to apologize to Ellyn and to those foggy panes of glass and to the hallowed silence I had broken. I needed to tell Mom and Dad they were my best friends forever and ever and that I never meant to hurt them. But there was no escape. Not even a vein or fissure in those dull gray walls. Just a pile of jigsaw puzzles and a fake window that was mercilessly sealed shut.

superpowers

· ·

After Ellyn dumped me and *The Wiz* was over, I didn't have many friends to hang out with. Still, my afternoons were pretty hectic. I don't know quite when I started working on my collection of dangerous litter, but by Christmas break of seventh grade I had ten paper clips, eighteen pieces of glass, a handful of wood chips, three safety pins, a plastic sword from a cocktail glass, a thumbtack—that was a big find—and about twenty-two nails. Sometimes I counted twenty-three, and then I had to start over, beginning with the paper clips again. I loved math class in school, but counting up my litter pile was different. It wasn't just random numbers. It was a matter of life and death.

Our junior high had a big circular parking lot that was teeming with shards of glass, bicycle spokes, and bobby pins. I'd found a razor blade outside the video store. Once I made it past the crosswalk, there were scattered Hostess cupcake wrappers (that could get caught in an exhaust pipe), empty matchbooks (still highly flammable), and armies of soda bottle caps (jarringly slick under a wheel). If my hands were full by the time I'd reached the mesh garbage cans by the Super Stop & Shop, I'd drop in the wrappers and bottle caps. But I didn't trust those cans with anything sharp or combustible. The pins and glass could easily pierce the garbage bag or shoot through the metal grating.

Every day on my walk home from school, I filled my hands with litter, stuffing all my finds deep into my pockets so they couldn't leak out again. When I was safely home, in my bedroom with the door shut, I counted the pieces up, laying everything out on my radiator. Then I washed my hands in extra-hot water with at least two rounds of soap, because I knew metal and glass carried a lot of germs. Not that I was afraid of getting sick, but if I forgot to wash my hands and then played with the dog or handed Mom a cracker, I could potentially poison them. There were new diseases in the newspaper every day.

Mom didn't like *the hand-washing business,* as she called it. She also didn't care for my dangerous things pile and tried to make me throw it out each night, but I would just collect a new stash the next day. I had a metal trash can, and I tried to empty it regularly so I could hear the heavier objects clink on the bottom when I dropped them in, but the twigs and pointy leaves didn't make much noise. Sometimes I counted everything again while it was in the can. Though they were lying inert on the bottom, I knew disaster was still looming. Those razors and paper clips would never be gone completely. Our garbage was collected on Tuesday and Saturday mornings, and every time I heard the sanitation trucks sputter away, there was even more work to be done. At each bump in the road, the trucks regurgitated more of their load, leaving a thorny trail that I'd have to pick up all over again.

Mom grew increasingly impatient with the piles. I often made her count with me as I dropped each object in the can so I could have a witness to its disposal.

"Come on, Ab. A Band-Aid? That's disgusting."

"I'm going to wash my hands afterward."

"But why can't you just leave it alone?" Her lips creased in a confused pout. I knew my actions didn't make a ton of sense, but I didn't have words to describe what I knew to be true: that every second of every minute of every hour people were dying because of stray Band-Aids and safety pins, forgotten wrappers and overlooked twigs.

I knew this because of Mom, actually. She had explained it to me a few years ago, and now that I had more time by myself, I was finally uncovering some important memories.

I don't know how old I was. It was a summer night—everything earth-shattering and important happened in the summer, as far as I was concerned. This summer night, Dad had come home from work early so the whole family could go to the local pool for a swim. It was my favorite kind of night, the sky wild and reeling with an oncoming thunderstorm and my tongue scratchy from gulping too much chlorine by mistake. After Dad finished his laps, he threw me up into the air again and again and it didn't matter how much I splashed because we had the pool mostly to ourselves. Betsy showed off her new dives from swim team practice and we teased Jon about having a crush on the bouncy-chested lifeguard. Mom said that for a special treat we could pick up a pizza on the way home and I got so excited I snorted pool water up my nose and Mom wrapped me into a green beach towel and said I was her sniffly string bean.

But the whole night cracked in half when we walked out to the parking lot and found that our station wagon had a flat tire. We sat in the crabgrass at the edge of the darkening lot while Dad got the jack and the spare tire out of the trunk and went to work on it. Jon tried to help but he got in the way and it was the first and only time I ever heard my father cursing under his breath. I had to go to the bathroom so badly that Mom told me to pee on the side of a weeping willow.

By the time we picked up the pizza and drove home Dad was in a nasty funk. As he rinsed off the brown-gray sludge from his hands he stained the sink. I wanted to wash my hands next to him but he grumbled, "C'mon, now. Give me a sec, will ya?"

Mom took me aside and said to give Dad some space. She also explained that flat tires could be very upsetting and very dangerous. That's why it was so important not to litter and leave jagged objects in the street where a tire could roll over them and be punctured. It was particularly hazardous if the tear happened while you were driving because it could cause something called a blowout, which was a devastating accident. I asked what does that mean, what kind of devastating? But Mom was too busy setting out napkins and cups to explain any more, and she said everyone should come to the table before dinner got cold. We rarely picked up pizza, so Betsy and Jon raced to the table and the dog was jumping and barking because she thought it was time to play and I wish the memory ended there, but it doesn't.

In my head, a blowout is vicious and fiery. I see the tires, then the metal, then the bodies ripping open. I imagine that inside the car were teenagers on their way to the prom, giggling and singing through piles of hair-sprayed ponytails and taffeta. Or a lone trucker, distracted by a bag of potato chips that won't open; on his flatbed are hundreds of gallons of oil, gas, anything flammable, always flammable. A mother with a pinecone air freshener and her new baby swaddled in the backseat. Or a whole carpool of kids dressed in leotards and tights, fixing their bobby pins.

Even worse is when I see no faces, no skin, just empty seats, still dented from permanently lost limbs. When the sun comes up the next day, those decaying cars are all that is left on the side of the highway, tipped into a patch of flattened scrub. The windows are gone and the air is sore with blood and rust. The mangled human remains have been carried away on stretchers; pulled out in a swirl of lights—red, white, yellow, into the night, howling. And it's the sirens howling but it's also the people howling, begging for one last chance because they are dying and they can't stop it. I can't stop it. There is no beginning or end or even a final horizon to stagger toward, a hope that this could resolve peacefully. The destruction is bottomless and inescapable. There is no length, width, height, depth to measure how far and how devastating it can become. There is no way to hold it in.

After pizza it was bedtime and I was scared that Dad still needed his space, so I told Mom to kiss him good night for me and also to say I was sorry that I'd gotten in the way.

"Don't worry about it, Chicken," she said.

"But it was good that the flat tire happened while we were parked and not while we were driving, right?"

"Yeah, I guess so."

"A blowout is worse than just a flat tire, right?"

"I suppose. But neither of them are fun."

I needed to ask her more about how often blowouts happened, what kind of damage could occur, which tires were the soundest investment, and how much time there would be to yell between the actual point of contact and the fatal rupture of all life inside? But as I debated where to begin, Mom was leaning in to kiss me on the forehead and then heading toward the door.

"The Shema!" I insisted.

"We just did it, Chicken. Come on, it's late."

"Only close the door halfway," I reminded her feebly, so I could see the triangle of light from the hallway sketched into my floor.

It didn't matter. As I lay there in the stippled dark, everything was detonating inside me again.

I see it still. The stretch of highway where everything collides and breaks in a thousand directions. The spot where the tire rolls over a nail, a crescent of glass, a razor blade. Misshapen paper clip. Hairball. It doesn't matter what. Only how. It skewers the rubber tire side-walls, splitting open treads and chewing through the inner lining, as if it were loose taffy. The car swiveling in a spasmodic, deadly dance. The passengers veer and spin, bucking on a demonic roller coaster.

Maybe there are three children in the backseat, like in my family. A father who is sturdy and honorable and usually a steady driver. A mother who is humming bits of a concerto strung loosely into a new melody when she hears a *pooooosh*.

There's a loud hiss as the car and the night are simultaneously impaled or it may also be completely silent—faster than the speed of sound. The crash is appallingly quick and in slow motion at the same time. It rips through all the stars and all the nights that ever were. Even though the driver is smooth and cool and a good father and he's supposed to be in charge. Even though they worked so hard on those jungle-themed prom decorations and his delivery of flamma-ble materials is due in Des Moines in less than an hour. The gasoline explodes; the corsages erupt; the conflagration eats all the taffeta, air fresheners, and bobby-pinned buns in a single flamey gulp. Every-one and everything snaking, lurching, crashing into this rudderless, gravityless, too-deadly-to-survive blowout.

Every time I tried to step around a staple or a broken pencil in the street, I saw another lifeless face tipped up into the flashing lights. Each time I walked the dog, I found more life-threatening trash. Needles, broken buttons, and pinecones creeping out of the cracks in the sidewalk, bubbling up from the curbs and gutters. And if I walked by without doing anything, the next tire that rolled by could be zooming toward its end. I saw those frozen stares, the windshields splintered and bloodied. One evening I circled the block three times. The streets revealed glints of metal and glass, winking at me treach-erously. I kept stopping to scrape at a square of cement that looked particularly threatening. I knew it would come loose and tear into the next car that drove over the hill. By the time I got home, I'd grazed a hole in my fuzzy white glove and the tip of my middle finger was five different shades of blue. Mom made me put it under the faucet and my whole arm was shaking and she said it was frostbite and what was I doing out there for so long?

"Just walking!" I moaned, even though I knew she wouldn't be fooled by me. I tenderly kissed my injured finger all night, secretly delighted and ennobled. It was better than the ripped piece of cloth Rabbi Poller had fastened to my chest for my father's funeral. A true medal of honor for suffering and service.

Mom wanted me to tell Dr. M. about the hand washing and the litter stockpiles, but I told her I didn't have time. Mostly when I went to see Dr. M., I talked about homework or how Ellyn was still more popular than me. I tried to speak rapidly so Dr. M. wouldn't just sit and look at me, but sometimes I ran out of things to say. A couple of times she asked if I had any more memories of Dad to share yet and I told her he was a good driver and one time I got to ride in the backseat by myself after the circus. But I couldn't say more than that because all the cars I envisioned were swerving and imploding, choking me with their burnt exhaust. Each time I visited Dr. M., Mom rewarded me with an egg cream or Peppermint Patties from the hospital gift shop. But I still felt wretched the entire way home, the sugar and sirens hurtling together inside me.

I didn't know why everything had to be so complicated and hazardous. One night my mother caught me kissing the four nails, two leaves, and eight paper clips I'd dug out of my jeans pocket. I hoped kissing them would ensure their safe end. This time Mom's face went from mad to crumpled. She held out her hand so I could put the items in it. Then she held me while I cried.

"Abidab. You're not in charge of the whole world, you know that?"

I wanted her to be right, but her words couldn't unravel the clamor in my chest. She couldn't take away those cars from the side of the road. I wept for her and for me and especially for all the litter that I'd left behind.

"Oh, Chicken. What if I call Dr. M. and tell her for you?"

"No, I'll do it," I bleated into her chest.

The following week, I waited until there were only five minutes left of my session before offering a rehearsed yawn and casually tossing out, "Oh, yeah. I guess I told my mom that I would tell you I like to pick up stuff sometimes."

Of course Dr. M. had a million questions—what kind of stuff? How often? Where? Why? When?

"Just stuff. You know. Sometimes." I was furious at Mom and at Dr. M. for acting as if saying it aloud was going to solve anything. It didn't. It only made me want to go outside and tip the entire street into my mouth and swallow every last pin until my insides were shredded.

"Thank you for telling me this, Abby," she said. "Let's keep talking about this next week, okay?"

Next week was significantly worse. Dr. M. was exasperatingly inquisitive and thorough. She wanted to know why a paper clip was dangerous and I had to describe how even the smallest piece of metal or plastic could spear the most resilient tire.

"What about the things on the sidewalk?" she persisted. I knew it sounded illogical, but I had to map out the path of any unsuspecting pedestrian as he slipped or stabbed himself in the foot and then wound up in the street. A driver could come around the corner too quickly. The routes to undeserved and cataclysmic death were infinite and I didn't know why she was making me go through them all but I was definitely not coming back here next week.

"Do you feel better after you pick these things up?" she asked.

"I don't know." I hated her and I was done talking.

"Or do you feel like you need to pick up more?" she prodded. I stared blankly past her at the sealed window.

And then Dr. M. gave me the greatest gift I could imagine.

"You know, I have another patient who likes to pick up things. She also sometimes says little prayers. Do you pray at all?"

I shrugged.

"Well, this other patient of mine, when she hears an ambulance go by, she says a little prayer so that everything comes out all right. What do you think of that?"

"That's . . . nice?" I said, barely able to contain myself.

"I just thought you might like to know there are other people who think about these things like you."

I walked out of her office determined and breathless. Marched right past the gift shop and waved victoriously to the nurse at the front desk. This was the escape hatch I'd been searching for. This was the answer. It was the greatest homework assignment ever and nobody else knew about it except for me. I felt as if I'd just been knighted or bestowed with the most fearsome superpowers. I was slightly ashamed I hadn't thought of the ambulance prayer myself—it seemed so fundamental, so crucial. But there was no time to wallow in the past anymore. I had to start praying for those ambulances. I finally had a chance to rescue everyone and everything from their unforeseeable and irreversible demise; from all those shards of glass I hadn't picked up yet and all those looming garbage cans. I could pray for those hollowed cars and faces. Instead of fearing the spinning lights I could carry them forward. I could save everyone and everything.

I chose these words: *I hope you get there in time.*

I hope you get there in time. I hope you get there in time. I hope you get there in time. I hope you get there in time.

I would whisper this twenty-five times. I chose the number twenty-five because I could do five repetitions for each finger, an odd number for each finger and an odd number in total. I didn't trust even numbers anymore. They all seemed to add to or be divisible by six. I made sure my words were enunciated perfectly so the message was clear.

No matter where I was, what I was doing, saying, eating, thinking. *I hope you get there in time. I hope you get there in time. I hope you get there in time. I hope you get there in time. I hope you get there in time.* First I said it whenever I saw an ambulance. Then police cars and fire engines. Whenever I heard sirens in the distance or saw those warning flashes of red in the sky. My words ushered them forward quickly, smoothly, safely. In time to save the day. To put out the fire, stanch the blood, pry open the doors, pump air back into stone-cold lungs. I had to say these words. It was that simple. That immediate and imperative and binding. I whispered fiercely, full of purpose and righteous resolve.

If I didn't say them . . .

The tire explodes.

Steering wheel crushes ribs, spleen, kidneys.

Everyone and everything gobbled in unforgiving flames.

He is dead, she is dead, it is dead, there is blood and fire and screaming and ruin.

Saving them was up to me. It was my responsibility. My mission. My reason for being.

WHAT NEEDS TO BE KISSED
AND HOW MANY TIMES LIST

1. G-d's name (twenty times each time it appears any-where on any page . . . textbooks, library books, newspapers, magazines. ANYWHERE. If it's not hyphenated, see if I can take it home so it doesn't get thrown out)
2. AbYn shampoo (twenty-five times before each use)
3. Daddy's picture (one hundred times anytime I go past it)
4. Mezuzah (Jewish prayer scroll that's on the door as I come into our house—one hundred times any-time going in or out)
5. Prayer book (one hundred times after each use, one hundred more anytime it is accidentally dropped)
7. Sharp objects (ten times each before placing them in garbage)
8. Bicycle (one hundred times before locking it up at each destination)
10. Mom's or Dad's sheet music (twenty times any-time I come across it)
11. Pictures of Yul Brynner (same)
12. Air kisses (twenty times each) for funeral homes, synagogues, anyone with a yarmulke, anyone who looks handicapped or retarded

sue simmons cannot be trusted

The rabbi kept my father on the Dearly Departed list for an entire year after his death. Mom and I went to services at least once a month—Betsy was too adamant about her agnosticism and too engrossed with field hockey and her newest boyfriend to be bothered. Which was just as I wanted it—that meant more sorry attention to be lavished on me and Mom after the Kaddish. Terry Jaffey said I was so mature and graceful that we could pass for twins. Slow-motion Beverly sidled up to offer both of us butter cookies off her plate. It felt good, especially when someone from my Hebrew school class had to come over with their mom to say how sorry they were. I acted like it was no biggie. I'd read Anne Frank and watched Mom put on her fake smiles and frilly tops enough to know that true martyrs were silent in their misery. If the person offering condolences was someone like Suzy Marks, who was normally too popular to talk to me, I liked to say, "Don't be *sorry*. You didn't kill him." I thought it made me look pretty tough and clever and nobody knew what to say to me after that.

My own DD list kept growing. I had to add to it practically every day because people were dying all around me:

1. Yul Brynner. After Yul Brynner died, Mom sat me down and read his obituary out loud from the paper. It was one of the few nights I can recall wishing my sister was there to divert some of Mom's attention from me. She showed me his picture and asked if I'd ever seen such an exotic hero, all the while shaking her head at his crazy eyebrows and hoop earrings. During supper, she listed Yul's important film and theater credits. He was Russian, like her parents,

and he was one of very few people to ever win a Tony and an Academy Award for the same role. Most important, she said, he was a smoker and that was his fatal mistake.

"It's just not fair," she growled. Then she lowered her voice to tell me that my father had made a deal with her that he would try to live as long as Yul Brynner did. I wasn't sure if it was unfair because Dad didn't hold up his end of the deal or because they were both dead now. Either way, she blinked hurriedly while she sipped the end of her scotch. The rest of the night she hummed "Shall We Dance?" Mom's humming was usually similar to Dad's whistling—it started in one song and then slipped into another and often it climbed from marches to waltzes to the anthem for the eleven o'clock news. But that night it just looped over and over again, back to the King of Siam.

2. Mr. Hughes. Mr. Hughes had lived next door to us since before I was born. I named my first teddy bear after him. He was as thin as a telephone pole and almost as tall and loved to talk about life before the Model T and how when Hurricane Gloria blew through our town he trooped down to our local harbor and helped pull in the dinghies that were hurling themselves against the rocks. Mom said he'd outlive us all. But a few weeks later he was gone and I kissed my teddy bear a lot after Mom told me so that Mr. Hughes would know I loved and missed him. I tried not to look up as I passed his house in the morning, its face pockmarked with empty windows, its hedges thirsty and forsaken.

3. Mr. Pultz. Mr. Pultz was one of my teachers from grade school who got brain cancer and when I saw him downtown his face was swollen and pink and he was sweating all over his shirt. He tried to keep teaching through the year but he had to go home one day and die.

4. The Robbins family from the pool. The Robbins were in a tragic car accident, and two cousins, a brother, and an aunt died. Mike Robbins was in my grade and he survived, but he got burns up and down his arms so he came to the pool just to sit with his mom. He couldn't join the swim team or wear a bathing suit the whole summer. I tried not to stare at him when we were both standing on line for French fries, but I wondered how many ambulances his family needed and I was mortified that I hadn't been there to whisper at them.

5. Mr. Diamond. I was taking piano lessons from a different

teacher by the time Mr. Diamond died, but still I dreamed of finding him in that chair, fading in the afternoon sun. I hope he died listening to his favorite composer, Chopin.

7. This girl from the high school named Mara, who didn't wake up one morning and it turned out she had Addison's disease. When Mara died, they played a sleepy song over the loudspeaker instead of morning announcements and told us we could talk to counselors if we wanted.

8. Mrs. Ashner. Mrs. Ashner's death was a rough one. Mom knew Mrs. Ashner from the synagogue Sisterhood. She was extremely attractive and British, and her kids were in the grade above me and below me, and one day she went to pick up her husband at the train station after work the way we all did. But a storm was gathering off the coast and a tree fell down and smashed her car and Mr. Ashner got off the train and waited and waited but she wasn't there because she was dead. When Mom told me about Mrs. Ashner I started laughing out loud. Then I kept on telling Mom I was sorry and I didn't know what was wrong with me. I wasn't laughing *at* Mrs. Ashner's being dead but I wasn't sure what I was laughing at and maybe if I could laugh it meant I wanted her dead too. I begged for Mom's forgiveness over and over again and she said it was okay but I knew it wasn't.

10. Christa McAuliffe. I was on my way to Mrs. Troy's history class when the *Challenger* burst apart in the sky. Larry, this kid in my class who was really overweight and not that popular, was running through the hall yelling, "The spaceship blew up! The spaceship blew up!"

A lot of people told Larry to shut up and that he wasn't funny but it was *really* not funny because it was true. For the rest of the day and the week we watched the replays of the sky splitting open; the cumulus of death with billowy tentacles cascading all over the globe. People as far away as England crying into their tea at the smoke and devastation and everybody so sad, especially for Christa McAuliffe, because she thought she was just going on a ride. And we watched the TV in class and stayed very solemn and it was sad, but I have to admit that even though it was pretty selfish, I was kind of mad at Christa. Because she was definitely more of a martyr than me. She'd made it onto a worldwide DD list and was getting all this adulation and I wanted to say *Oh yeah? Well, my father died and so did my aunt and so did Yul Brynner and no we're not related but my dad and he were having a who-can-live-longer contest and they both lost.*

On November 22, 1986, I got to be a celebrity. At least in the Jewish world. I had my Bat Mitzvah, which meant I was officially a Jewish woman, but basically meant I wore a fancy black dress with a lace collar that looked like a neck brace and I got a bunch of treasury bonds and a locket with a butterfly on it. I also led most of the service, including the Torah part, and then I had to give a speech. The speech is what scared me the most. I knew that I needed to say something praising G-d. The synagogue was His house, after all. I had been feeling particularly nervous about G-d lately. I didn't understand why so many people were dying and I no longer thought it was because of something bad they did. It was something I'd done. Under my labyrinth of paper clips and soda bottle tops was a naked fear that gripped me as I watched Christa and her crew die, over and over again. I didn't know how exactly, but I was responsible for each of these additions to the Dearly Departed. I still hadn't told anyone about possibly willing my father to death, but I knew G-d could hear and see the whole thing. He saw all my venomous thoughts, all my overlooked litter, and I didn't know how to ask Him for forgiveness. I would do anything to make Him happy.

My Bat Mitzvah speech was about never having to fear because G-d will provide. I said that my father had died just a little while ago and that even though I was sad, I knew The Big Guy would take care of me and my family. I puffed out my lace-covered chest and spoke as loudly as I could. I needed Him to hear my declaration of love and devotion. I was so relieved when the speech part was over, I almost clapped for myself. After the service, all of the adults blew their noses and told me I was very brave. Then we went to the beach club, where my mom threw me a party with limbo and pizza bagels and two girls in my class got caught smoking cigarettes in the phone booth. My cousin Steve sang a song just for me about climbing new mountains and then Mom gave a toast saying how proud she was of me. I was fairly certain He was pleased too.

But a few weeks after I announced my loyalty to Him, my DD list took a horrible turn:

11. The lady in the Finast parking lot.

Her death is harder to explain. Mostly because it keeps recurring right behind my eyes; her final breath still drawing me into its wake. Her abrupt ending wholly defines the pre-existing condition of being me.

Mom and I were doing errands in town. It was a Saturday, so the post office and the cleaners were fairly crowded, and I was dreading running into someone from school because I should've been doing something cooler like hanging out at Cook's arcade or smoking on the Bonnie Briar golf course. I only had a handful of girls I could call friends, and we rarely saw one another outside of class or band rehearsal (I'd halfheartedly taken up the flute). Betsy and her friends were experimenting with either drugs, guitar riffs, or both. Mom had become the only person I felt comfortable spending time with, and we had grown almost inseparable. She didn't care that my hair was a cloud of frizz and that I still didn't have boobs or my period. Plus, whenever I tried to pick up litter she caught me and said, "C'mon, Ab."

And I usually said something like, "But there's a broken bottle . . ."

"Enough!" she would snap, and I loved it when she yanked me up by the elbow too. Somehow it jostled my brain into a momentary lull, shutting off my mental static like an Etch A Sketch that only she knew how to sweep clean.

But the day I killed the woman in the Finast parking lot, there was nothing Mom could say or do that could erase what I'd done.

It was a simple crime. Almost untraceable. Mom and I had just finished getting groceries. We loaded up the car and then Mom asked me to put the empty grocery cart in the metal cage with all the others. A woman in a blue Subaru was rounding the aisle of cars at the same time. I saw her, but she didn't see me. I left the grocery cart and walked away.

A mess of wire baskets. A *PennySaver* caught under a rusting wheel. I feel the cool of the plastic handle even now. I could've made sure that the cart was firmly anchored with the others, but I didn't. In fact, I didn't even give it a shove so it could hook on to another wheel or bump up against the guardrail. I just let it go.

And as I turned around, I knew without looking what would happen next. I felt my cart coming unmoored from the pack, working its way out, inching slowly backward. It was just a matter of moments before the blue Subaru was in striking distance. Just long enough for the cart to gain momentum and then crash into the driver side door. Metal ripping through metal, fiberglass, steel, velour seating, flesh.

I stayed icily composed as I walked back to Mom's car. I waited until we had passed two stoplights before I told her that I'd just caused a devastating accident. As bad as a blowout. Worse.

"What? How?"

I described the crash with lots of *um*'s and *I think*'s, but they were just for show. I knew exactly what I was talking about. The whole scene was hideously detailed, scored into my retinas in full, precise colors and shadows. I didn't secure the cart carefully. It rolled back just as a car was approaching. The woman in the blue Subaru wasn't looking. Why should anyone be on the lookout for a stray grocery cart?

She had no time to get out of the way. She was so startled that she lost control of her wheel and plowed into a steel pole. She could be dying right now, I told Mom. *She* is *dying right now. We need to turn around and go back to Finast.*

Mom was sure it would be fine. She patted my knee and hummed while steering us home, looking straight ahead. Or, not exactly straight ahead because she shook her head ever so slightly from side to side. She'd been doing this a lot lately—especially when she was driving. Her hair sprayed out from the nape of her neck like a duck's plume while she wobbled back and forth. As if she was trying to see everything at once. Or maybe she was saying *No no no no no.*

"Please, Mom? Can we please go back and see?"

She said I was just imagining things. If I had actually caused an accident we would have heard it. I wanted so badly to believe her, but I just couldn't stop seeing that woman's permed hair, her sunglasses thrust back into the flesh of her cheeks, her jaw wrenched unnaturally over her right shoulder. The farther we got from the parking lot, the more the picture came into focus, its edges and textures, its sky. Mom asked how this could happen in such a short space of time.

"I don't know," I groaned. "But it did."

We were in our driveway now. The engine was off. But Mom was still shaking her head, and I was too, trying to knock this dying lady, the sirens and blood out of my skull.

"We have to go back." Really, I wanted to run as far as I could away from there, give myself a new name, reconstruct my face and my past, and live in quiet unknowing on a forgotten hillside in Mexico or Montana.

"Please," I begged, not only of Mom but of the deafening swarm of ambulances collecting in my mind's eye. Mom told me to help her take in the groceries, and then we could figure out what to do.

We carried in packages full of meat, milk, juice, eggs. Mom said, "Make sure to put the carrots in the drawer," and "Look at that. We already had sour cream. Oh well, just let's make sure to use the old one first."

She acted as though she wasn't standing next to a murderer.

We sat down in the kitchen with cups of mint tea and she asked me to tell her the story again, which I did, slower now, surer. Mom listened to the whole thing without interrupting, which made it even worse. She folded her eyebrows together, trying to see what I saw too.

"I'm sure it's okay, Chicken," she said at the end, reaching for my clenched hands. "Even if it rolled backward, it—"

"I'm pretty sure it did."

"Even so."

"It did! It *did*!"

"Okay, let's say it did, it couldn't have been fast enough to kill someone."

"But how can you be sure?" I insisted.

"It would have to go very fast."

"It was going very fast."

"Well . . ." Her head shook more vehemently now. I wanted her to have an answer, I really did. But then my mother let go of my palms and asked me the worst question of all:

"If you thought the shopping cart could be loose, why didn't you go back and push it in again, Chicken?"

Her words still feel ominous and unanswerable as I watch that woman dying over and over again. *Why did you do this? What did she ever do to you?* I continue to see the steering column goring the unsuspecting woman through her stomach, her insides spilling out while her family waits for their groceries at home.

"I should've gone back," I wailed miserably. "I should've!"

"Okay, shhhhh," said Mom. "You're still my little girl and no matter what happened, I love you. Hey, how about some turkey salad?"

"I can't . . ." I couldn't accept her complacency. I couldn't shrug off this woman's disfigured form.

"Then how about this?" Mom gently offered. "We'll turn on the local news in a few hours, and if something bad happened, we'll hear about it."

Somehow this suggestion quieted me for the rest of the afternoon. I'd always trusted Sue Simmons, the pretty anchor lady on our local NBC newscast. If anyone could find the truth and exonerate me, Sue could. I made my mother promise to watch Sue Simmons and read the newspaper cover-to-cover for the whole week. Mom swore she would. Each morning she reported that I was still clear of any wrongdoing.

But Mom and Sue Simmons couldn't stop anything. Not the nightly visitations from that grocery cart. Not the shriek of metal scraping and the permed hair stuck together in bloody coils.

Worst of all, they couldn't stop me. The rest of eighth grade was a gruesome spree of unresolved crimes and senseless murders. I made sure to look harmless in my corduroy shorts and braces, but in my heart and mind I was ruthless and bloodthirsty. I slinked home through the streets after school, my fists heavy with daggers of glass, rusty thumbtacks, and safety pins caked with dried mud. Stuffed with my dirty secrets.

I trampled baby birds, poisoned squirrels, and sent a lady in a down vest running into the street by Tony's Nursery so she could be plowed down by a minivan. Another day it was a Hispanic boy wearing a Walkman. I shoved him into the crosswalk just as an armada of eager cars raced over the hill. Then I walked away as quickly and naturally as possible so no one could suspect me. All the while depositing a trail of razor blades and cocktail swords to stab the next unfortunate tire or foot.

Behind sealed lips I was constantly screaming racial epithets at black people and grabbing walkers and wheelchairs from anyone impaired, cackling as I announced that they would die soon. I walked past the highway and smiled at the fractured windshields and gnarled bodies. I poisoned dogs that were sleeping in their backyards and I stomped on flightless animals. When I ran across the street, two cars behind me swerved and collided and I heard sirens but I kept running. Only it was never fast enough to escape the parade of angry dead faces that roved through my brain. I didn't mean to kill them and I didn't know whether I in fact *had* killed them, but I couldn't see past their twisted faces and broken necks. Their last gasps strangling me. When I got home I would lock all the doors, trying to barricade myself from the leering corpses. I scoured my hands and face under searing hot water, but still I couldn't wash clean.

By the time Mom returned from work, I would be crippled with fear and remorse. We would sit on the blue couch in the living room while I listed everyone I had killed that day. Mom called it the *confessional*. Besides the squirrels, birds, vest lady, and Walkman boy, I'd also crushed a poodle on Maple Hill Drive. I yelled *Ugly! Fat! Black! Retard!* at people waiting for the traffic light by St. John's and Paul's. Then I ran into Murray Avenue just as a car was coming and laughed as it careened into a white picket fence in order to avoid hitting me.

"All right, all right," Mom would intone, pulling my hair from my face, trying to still me. She would unbutton her ruffled blouse so we could both breathe better. We sat on the couch as the night sank around us. I listed my sins mournfully, my whole body shuddering. Mom listened to it all, her hands thick and warm rubbing the small of my back.

"I stole candy from the drugstore caramel bins."

Mom sighed. "I'm sure you didn't mean to."

"I cheated on my English test and rammed a girl into her locker."

"Ssssh. It's okay. Really."

"I had sex in the back of the video store."

"Really?" She sucked in her lower lip and I didn't know whether she was about to laugh or cry. "With whom?" she asked slowly.

"Someone you don't know."

"Well, did you like it?"

"That's not the point!" Didn't she know that I was only thirteen and I shouldn't be having sex and cheating on tests and mowing people down in halls and parking lots? I was baffled and horrified by her nonchalance.

"Well, listen, Chicken. I need to get going on supper, so . . ."

"Wait!" I whimpered.

"What? What?!" She was becoming weary and exasperated. We were both so helpless.

"Never mind," I said, releasing her.

"There's more. Just so you know," I muttered when I knew she couldn't hear me.

After a while, Mom gave up on arguing with me, even when I had to restart my confessions in order to fill in the gory details. She just rubbed my back and shook her head. She vowed daily to study the papers and watch the nightly news.

"But Sue Simmons doesn't know the whole story!" I protested. Every once in a while, when I was too frantic to speak, Mom drew me in to her bosom and murmured, "Really, Ab. You're just not that powerful."

Which soothed me for a breath or two, but I knew better than to attach myself to this brief respite. Soon the fixed march of cadavers would invade again and I had no way to silence them. Nobody knew the evil I was capable of, including myself.

Every Wednesday after school, Mom drove me to see Dr. M. Ever since she'd cajoled me into telling her about kissing the shampoo bottle, I was extra cautious about what I told her. I had the feeling that if I listed everyone I'd killed, even more people would die. Not to mention, she'd have to report me to the police.

Occasionally, though, I couldn't help it and I blurted out that I thought I *might've* caused an accident, and she caught me in conversation loops that made me dizzy.

"You *might* have?"

"I'm pretty sure I did."

"Do you think it really happened or are you maybe imagining?"

"I think it really happened."

"You know that for sure?"

"Well, I'm pretty sure and I think so. Yeah."

"You're *pretty* sure? Or you *know*?"

Everything I said seemed like a flimsy alibi and none of Dr. M.'s words could come near the thrumming and thrashing in my chest as I envisioned the hospital parking lot where I'd left pins under ambulance tires and lit matches in exhaust pipes. It was easy for Dr. M. to sit there with her flawless skin and her poster of hypnotic houses on the wall and ask these questions as if they were simple math equations. Her experience of this real or imagined massacre ended in forty-five minutes and she didn't have to go home with the stink of death in her hair. But for me, there was no right or wrong answer and no way to bury these slain bodies and no way to prove that I was innocent or guilty. That was what I hated the most about my path of destruction—I was the only one who knew the true story and so it was up to me to decide what had really happened. The more I foraged through the wreckage for answers, the louder the sirens screamed, the thicker the blood ran toward me. And I couldn't say *I hope you get there in time. I hope you get there in time. I hope you get there in time. I hope you get there in time. I hope you get there in time* fast enough. I couldn't sing the songs "White Christmas" and "My Heart Belongs to Daddy" (my newest additions) soulfully enough on my walks with the dog. Often I devolved into a refrain of *I'm sorry* and *Please forgive me*. I chanted it in multiples of five as I trudged around the block again, searching for spiky pebbles and sharply notched leaves.

I wasn't sure if I was repeating these things for my father, because his death was my fault; for my mom, who kept my vicious secrets safe and because it was only a matter of time before I subtly murdered her, too; to my steadily multiplying mass of dead bodies, to Sue Simmons, or to G-d.

Now I knew this for certain:

G-d has been here the whole time, watching me. He is hovering just above the thickening trees in our backyard. Creating sparks in my bedsheets at night. He conducts all of the oceans to match the moon's pull. He is the Grand Designer of those squiggles and polka dots in my wallpaper. He is inside every pink branch and each speckled blue leaf leading up to His home base in the sky. He is propelling the ambulances forward so they *get there in time get there in time get there in time*. He is inside the wheels of every shopping cart. He and

He alone knows my capacity for cruelty, and I have to prove to Him that I am really trying to be a good girl and I didn't mean to hurt anyone and beg Him to please give me another chance to make up for all the sins I have committed and vow to Him that I love Him the most always. Always and forever. Forever and always. Amen.

Amen.

Amen.

PRAYER FOR DIET COKE*

Ba-ruch a-tah A-do-nai, E-lo-hei-nu me-lech ha-o-lam, bo-rei pe-ri ha Diet Coke.

Blessed is the Lord our God, Ruler of the universe, Creator of the fruit of the Diet Coke.

*Must be repeated in Hebrew and in English every time Diet Coke is drunk.
**It helps to say it in front of someone else so I can make sure I'm saying it correctly.
***If I don't say it correctly, must do it again until I get it right.

walter's world-famous hot dog stand

Walter's hot dog stand was world famous. It was on Palmer Avenue in Mamaroneck and it was impossible to miss because it was shaped like a Chinese pagoda and there was always a long line outside its *Order Here* window. Postcards from loyal customers were taped to the greasy tiles along the side of the counter.

> *Dear Walter's, came all the way to Brussels but still couldn't find a wiener half as good as yours!*

> *Dear Walter's, Monica and I are trekking through Bali. Can't believe the sky here! Send relish!*

> *Dear Walter's, so if I swear on all that is holy not to tell, what's the special ingredient?!*

Everyone knew Walter's toasted and buttered their buns, split the dogs in half, and broiled them over an open flame. The secret was in the mustard—they had some recipe that Walter himself or maybe some Chinese monk passed down long ago and that no one who worked at Walter's was allowed to tell.

Walter's happened to be right across the street from a big hill and on top of the hill was Mamaroneck High School, where I started my freshman year on a deceptively clear-skied day in 1987.

Even though MHS (that's what everyone called it) was only a few blocks down from the junior high, it felt galaxies apart. Or maybe it was just that I was so different. I didn't blow-dry my hair or wear turquoise eyeliner anymore. I had given up trying to be in the popular crowd. Sometimes I saw my sister smoking by the wooden gazebo or the performing-arts crowd laughing in their paint-splattered jeans and leotards and I felt incredibly lonely and dull. But I also knew that my purpose on earth was much larger and if I didn't accept my calling, countless lives would be lost.

I had to pray.

After the Finast slaying, it took me months to realize that neither Mom nor Dr. M. could absolve me as I continued to sin. The only one who could possibly offer salvation was the Redeemer. One morning in the summer before ninth grade, I sat cross-legged in my closet with the door shut tight, kissed my Sisterhood prayer book ten times, and began. The first prayers I offered to Him were ones I knew from synagogue. The Shema. The Eliyahu. The Kaddish. I said them each three times. Then five times. Three and five were good numbers. Nobody could get hurt from them—I hoped. Then I recited my list of people who were currently sick or in need. Mr. Merrobs, who'd broken his elbow and then it turned out to be brittle bones because he had cancer. The girl in my grade who had Lyme disease and couldn't leave her house and was possibly going blind. Aunt Doris, who was forgetting words and falling a lot. Mom's friend Kay, who had something wrong with her lungs.

Please let them heal completely painlessly soon.

Did that sound like painfully?

Completely painlessly soon.

Maybe that was too dramatic. I didn't mean *less* soon. I meant less *pain*. But *very soon*. As soon as possible. *Completely painlessly soon. Please.*

I went back to the beginning to make sure I hadn't made the words confusing or offensive to G-d in any way. I was petrified of making Him mad or accidentally praying for someone to perish. I was responsible for the health and well-being of all these people, and the lists kept getting longer. I also needed to pray for people who were traveling.

Uncle Murray and Cousin Steve and Helena's dad and Mom's friend Lynn. May they return safely soundly happily healthfully.

I tried to always end my prayers by asking for forgiveness.

Please forgive me for all my transgressions. Please forgive me for fighting with Betsy and for taking Your name in vain and I'm sorry if that lady by the gas station got hurt please do not let her get hurt I'm so sorry. Please forgive me. I'm sorry. Please forgive me.

I hoped He was listening. I didn't need any signs or miracles. I just knew that I had a lot for which I needed to atone. I also knew that if I didn't say the prayers right or enough times, someone else was going to die too. Whenever I wasn't praying, I was killing people with my storehouses of thumbtacks and lethal thoughts.

I was determined to keep my newfound faith secret. Betsy was busy with field hockey practice and college applications, so she never noticed the blockades I set up in front of my closet door. At night, I continued cataloging for Mom the pettier crimes I was sure I'd committed, like stealing and cheating, but my murders I saved for the sanctity of my inner chamber confessionals. Only Mom must have figured it out—she started repeatedly knocking on my door just as I was counting out my Shemas. First I tried pretending I wasn't in my room at all, but then she barged in, and after a few weeks of this routine I ran out of excuses for why I was on the closet floor. Even saying His name out loud in front of Mom felt blasphemous and scary. Mom said it was okay to pray as long as it made me feel better and didn't interfere with my schoolwork. She called my prayers *quiet time*—as in, "Don't bother your sister right now, she's doing *quiet time*." I told my sister she was not allowed to mention *quiet time* to anyone. She told me I was "high maintenance."

I couldn't let my mother or my sister know the scope of my responsibilities. More and more people were traveling or getting sick or dying and I had to keep track of them. I couldn't write down any of the names I prayed for, either, because someone could find my words and I didn't think He'd want it known that He was cutting a deal with a mortal; bestowing life-saving powers on a girl from the suburbs who could only say *peace, table,* and *Shut up, children* in Hebrew. Everything about my prayers felt terrifyingly potent. My feverish utterances channeled directly to His ears. He who is All-Powerful and All-Knowing, providing manna from heaven and parting the seas for Moses and giving us music, especially the reverberating minor chords of the synagogue organ. I had begun to hear these chords even when I wasn't in His house. Especially when I was scared I'd mispronounced *completely* or *painlessly,* sentencing another innocent to a life of pain or a torturous demise. I heard these chords as a swelling funeral dirge, shaking the earth to its core with its unremitting sorrow.

I had to get it right or else Aunt Doris and Kay would surely die.

I repeated it. And repeated it.

Completely painlessly soon. Completely painlessly soon. Hear, O Israel, the Lord is Our God, the Lord is One! Blessed is His glorious kingdom forever and ever! Forever and ever! (Sometimes I said that one louder too, because it sounded a little bit like *never* and I didn't want to make that mistake.)

Sorry. I meant Forever and ever always. Always *forever and* always *ever forever* always. *Thank You, Amen.*

Sometimes it didn't matter how many times I started over and how careful I was with my enunciation. No matter how many times I parsed each syllable, I still couldn't stop myself from killing.

On the first day of high school, I set the alarm clock for 6 a.m. so I'd have plenty of time to pray slowly and thoroughly. I had to repeat them again and again that day, because I was distracted by thoughts of navigating the new halls without tripping or maiming anyone. By the time I went downstairs, my mother wasn't happy. There was no time for me to eat breakfast.

"This is how you're going to start your high school career? On an empty stomach? Your sister already left. I tried calling up for you but I guess you didn't hear me."

"Sorry."

Of course I had heard her, but I didn't tell her this because I was afraid that maybe I had stopped in the middle of prayers when she'd yelled and if I had stopped, then I should go back upstairs and start over again. But Mom was handing me my backpack and forcing me out the door and all I could do was hope that I had said all the prayers I was supposed to say and that G-d wasn't mad at me.

I quickly decided that my favorite class was going to be English with Dr. Scaladino. I was almost two inches taller than him, mostly because he pitched forward awkwardly as if his brain weighed too much for his spindly neck. He had us take turns reading "The Love Song of J. Alfred Prufrock" out loud. Then he wrote two lines on the board:

Rosy-fingered Dawn

Rosy fingered Dawn

And he said, "Can anyone tell me why hyphenation is so important?"

Once I figured it out, it was pretty hilarious. I'd always been a big fan of hyphens.

I had plans to meet Jessica at Walter's hot dog stand for rolls with mustard—hold the dogs—at lunch. Whoever got there first after the lunch bell rang had to save a spot on line. Jessica and I had met in social studies last year and we were in five out of eight classes together this year, too, which I was grateful for, despite the fact that she got 100 percent on all of her tests. She was a good friend to have because she was kind and thoughtful. Plus she was Conservative Jewish and kept kosher at home. I could learn a thing or two from her. I knew her family said prayers over their food at the dinner table, so at lunch I asked her what the proper Hebrew would be for a prayer over Diet Coke and rolls with mustard.

"Just—hypothetically," I added. After she told me the words, I whispered them into my napkin when she wasn't looking.

When the last bell rang, I was surprised at how quick and easy the whole day had been. The halls of my high school had been cleaned and waxed over the summer and I had found only a few candy wrappers to pick up and had avoided poisoning anyone in class. I had even made plans for later in the week with a girl named Lizzy from my physics class. Only, I had to be extremely cautious when it felt as though everything was going well. That's usually when disaster was stalking me.

Although the afternoon sun was bright, when I stepped through the school's doors, the swirling red lights were all that I could see. The ambulances were frozen in a triangle outside Walter's world-famous hot dog stand. In the teachers' parking lot, students clustered together, watching. Someone said it was a kid from the junior high. Another person said it was a Rollerblader with a German shepherd.

I hope you get there in time. I hope you get there in time. I hope you get there in time. I hope you get there in time. I hope you get there in time. I hope that everybody and everything involved in that accident gets all better completely painlessly soon. Please let everyone and everything involved in that accident heal completely painlessly soon.

The crowd was knit closely and stank of BO, but I pressed further in. I needed to know how many bodies there were, what kind of bloodshed lay below.

"Was anyone hurt? Excuse me, do you know if anyone was hurt?"

No one answered me.

"Excuse me, did you happen to see . . . ?"

There was too much blathering and bubble gum snapping and not enough information. *I hope you get there in time. I hope you get there in time,* I incanted five, ten, twenty more times as I strained my neck to get a clearer view. A policeman was directing traffic around the crimson flares.

Please let everyone and everything heal completely painlessly soon, completely painlessly soon. The longer I stood there the more certain I was that something was seriously wrong and that I had caused it. I felt dizzy and panicked. I wanted so badly to run away but I couldn't risk being seen as suspicious.

At last, the sirens moved on. Backpacks and jean jackets thinned out, drifting to the bike racks, huddling by trees to smoke and flirt, exchanging telephone numbers. For them the world was somehow only as big as the next math assignment or weekend plans. But I couldn't take my eyes off the neon traffic cones the emergency workers had left in the street—five pieces of hollow orange plastic that knew every grisly detail of what had happened.

I had to run most of the way to Mrs. Roman's, but I was still late and she squawked at me. Mrs. Roman was my new piano teacher.

"You know I've got someone in at four thirty! Did you eat a snack? I'm having turkey on a kaiser roll—we'll split it. Begin with the scales. You've been picking at your face again, haven't you? Beige book! We're starting the Debussy today! It's hard but you'll get it. Go!" Mrs. Roman was part of the deal I had made with Mom at the end of the summer. I'd assured her that I didn't need to go to Dr. M. anymore because I was feeling better about Dad and Ellyn and I would need my afternoons for piano and studying now that I was in high school. The truth was, I'd run out of things to say to Dr. M. and I couldn't tell her about praying or I was sure He'd be mad. Mom agreed, but not without stipulations.

"If I see you collecting trash again, we're going back, you hear?" So I hid all my litter piles and tried to keep my bedtime confessions short and sweet. I think my mother was silently relieved that she didn't have to hear about my daily transgressions. Besides, she loved it when I played the piano for her. When she was young she'd studied Debussy and Chopin for almost fifteen years. Sometimes I felt she wanted me to continue where she had left off.

When I came home from Mrs. Roman's that day, I knew I should go upstairs and pray for the Walter's people, but I was too scared of being alone with those sirens and traffic cones spinning in my head. Instead, I showed Mom my new piece of Debussy, *Clair de lune*.

"Bravo!" she cheered, pulling me toward the cabinet by the fireplace.

"I was hoping you'd get to this soon. Oh, Abidab, your father would be so proud of you." Her knees creaked as she squatted down and hauled out a sheaf of yellowing sheet music. Ballads and mazurkas, the score for *Oliver!*, and two anthologies of Cole Porter's tunes. It was disturbing but also exciting, seeing these vestiges of my father stacked among the yarmulkes and candy dishes. After he died, we had never discussed what to do with his belongings. I knew my mother had given some of his clothes to my brother and donated a fair amount to the synagogue bazaar, but many of his coats still hung in the closet, two years later. His watch and dish of loose change remained on the bureau upstairs.

Mom picked over the music reverentially, pausing every few moments to linger in its unvoiced melody. I realized many of these books were hers, too—her signature sprawled across the prehistoric-looking covers. Music for violin. Flute. Trombone. Full orchestra.

"Aha! Knew it was here!"

Mom lifted up a sky-colored book. A pamphlet really—maybe four pages thick. *Claude Debussy: Claire de lune* the cover read in big, chunky letters. She opened it so delicately, as if it might float away, running her hand over the edges, the places where her teacher had written in a steady cursive, *Not too fast* and *Pedal.* In the corner Mom had scribbled *June 12, 1946.* All of the fingerings and accents were still there, starring the page with fuzzy pencil marks like loose confetti.

"Shall we?" asked Mom with a wink.

Though she stumbled at first, the notes were soon moving by themselves. I couldn't tell if it was the piano or her humming that was leading us, lifting the whole room into this plaintive lullaby. We had never met at the piano bench together like this before; she wasn't teaching me, she was simply giving me everything she knew. As she played, she sounded so naked I could only bear to look at the floor. When she was done she thumped me on the back triumphantly and said,

"Oosh. Needs a little work, but that was fun, huh? Now you try."

I put my hands on the keys, but they wouldn't move.

"Ab?"

I couldn't look at her. I felt my whole body cramp into an airless knot. The ambulances encircled me, the flares lapped at the sky, and now there were lifeless bodies being carried away too. Mom could sense something was up. She always could. I felt her hand slowly kneading my back, softening, trying to calm me down.

"What is it?" she whispered. I longed not to tell her but I couldn't get out of that mess of knapsacks on the hill, where I had pressed forward, craning to see the carnage.

"It's just . . . something that happened at school today." My breath was thin and choppy as I described the traffic cop and the stink of bubble gum and sweat. My leaving the scene of the crime just behind the emergency team, which was traveling at approximately forty miles per hour—not necessarily life-and-death speed but probably meant there were serious injuries. There were stretchers, though. At least two.

She closed her ancient music. "And you caused this, of course," she said, defeated.

"I'm pretty sure. Yes. I mean, yes. I was standing at the top of the hill by the parking lot and I had on my purple shirt, which is really bright, and I was waving and the car was going so fast and the driver looked up and saw me and he got distracted and I kept waving and they were crossing the street while he was looking up at me and there was no—"

Mom stopped me with a firm palm on my leg. "You know what? I'm sure everyone is going to be fine and the driver should have been looking at the road, not at you."

"No, but I was running toward him and waving my arms. I was—"

"Ssssh! I'm not done!" Her voice tightened with frustration. The same room that moments before had sung with her music now shriveled with our common uncertainty. "First of all, it's a bad inter-section and they need to have a crosswalk with a light. We've brought this up at PTA board meetings countless times. The point being, I'm sure it wasn't your fault and everyone is going to be *fine* and it's been a long day. How about helping me chop up some salad?"

She pulled me into her chest and smoothed my back again, but we were both flushed and panting now, both trying to escape those sirens and lights. There was no more Debussy and there was nowhere to go that didn't flash red and I still had more details to confess but she was whispering into my ear *Ssssh ssssh,* as if she was trying to blow all my thoughts out the other side of my skull. Whenever I said "But—" she held me closer.

"It's okay. It's all right."

"I didn't mean to, but I was standing—"

"You didn't hurt anyone. Ssssssssh."

We sat on the piano bench until it was night outside. Until my neck felt wet from her shushing.

"Sssssssh."

Sweeping through me, shushing all the wails, extinguishing all the flares. Until there was nothing in my head except empty space.

walter's world-famous hot dog stand is not all right

Mom was wrong. Everything was not okay. Everything was not all right. I swore I would never go to Walter's world-famous hot dog stand again.

Two girls from the middle school—the Miller twins—were crossing the street to beat the after-school rush for French fries at Walter's. Maybe they were running against the light—we all did it. Sydney was hit by a car while her sister Pam hopped onto the curb. Sydney was in a coma for a week before she died. A week in which I prayed, *Please let Sydney Miller recover completely painlessly soon.* Five, ten, a hundred times.

It didn't matter how many times I said it. It was too late. They lowered Sydney into her permanent resting hole while Mom tried to assure me I wasn't at fault and Sue Simmons turned to the weather report with a smile.

A week after Sydney died, Jessica and I were sitting on a rock on the Post Road side of the school—we were both too creeped out to sit by Walter's anymore. But our reasons were very different.

Jessica's little sister had been best friends with Sydney, so Jessica's whole family had gone to the funeral. She said Sydney's mom looked like a ghost. I took a bite of my buttered roll so I could keep my lips from quivering.

"It's just so . . . I just can't believe it." Jessica closed her wide eyes delicately, the lashes budding with tears.

"Yeah," I murmured in agreement. Sydney's corpse danced and

shook, rattling at my rib cage like prison bars. I didn't know how to keep it all inside. I couldn't confess to Jessica or I'd lose my one friend in the high school and again I didn't have proof or witnesses to my crime but I knew I'd done it and a little girl was gone because of me. I was homicidal and heartless and somebody needed to stop me before I struck again. I pushed my soda straw into my mouth and bit down hard, snipping the tip of my tongue.

"Oooouch."

"You okay?" Jessica asked sweetly, wiping a tear from her nose.

"Yeah."

I brought my finger to my mouth and found a small bead of blood on my tongue. Maybe it was proof that I was human.

More likely, it was G-d's way of saying *I saw you shove Sydney Miller into that street.*

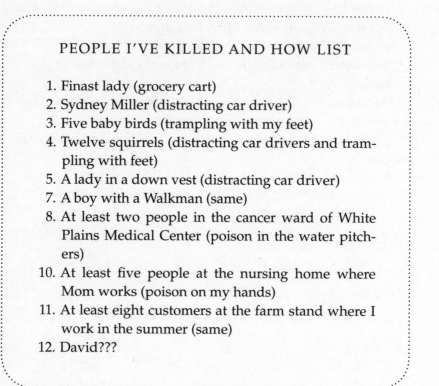

PEOPLE I'VE KILLED AND HOW LIST

1. Finast lady (grocery cart)
2. Sydney Miller (distracting car driver)
3. Five baby birds (trampling with my feet)
4. Twelve squirrels (distracting car drivers and trampling with feet)
5. A lady in a down vest (distracting car driver)
7. A boy with a Walkman (same)
8. At least two people in the cancer ward of White Plains Medical Center (poison in the water pitchers)
10. At least five people at the nursing home where Mom works (poison on my hands)
11. At least eight customers at the farm stand where I work in the summer (same)
12. David???

love puffs

. . . .

I took a job babysitting after school until I convinced myself that I was molesting the children and quit.

I worked at a farm stand and scooped ice cream downtown but each day I knew people were dropping off because I was lacing their treats with arsenic.

I started going to confirmation class at the synagogue, where we studied Martin Buber and Elie Wiesel. I cried every week after class because I had a crush on the new rabbi and he was married, so I had to pray for his wife to be okay in case I smote her with my jealous thoughts.

On Saturday nights I climbed into bed with Mom and we did the Sunday crossword puzzle together with erasable pen until Sue Simmons came on. Betsy was living at Penn State with her boyfriend and Jon was already in law school and I told Mom I was going to be the loser who never left home and still couldn't sleep with the door closed all the way. Mom said to give it time and that she was a late bloomer too. I prayed for Mom the most—that she would stay *completely happy, healthy always*.

It wasn't until junior year of high school that I began hanging out with people my age again. I joined the performing arts program and was cast in a play about a woman whose husband tried to kill her on Christmas Eve. I played Psychiatrist Number Two and all my lines were monosyllabic. If I said my lines clipped and cleverly enough, the auditorium echoed with laughter. I felt a new hopefulness bubbling in my chest, like the audience was tickling me with their warm breath.

101

I felt that same tickle when I was near Psychiatrist Number Three, played by Will McIntire. Will was tall and had thick brown curls and chapped lips and I especially liked to watch him chew on the strings from his hooded sweatshirt when he was thinking. I knew for a fact that I wasn't the only one watching Will. Maria mentioned that she thought Will had gotten cuter. Lucy said Will should get some ChapStick, and Dina said she was really sorry she told him that his breath stank. Will was dating Anna, who was a year ahead of me and had recently been accepted for early admissions at Harvard, had hair spun from chocolate silk, and starred in all of our school dance recitals. So she and Will would probably elope or at least last through prom. Still, I felt that Will and I connected on a pretty intense level. I'd play-punched him at least four times during rehearsals and I was also the only girl in our cast who knew how to belch really loudly, which made him laugh.

But I would never be with Will. And it wasn't because of Anna.

I knew, though He hadn't told me specifically, I *knew* that I wasn't supposed to be with a boy. I'd known this for a long time. Ever since my dad died and I started kissing his picture (which I still did, but I kept it to one hundred light kisses and hugs just before bed) and writing in my journal.

Daddy is my best boyfriend and Mommy is my best girlfriend. I love You G-d most of all forever and ever.

I would love the three of them and only the three of them for the rest of my life.

Daddy is my best boyfriend. My father was the last man to see me undressed. That was before I had breasts or armpit hair or my period. When the landscape of my thoughts was simpler and I truly was blameless. I wanted to stay in that time, on his lap with his corduroyed knee bouncing to his newest jazzy riff. I longed for him every time a cement mixer passed, my stomach and throat constricting as I sang his songs urgently, guiltily. I couldn't change the fact that he was dead, but I could dedicate myself to him. I owed him that much. I also stayed away from boys and consecrated my body to my father to fool myself. If I could sing that Cement Mixer song enough and wear pigtails with ribbons in my hair I could go back to being ten years old and stainless instead of this monster who molested and killed.

Mommy is my best girlfriend meant that I would always be her little girl. I knew she loved Jon and Betsy, too, but I was determined to be her favorite. I gave her pet names and swore she was my best friend forever and ever and even though she usually said "That's nice" I convinced myself that she felt the same way about me.

I love You G-d most of all forever and ever was the part I had to repeat daily. My prayers were up to about thirty minutes in the morning and twenty at night. But sometimes I'd fall asleep in the middle of them and dream about being chased. I often woke up wheezing and exhausted and then I had to start with the Shema all over again. I was scared G-d was losing His infinite patience with me and each night there was more for which I had to thank Him and ask forgiveness and yet it never seemed to be enough to flatten out the spikes of terror, the nightmares of running. Promising Him my celibacy was the only right thing to do. Nobody had told me sex was bad, but I had decided somewhere in my sixteen years of existence that any urges below my waist were base and crude and must be ignored or stamped out. Plenty of people in my grade were having sex, but most of my close friends were still waiting to be kissed. Betsy was the only person who talked to me about sex and now she was living with a boy and I imagined her having sex with him all the time—on the kitchen table and in the driveway and under their burbling fish tank in the living room. Betsy had lost her virginity the summer she went to photography school five years ago and loved it. It had happened just a few weeks before my father died and the connection between sex and death was clear enough to me. I didn't need Him to spell it out. I just had to keep my body chaste so no one else's life was endangered.

After our play closed, a bunch of us from the cast usually went to Will's house to watch movies on Saturday nights. It was mostly Will and Anna, Will's friend Dan and his girlfriend, Lara, and girls who had a crush on one of them even though they were both taken. For most of my junior year, my social life followed a fairly predictable routine: Will told us to come over around 8:30. I got into my mom's car at 8:20, drove around the corner, and turned off the engine. I had to do extra prayers on the nights I went to Will's to make it clear I was still wholly and completely devoted to Mom and Dad and G-d, no matter how electric Will made me feel. I did the healing and traveling prayers. I was always hearing about more people who were sick or planning vacations whom I had to add, so these took a while. Then I prayed for forgiveness. I was careful not to mention that I was going to Will's house, although that's what made me sorriest of all, because I still loved Daddy the most and Mommy the most and G-d even more, of course. *I love* You *the most for always. Thank You, Amen. Thank You, Amen. Thank You, Amen. Thank You, Amen. Thank You, Amen.* My heart drummed loudly as I neared the end. My fingers shook from worry and cold as I counted out my final *thank You*'s. I was sure I hadn't prayed enough and also that going to Will's was greedy and immoral, and if I didn't start my car prayers over, Mom or Will or all the squirrels in the road would die that very night. I started over. And then over again. By the time I rang Will's doorbell, it was often after ten. I was grateful Mom didn't give me a curfew.

"Oh! You came!" Anna smiled. Her hair was always extremely shiny and she wore a subtle rose lip gloss. I hated how pretty and kind she was. Which meant I had to get to Will's bathroom and pray for her again so she didn't get hit by a car on the way home.

Will's parents had usually rented us some movie from the sixties that was supposed to be famous and absurdist and good for us to watch. They were both professors and had very refined taste in clothes and food. Their house smelled like fresh-cut wood. I would sink onto the floor cushions by the fireplace and try not to stare while Will and Anna snuggled two feet away from me. Frequently it was past midnight when I'd call Mom.

"Mom! Is it okay if I stay a little longer?"

"Sure. You having fun?" she'd ask hopefully.

"Yeah, you?"

"We're almost done with the crossword and . . . what's that? Oh, David says when it's time to look at schools he'd love to take you to Bucknell."

"Great."

David was the other reason I finally left the house on Saturday nights. I don't know who came first, David or Will. All I know is I wanted David to be gone.

Mom had met David at a dinner party. I bet he was passing out mints or making his revolting snort-laugh. He was shaped like a pear. He loved to take my mother to concerts and expensive restaurants and he bought her flowers and jewelry all the time. For her birthday he gave her a pink suit. When she showed it to me, I told her I didn't think she liked pink—we both didn't like pink. But Mom said she'd changed her mind and she'd never had such a fancy outfit before.

I didn't say anything after that. Especially not "Pink is for stupid people" or "You look like an idiot" or "If you really loved Dad you wouldn't be doing this." I soon learned (by snooping) that David had two plaid shirts in Dad's closet and a pair of tan pants (size: Bartlett) for when he stayed over. Nobody had asked me if he could do that.

I was disgusted and disappointed in Mom. I didn't know what she saw in this man. He was nothing like my father, who grew more saintly each day. It wasn't only that David couldn't sing or dance or that his nose was the size of a small bird; I couldn't comprehend her willingness to kiss *anyone* besides Dad. Of course I never told her this. I'd never openly disagreed with my mother. Not even when she put an answer in the crossword puzzle that I thought wasn't right. That was part of our indestructible mother-daughter-best-friends-forever bond—her infallibility and my unshakable loyalty. I prided myself on never getting in trouble, either. She had yelled at my brother and sister, but I made sure always to follow her obediently. As our house slowly emptied, Jon and Betsy called home less and less, their sleeping bags and sweaters were stuffed into the attic, and Mom and I were the only ones left on Team Sher. I was determined never to lose her.

David was the worst kind of intruder. Breaking and entering in full daylight and stealing my mother, my best friend and confidante, from me. Snorting and smiling the whole time. When Sydney Miller had died, I'd begun confessing more vehemently to Mom again as she tucked me in at night. But with David around it grew harder and harder to find time to clear my conscience and I felt my body getting heavier with the weight of those dead pedestrians and squirrels. Sometimes when Mom came in to say good night I tried to punish her with my silence.

"Anything happen in school?"

"No. Are you going out with David again this weekend?"

"I don't know. Probably."

"Really?" I countered, often throwing in an oppressed-sounding sigh before starting the Shema. *"Ayl me-lech ne-men She-ma . . ."*

Those nights felt the worst. I had so many sins to atone for and now I'd added anger to the expanding list. I prayed, *Please let Mom be happy healthy and David happy healthy too. And I'm sorry for anything mean I said or thought or did or tried to do to them, please let them both be completely happy healthy always.* My wrath put them both in the gravest danger.

One day, a few months after I discovered David's pants in the closet, Mom and I were on our way to CVS. Going to the drugstore had always been my favorite thing we did together. We sprayed each other with imitation perfumes and laughed at all the different ways panty hose companies printed the word NUDE. We were circling the block for parking when she offhandedly remarked, "So, I think David and I are getting married."

I was instantly winded. "What? You *think*? You don't know?"

"Well then, yes. We are. What do you think of that?"

We stopped at a light. I refused to look at her.

"What do *you* think? Are you in *love*?" I snarled.

"Sure. David is a very nice man and he cares about you a lot."

"That's nice. If you're in love, that's good then . . . that's nice."

The traffic light had to be broken. It was taking forever to turn green. My skin, my scalp, even my tonsils felt irritated and inflamed. I wanted her to know how much I hurt all over.

"Mom, you know, you still shake your head a lot. Especially when you drive. You should get that checked out by a doctor. It's pretty disturbing."

It was the cruelest thing I could bring myself to say to her. She wasn't shaking her head more than at any other time, but I felt my brain overheating. Mom falling in love and remarrying was definitely not supposed to happen. She had to know this was inappropriate. Disrespectful. Whorish. It hadn't even been a full five years since we threw dirt on my father's coffin. If she was trying to fill some void, she was doing a horrendous job. I wanted to point out

that David was a hideous driver and every time he took us somewhere I got motion sickness because he pumped the pedals back and
forth. Or that he never knew what to order from the Chinese food
menu. He was so *not* my dad in so many ways and why couldn't she
see that?

I continued to seethe as she addressed the wedding invitations and
gritted my teeth as we tried on dresses together. But I couldn't admit
to her or to myself that it was she, not David, I was truly mad at. I
couldn't let myself even *think* that Mom was at fault without killing her too. I knew my anger brought on devastation. My father's
death had followed on the heels of my incensed premonition to my
cousins. I was sure there was some hidden rage that led me to strike
at Finast and Walter's too. This unholy marriage was obviously my
punishment for all the lives I had already taken.

The wedding was held in our living room. A handful of neighbors and relatives draped themselves over the arms of the couch and
toasted Mom and David with champagne. They grinned at the happy
couple and left crumbs and fingerprints next to our family photographs without ever looking at them—frames holding our trip to the
Grand Tetons and my father's tanned face winking under a cowboy
hat. I was mad at the rabbi, at Terry Jaffey and the ever-present Sisterhood, at our neighbor Estherann for loitering and applauding this
disgraceful union. I wanted to punch and scratch the sloppy smiles
off their faces and shred their cocktail napkins into thousands of
pieces but I knew it wouldn't make me feel any better. Every vengeful thought would only make my prayers longer and more desperate.
I was playing a cruel game of hide-and-seek with myself, chasing my
own fury. I needed someplace safe where I could scream my resent-
ment and grief without worrying about everyone in the room being
snuffed out.

Mom and David went on a honeymoon. They left us a ton of
leftovers. Roast beef, mushroom chicken, and little heart-shaped
quiches my sister made, calling them love puffs. Betsy invited her
friends over and they drank the extra booze, their laughter sluggish
and garlicky, their fingers oily from crab cakes and balls of mozza-
rella. I could hear them from my room, sitting with my back against
the door. I repeated my prayers louder and louder, my throat grow-

ing raw and my neck cricked. I pressed my hands into my ears so I could concentrate. I prayed for Aunt Doris and Uncle Morris, the girl from math class who looked like she had a skin disease, and Mickey, the retarded boy who stood by the Exxon station and tried to kiss anyone who stopped to talk. I prayed most of all for my mother's new love and that they traveled safely, soundly, happily, healthfully.

But G-d saw through my façade. He smelled my hatred. It took approximately eight months, three days, and ten hours for me to kill David.

I was a senior and had just been cast as the manipulative temptress Abigail in the fall production of *The Crucible*. I had to take it seriously because it was my first big part in a play and I wanted the acting teacher to like me and say that I had a lot of talent and unharnessed energy. Each day in rehearsal I bellowed my lines louder, trying to visualize my blood coursing with abandonment and forbidden lust. But most of the time I could focus only on not looking at Will. He was playing Abigail's uncle, a pious and troubled colonial man whom she respected and admired. I couldn't stop staring at his cracked, red lips.

Will and I had been spending more time together. As friends. Anna was at college but he was still committed to her, and I was passionately in love with my mother, my father, and the Ruler of the Universe, so each of us understood that we were just good buddies who appreciated each other's company. The day that David died was a Friday. Will and I had plans to go to hear *La Bohème* together that night—*not* as a date. We were going with his parents because they had an extra ticket and I wasn't even dressing up because it was at the local community college. But I still felt jumpy and restless through all of my classes.

Last period of the day. I was struggling through a math quiz when Mr. Ramirez, the assistant principal, knocked on the classroom door.

"Ms. Sher, would you mind seeing me when you're done with your exam?"

"Ooooooh," said Andy C. under his breath.

Mr. Ramirez had a tiny office that was stuffy and thick with his spicy cologne. He sat with his hands folded, his pit stains inching up toward his chin, at a desk that reached from wall to wall. He nodded toward a chair, but when I turned to take a seat, my mom was sitting there, slouched in her plum-colored suit.

Mr. Ramirez cleared his throat.

"There's been an . . ." Accident. Incident. Just after breakfast, where David had asked me again what I thought of Bucknell as a possible safety school and I had given him the silent treatment because breakfast was not talking time and only pear-shaped losers went to Bucknell. David, of course, was unfazed and waved cheerily before he left for the train station.

"Have a nice day, ladies!"

He made it into Manhattan on the 7:55. Took the Vanderbilt Avenue exit and greeted the October sun before collapsing on the sidewalk. A heart attack. Someone called my mom from the ambulance.

I wondered why Mr. Ramirez was still talking.

"So, what hospital is he at?"

Mr. Ramirez smiled. His collar was soaked with sweat.

"He's not at a hospital, sweetie," said Mom. "He's . . ."

The three of us sat in the gaping hole of her unfinished sentence.

"Does this mean I can't go to the opera with Will tonight?"

I didn't intend to be cold or unfeeling, I just couldn't think of anything else to say. I was thankful I hadn't laughed as I did when Mrs. Ashner was killed by a tree. But as Mom and I drove home, I felt David's hulking form, cutting out the afternoon sky, throttling me. I needed to be sure that I couldn't be implicated in this abrupt fatality. Though I'd never accepted him or treated him kindly, the fact was I hadn't slipped any cyanide into his coffee and I was nowhere near Grand Central that morning.

At least, I'm pretty sure I wasn't.

I wanted so badly to tell Mom I killed him and for her to say that was impossible and that I wasn't responsible for the world and then for us both to watch Sue Simmons with cups of mint tea. But Mom looked too sad and spent, her head wobbling *No, no, no, no, no.* I knew she couldn't cool the blaze inside me.

When we got home, Betsy was already back from Pennsylvania. We were put in charge of cleaning out the freezer to make room for the lox and kugels that would soon be coming through the door with the first wave of shiva callers. Less than nine months had passed since the wedding, so we still had love puffs in the freezer that we could defrost and put on the table with a little fresh garnish.

Mom started her list:

1. Parsley
2. Milk for coffee
3. Tablecloths

She was worried because all the tablecloths looked dirty. She made me take them out of the linen closet and lay them out one by one.

"I just don't understand!" she groaned miserably. "Who put these back stained?!"

But the tablecloth issue was easily resolved. Terry Jaffey and the Sisterhood brought their own tablecloths. Mom's friend Lynn came over and began calling everyone in Mom's address book to tell them the news. David's suit was being pressed, the cleaning lady was coming to polish our candlesticks, and Mom, Betsy, and I had haircuts scheduled for Saturday before the limo picked us up for an afternoon funeral. Jon promised he'd shave before getting on the plane home. We were very efficient mourners. Mom said she couldn't do anything without us.

She had no idea.

While Will and his parents got lost in arias about a fictional turret and ill-fated lovers, I lay on my bed, chilled by the all-too-real creep of death around me. There was nowhere to go with my fingers or eyes. I was just watching, waiting. It seemed so childish now to think Aunt Simone had caused her own death. I knew it was much more complicated. The fields and polka dots, the passageways I had tried to follow to find the answers, were all gone. Mom had finally let me take down that wallpaper when David moved in and I was allowed to pick whatever I wanted for my walls. I'd chosen a bucket of cool light blue paint. The color of a clear sky in every direction.

I'd never felt so exposed before. I had wanted David to be gone and I had thought it and then *poof*—he was obliterated. I felt the kind of fear where everything shook from straining so hard to be still. I couldn't piece together exactly how I had done it. I had silently cursed David at breakfast. I had furtively slipped him the dirty silverware last night at supper. The details of how it happened were irrelevant; I knew that I was culpable. My infatuation with Will. My untamed anger. I had destroyed a good man simply by imagining it so.

I stared up at the terrifying blue of my walls for hours. Outside was the sky. And beyond the trees was Him. I didn't know where to begin praying tonight. I didn't know how to be penitent enough. There was nowhere to go and no way to trace or shred or count my way to safety. By taking away that patchwork paper I'd also taken away any path to softening this brutal tightness in my chest. There was no squiggled road to travel with my finger, no way to scorch through the smog of fear pinning me to the bed. There was no release valve and no Mom to blow it away with her shushes. It was just me and Him. And nowhere left to hide.

WORDS I NEED TO AVOID SAYING OUT LOUD

G-d (could sound like I'm saying it in vain even if I
    don't mean to)
G-dless
G-dliness
G-dness
god(s)
goddess(es)
Lord
lord(s)

guard (sounds too much like His name)
guardian
got
gotten
landlord
Laura
Lori

Allah (in case it sounds like I'm worshipping someone
    besides Him)
Buddha
Jesus Christ

lucky (sounds like He's not in charge, and He *is*)
luckier
luckiest
fate
fateful
free will
predetermined

the cure

· ·

After David's death, my mother and I were the only ones in the house again, but there was a third presence that was much bigger than both of us. A weariness that leached through our walls and made even our tap water taste stale. Mom was working a new job as public relations director of the American Jewish Federation and in her spare time she began redecorating. She said she wanted to do as much of it herself as possible but she had never been Betty Homemaker and her attempts involved multiple staple guns and, often, heavy Scotch tape. Every piece of furniture was reupholstered in a different pattern; each material she brought home was brasher than the one before. The dining room was papered in thick cobalt stripes, the drapes hung in oozing brown paisleys. Her night table was buried under swatches of blues, mauves, and maroons. At dinner she lined them up in front of our plates and asked me my opinion. But I soon realized she wasn't listening to my answers. The stairwell was painted an unsettling bloodred. The couch was smothered in tropical flowers. Worst of all, my father's easy chair went from a worn gold velour to pink-and-peach checkerboard.

"What do you think?" she asked me eagerly.

"It's not exactly my favorite," I responded. Which was what she'd taught my siblings and me to say if we thought something was disgusting. Only now, she smiled brightly as if I'd just paid her a compliment.

I'd hoped David's death could draw us together again. Each night I helped dish out leftover kugel and sat down, wishing we could hatch a plan to run away together and reinvent ourselves. But my mother and I rarely spoke candidly to each other anymore. I knew that she was

113

suffering, only I could never bring myself to ask her about it. There was a certain formidability to her silent mourning that I dared not touch. She reapplied her lipstick constantly and fastened her lips shut, sealing herself off. Each night after dinner, she sat with her tea and filled out *Thank you for your expressions of sympathy* cards. She brought David's sweaters and suits to the synagogue bazaar, arranged her bottles of Jean Naté bath water on his side of the bureau, and moved her longer skirts and dress shoes into the closet that was once my father's, then David's, and now held home décor magazines and bits of extra carpeting. There was nothing more to discuss.

My mother valued poise, thrift, and intelligence above all. Joan Miriam Lear Sher was born during the Depression, the youngest of four girls. Her father worked open-to-close at his drugstore seven days a week so they could afford pineapple juice by the case and eggs when they were on sale. Mom was the only one who got to go to college, and she was tall in her independence. She loved to regale us with the story of her high school prom. How her mother had sewn her a peplum dress with a matching jacket so she could look smart next to her date at the prom, and though he wound up leaving with a lanky blonde, Joanie strutted onto the dance floor, blinking away all signs of distress behind her cat-eye glasses, and didn't stop shaking her peplumed hips until the gymnasium cleared out. She refused to stain her stylish ensemble with tears.

My mother rarely surrendered to her darker emotions, especially grief or anger. After my father was buried and we ate our way through his funeral cold cuts, I could count on one hand the number of times I'd seen her cry. When David died she just adorned herself with brighter and brighter scarves and matching blush as our house sank into its Scotch-taped stillness. Mom constantly stressed the importance of good posture, careful enunciation, and above all, restraint. *There's no need to air your dirty linen in public* was one of her favorite phrases, especially when her children threw tantrums. I suppose we each found ways to vent in our uglier moments—Jon's ceiling was permanently stamped with tennis ball smudges, Betsy's doorjamb was warped and chipped from mutinous slammings, and my stashes of litter grew exponentially in desk drawers and jacket pockets. But I was never as adept as Mom at concealing my inner tumult, and I was scared this disappointed her. Above all, I adored her and wanted to save her from any future sorrows. As we passed silent dinners together among the jungle of stripes and paisleys, I tried to quiet my mind as much for her sake as my own.

I was supposed to head to college in a few months, and the thought of leaving Mom made me anxious and teary. I'd been wait-listed or rejected from every school I'd applied to on the East Coast and I told her that was a sign I should stay home. She said no, I'd be miserable and what did I want to do, scoop ice cream for the rest of my life?

I started leaking out of my edges. I didn't want to involve any-one new in my chaos, but I couldn't face my mother's drawn face, her unbreachable stoicism. There was no way to douse the roar of guilt and confusion inside me. I explained to several befuddled teachers that I had possibly cheated on their tests and should get a lower grade. I enlisted my friends Gabra and Jessica to say Diet Coke prayers with me at lunch, because without them I was sure I'd curse G-d in a sudden fit of blasphemy. Once in a while I also had to ask them for help picking up a bobby pin when my hands were already full. Jessica often took the trash from me with sad eyes. Gabra said she would pay me good money to clean her bedroom too.

I became especially unhinged in the car. I was constantly checking and rechecking the rearview mirror for road kill and felled neigh-bors. I begged classmates to carpool with me so I could ask them at each stoplight "Did I hit something? Is that a limb under the wheel?"

When nobody was in the car with me, I often circled a street three, four, five times to see if I could find the struck body or the scratches and dents I was sure I'd left while pulling out of a parking spot. It was the same maddening circle I trod each night when I walked the dog, singing my prescribed songs. The same circle of fiery destruction that closed in on me every time I tried to walk past a paper clip. Sometimes the only way out of my dismal orbit was to leave a note on a wind-shield:

To whom it may concern:

I'm sorry but I may have accidentally scraped your car on my way out of the space next to you. If you see any scratches, you can call me at 914-555-0794.

Sincerely, Abby Sher

Miraculously, nobody ever called.

In the spring of my senior year, I was backing out of my space in the high school parking lot when I hooked the bumper of my mom's Pontiac on the rim of a silver Jeep's wheel. The scrape of enamel ran through my skin and groped at my neck, leaving me breathless. I was horrified by what I had done. It didn't matter that the Jeep was empty; I was seized by the idea that I had permanently damaged this car and its owner. I searched hysterically to see if there had been witnesses. If there were none, I was willing to abandon the car and run as far as my legs would carry me to escape. But there were too many students milling around. Maybe if I played dead long enough I could evaporate or at least block out the moment. Only, this was not a fantasy, this was not a floating corpse. This was terrifyingly tangible, metal entwined with metal, unmovable and unforgiving. More and more people were emptying out of the school. It was only a matter of time before I'd be discovered, spinning my wheels furiously, trying to unwedge the car.

It was my worst accident to date, even though no one died. I had to climb out of the driver's door and slog shamefully to the principal's office. A loudspeaker called, *Will the owner of a silver Jeep license plate 52A4V please report to the Post Road office?* The girl who owned the Jeep came out of soccer practice and scrunched her nose in annoyance. Her ponytail bounced as she gunned the Jeep forward to separate the cars. I wanted to curl up in the backseat and weep. I wondered what it would feel like to react as she had, to have that much uninhabited space in my brain that I could smirk and shrug it off.

As I sat in the driveway at home, I felt like I was being swallowed whole. The perimeter of my danger widened, the pressure in my chest spread and tingled in all of my limbs. There had always been a part of me—a splinter of light at the edge of a darkened door—that believed, or hoped, definitely prayed, that I was innocent. That's why I continued to watch Sue Simmons, so she could calm me with her facts. That's why I repeated *Amen, Amen, Amen* for Gabra and Jessica so they could stand guard and make sure I hadn't blasphemed.

Now everything was colliding. The real and the imagined were indistinguishable. No matter how much I hoped or prayed for my blamelessness, no matter how fervently I begged forgiveness from

Sydney and David and the Ultimate Creator, the scratches in my mother's Pontiac remained as incontrovertible proof that something had, could, and would happen. If I was capable of leaving the scene of this crime, there was no limit to what other massacres I could run from, and possibly had run from already. I had crashed into my own worst nightmare of myself and I knew the next time I struck there would be no survivors. I refused to get back in the car, slumping past the Pontiac's pitted fender every morning to run for the bus or get a ride from a neighbor. But I wasn't fooling anyone, least of all myself.

Gabra and Jessica took me behind the school cafeteria and asked what was up.

"What do you mean?" I sniffed.

"You're picking up stuff that isn't even dangerous, Abby. Like lint."

"Yeah, and we said prayers three times yesterday."

"Sorry," I whined defensively.

"That's not the point," explained Jessica. "Is there any way you could talk to that doctor again?"

I regretted telling them about Dr. M., and grudgingly agreed to go back. But after Mom scheduled me an appointment, she announced that she couldn't get off work early and I would have to drive myself. On the way to Dr. M.'s office, which was now in her house, I was sure I'd hit two horses at the riding stables near her house and three girls in kilts coming home from Catholic day school. I went around the block multiple times to check and then blasted the radio in the hopes that a string quartet could drown out their dying wails.

"Sorry I'm late."

"That's okay. Your mom said you might be having a hard time. Do you want to tell me about it?"

This was probably a pickup line in therapyspeak.

Not really. Last week I threw a woman into the street before putting razors in the candy at the drugstore and fondling a baby. I said landlord *three times just to rile the All-Merciful.*

"I'm okay," I mumbled.

I was disenchanted and annoyed with Dr. M. Her hair and skin and whole life were so calm and tan. Her private office was in the basement of her house. There was a leather couch and a low coffee table with tissues and a bowl of caramel-flavored candies and a fireplace big enough to hide in and go to sleep. Which was really all I wanted to do.

"Sorry, I've been picking at my skin a lot," I blurted. I knew she was trying to be polite by not mentioning it first. I tried to use cover-up but she had to see the scabs and divots where I had dug at my cheeks, trying to squeeze out my anguish.

"Do you know why you do that?"

I told her it just felt better. I told her about classes and tests and tried to fill up the session with whatever gossip I'd heard in the school halls. It was torturous sitting under her gaze, trying to match her calm while sirens and cadavers were chasing me. With five minutes left, I couldn't contain myself. I confessed miserably to the Jeep accident and how I wanted it to be a dream but it was so undeniably real. How the worst part was my need to run away.

"I almost did!" I whimpered.

"That's okay. It must have been scary," said Dr. M. She was still calm and tan; clearly she didn't recognize my deadly potential.

"How about your prayers? Your mom told me you were praying a lot. . . ." It wasn't a question, so I didn't have to answer her if I didn't want to. I was livid with my mom for divulging all my secrets, but I resented even more how easily Dr. M. could speak about something so intricate and hallowed.

"What would happen if you didn't pray for one night? Do you think you could do that?"

"I guess." I shrugged numbly. It was a bald-faced lie. There was no way I could skip a night of prayer. He would be angry and there were lives in danger and no one except Him knew all my evil secrets and no translation of these feelings into words she could comprehend existed. I could feel the tide of panic rising through my veins as I sagged farther into her couch.

"What are you thinking?" she asked softly, but I could only cry. Dr. M. was just as powerless, sitting on the other side of my sphere of pain.

The next week she jumped in with questions right away. "How long are the prayers now?"

"I don't know. Maybe twenty minutes." Another lie.

"And are you still collecting trash and washing your hands?"

"Just sharp things."

"Right." She chewed on her lip thoughtfully before speaking again. She told me some of my habits made her think of an illness—it was fairly common—called obsessive-compulsive disorder. Some people who had it washed their hands a lot, other people repeated phrases or numbers.

I smiled instinctively. I felt an odd lifting sensation, almost as if I had found another few inches of lung with which to breathe. I liked having the name of a disease to try out on my tongue—it gave me some sort of validity, some recognizable label for my suffering. But then she went on. She thought maybe I would like to try going on medication to help me. It might offer me relief and then I wouldn't have to pick up litter as much or worry about prayers.

My spine stiffened so quickly I flinched. I told her that I actually didn't wash my hands nearly as much as I used to and I didn't ever repeat numbers and I barely picked up things and most important I *liked* prayers—they were a *good* thing. There was no way that I could let her call faith a disease. In the wake of her suggestion, saying the word *prayer* out loud felt treacherous and irreverent. On the way home, even with the cellos bawling through the speakers, I could only hear His minor chords charging through me. I took out a jogger, a couple walking their dog, and a raccoon, and only drove faster, desperate to take flight.

*I'm sorry for all my transgressions please forgive me for my transgressions please heal everyone and everything ailing com*pletely*pain*less*ly*soon *com*pletely*pain*less*ly*soon *com*pletely*pain*less*ly*soon *com*pletely*pain*less*ly*soon *com*pletely*pain*less*ly*soon. Sending an entire school bus into a craggy ditch, beseeching His mercy above their Miss Mary Macks that devolved into death howls. How many more people dying around me would it take for Dr. M. to see that I *had* to pray? Prayers weren't an illness. They were actually the cure.

I prayed erratically that night. Falling asleep and running in hot pursuit of myself, waking and restarting the Shema only to find that the words had shuffled and I was repeating the traveling prayer too. I was so sorry that I had let Dr. M. speak impiously about Him. I would do anything to prove my loyalty. Each time I asked for forgiveness the words felt clumsier and more pitiful. The English language had nothing in it that could convey my remorse. I needed to apologize for all the fatalities, all the wicked thoughts and urges, the germs and poisons I was spreading. The car crashes real and imagined. And most of all this sin, which was a thousand times more horrible than bad—the sin of heresy.

me   Mom

mrs. shower door

Everyone at the University of Chicago had too much time. First of all, it was the Midwest, so there was an extra hour of night after I said the Shema over the phone with Mom. Also, we had to go to class for only a few hours a day. We spent eternities scrutinizing Marx's use of *the* and Descartes's *and,* comparing our struggles for self-knowledge to Plato's. In the basement coffee shops, the quads, the dining halls, students loafed and expostulated, chewing on new phrases like *experiential knowledge* and *categorical imperative*. When we got back to our dorms, the clocks moved in central-daylight-savings-the-world-is-your-oyster-you-have-no-obligation-except-to-learn time. In the common lounge someone was perpetually starting a debate about how we were the only generation left to change the fate of humanity.

Even with these added hours I was constantly running and always late. My morning prayers lasted longer and I missed most of my classes that met before 9 a.m. I often pleaded with the dining hall cleaning crew to let me in while they were vacuuming up after meals so I could grab some slices of bread or fill up plastic bags with dry cereal. Once in a while I made it to the library to study with some of the girls from my floor, but most of the time I sat Indian-style in my room, back shoved up against my locked door, with the lights off and my body rooted into the icy linoleum floor, my prayer book clutched tensely. I had a single, so no one knew I was there. I prayed about an hour and a half in the morning and another half hour at night, sometimes more. If anyone knocked to see if I was around, I started over. On weekends I stayed in my room praying until the afternoon clouds had already settled, then I crept through the echoey halls to see if anyone had snacks to share. My upstairs neighbor Ava was usually just waking up because her boyfriend was an insomniac-depressant and they made love and/or did finger painting all night long. Ava had wide gray eyes and flowing curls. Her walls were covered in nude photographs and fingerprints and she never asked me why I'd missed most of the day or why I looked so peaked and lost. She only stroked my hair, fed me Ramen noodles, and told me about her research on female mutilation in Africa. She had a Miss Piggy alarm clock, which made me even more tired because it was so rosy and cheerful.

At the other end of the hall was Marie. Marie had a life-size wall hanging of Jesus that she'd stitched by hand and a mirror that was embossed with a cross and the words *He died for us.* She'd never met a Jew before and I'd never felt so threatened by someone else's adoration for the Lord.

"Wow, so you follow the Old Testament?" Her eyelashes batted wildly behind her pink-rimmed glasses.

"Yeah."

"Even the fasting and all the sacrifices?"

"Sacrifices? No. I mean, we fast on Yom Kippur, but we don't slaughter anything. We have chicken instead."

Marie and I stayed up nights reading the Bible out loud on top of her fuzzy fleece comforter and she let me repeat the sentences I thought I might've said wrong. She already knew all the chapters and had notebooks filled with her questions and promises for Jesus. I had a lot of catching up to do. When I went back to my room and locked the door, I added new prayers about each chapter we'd dissected. Sometimes after Bible study it was too late to call Mom and I had to say the Shema by myself, which filled me with the most aching kind of loneliness. I never knew if I'd said it right, even when I repeated it ten times each in Hebrew and in English.

Five interminable weeks of freshman year went by before my mother came for Parents' Weekend. The first thing she said was, "Your room is so gloomy. Why don't you have an area rug? This floor is freezing!"

Then she saw the pile of wood chips, broken glass, paper clips, and silver gum wrappers on my desk that I'd been collecting since I'd arrived.

"Still doing that, huh?" She drew her eyebrows together disapprovingly and thumped me on the back. "C'mon, Chicken, stand up straight. Show me around."

"Well, this is my room. . . ." I offered blandly.

I don't know what we were both expecting from college. That it would change me. That I could be changed. I think my mom hoped a university setting would inspire or at least distract me from my *rituals and machinations* as she now called them. She ran her finger along my unopened volumes of Herodotus and Kant and purred appreciatively, "This should keep you busy, huh? My daughter is one smart cookie." But, looking back at me, she could see from my blank expression that I hadn't read a word. I scanned passages while my professors were lecturing in case they called on me, but there was only one book I was beholden to and it lay in my desk drawer, soggy and stained from ChapSticked kisses.

Mom held me at arm's length and brushed the hair from my face. "You've got to wear some blush, Abidab. You look so terribly pale." She went through her purse and pulled out her matching makeup bag. Led me toward the door where there was a full-length mirror flecked with pools of rust. She applied wide strokes of crimson blush to both of our cheeks and stepped back to survey us with a puckery grin. Then she added lipstick the color of ripe nectarines to her pursed lips.

"I know it's not your style, but just do me a favor and try it," she said, offering the lipstick authoritatively. She had found her way of coping with difficult times and it required smearing on a fresh coat of paint, constructing an unyielding smile. The lipstick was warm and slick and I folded my lips together to match hers. Mom was pleased. I remembered our Friday nights, preparing to say the Kaddish next to her, holding on to her tenderly crafted silence as the congregation praised us for our suffering.

"Okay. Let's go," she commanded. "We need to furnish this place now."

We trekked out against the Chicago wind, marching through the shedding trees of Hyde Park. It was too cold to talk, for which I was grateful. I just wanted to feel the solidity of her gloved hand in mine. She found a rug that wasn't on sale but bought it for me anyway. I'd never seen her do that before. Mom said it didn't matter; it wasn't a splurge, it was a necessity.

"Just take good care of it and use it in good health."

Back in my dorm room, Mom turned on the floor lamp and moved it over near the bed. Then she unfurled the rug with a flourish and carefully tucked the tag underneath, in case I wanted to return it.

"Can I throw these out?" She scooped the this-can-and-will-kill pile into her hand and I loved her so much in that moment I wanted to run into her arms and hide forever. Though I'd never admit it to myself, I had left that pile out in the hope she'd see it. It had been five weeks of counting and recounting, checking and rechecking, locking the door and recalling my victims for the day, shivering with shame and foreboding.

"Don't worry, I got it all," said Mom, holding the trash forward for my inspection. Her nails were trimmed neatly and painted with clear polish; she believed in looking her best for any travel. I wondered if she was already regretting her visit.

"Hey! Maybe we could throw it out together?" I asked with a forced grin, trying to make it sound like a fun activity.

I picked up each piece from her palm and dropped it into the metal trash can, enumerating out loud as they hit the bottom. Three safety pins, four pebbles of glass, two leaves (with pointy, dried stems), five wrappers, two razors, seven unidentifiable pieces of metal, two plastic rings from soda cans (which needed to be cut so birds wouldn't strangle themselves).

When we were done, we both washed our hands and Mom put some powder on her nose. Then we sat on the edge of my bed and let our stockinged feet travel through the new rug. It was soft and deep and I wanted Mom to gather me in its sturdy weave and carry me all the way home. I wanted to dive into her silk scarf and melt away. She was the only one who had ever been able to see all of me, to know me fully, and I felt I would suffocate if she left me here again.

"So!" She slapped my knee playfully. "How are classes?"

"Fine."

"Yeah? And you feel like you have more friends? Marie and Ava seem nice."

"Yeah."

"What do you think of those Clarence Thomas hearings, huh?"

"The what?"

"Oh, Ab. Have you even picked up a newspaper? How long is *quiet time* now?"

"I don't know. A half hour?"

I felt pathetic for lying to Mom. I was sitting so close I could feel my head shaking with hers. I longed to tell her about the Saturdays locked up in my room. The color of afternoon light seeping under the door as I listed my sins and recited the Kaddish. But I couldn't risk sounding ungrateful for all His infinite blessings.

"Sometimes it's a little longer," I confessed.

"Yeah, that's what I thought," she said with a sigh. She sounded worn out. "Well, I think G-d would be okay if you took a little time off this weekend while I'm here so we can have a good time, huh? What could happen?"

It was the only thing she could offer me, really. And I could only nod in response. Mom was so naïve it was scary. She already had two dead husbands, a job that was draining, and eyes that wandered nervously. And still she had no idea how dreadfully close she was to death herself.

"Thanks for the rug. I wish . . ." My voice wobbled and cracked.

"Just make sure to brush it out every once in a while," Mom instructed as I whimpered into her chest. "And if you get a chance, throw it in the wash—in cold water, though. Come on now, *ssssh,*" she blew into my ear, and though there was no way to empty my brain now, I silenced myself as dutifully and quickly as I could. She wasn't ignoring my pain; she just wanted me to rise above it— staple-gun and Scotch-tape a smile on if that's what it took. It was her way. After I saw her off the next day, I came back to my room, turned on the lamp as she had done, and sobbed deep and long into my new rug, clotting its soft threads with snot and drool, wretched and afraid for us both.

I don't know how I made it through that year. Most of my memories are of sitting on Marie's bed or waiting for footfalls outside my door to fade so I could begin my prayers over. I did make a few friends in my dorm and managed to get passable grades. I spent a lot of Friday nights at the campus Hillel House, where there were student-run Sabbath services. At the end of the year I even went to a dance at the Field Museum with a boy named Danny. I wasn't attracted to him and was sure he'd only asked me because his room-mate was going, so he posed no threat to Dad or to Him. But I said special prayers to apologize before and after the dance nonetheless. I spent most of the time at the museum tucked between the displays of stuffed marmosets and falcons, trying to squeeze in more *Thank You*'s and *I'm sorry*'s.

By the time finals had ended in June, I was praying about three hours a day, my hands were raw and bloody from scrubbing, and I left my rubbish pile in a drawer because I couldn't trust the numbers coming out of my mouth as I counted it. I went home for the sum-mer feeling bleary and skittish and told Mom that I had to be in my room for as long as it took in the morning and she shouldn't try to stop me. I took a job at a day camp and was soon convinced that I was hitting and groping the handicapped children. Mom didn't even ask this time. She just drove me straight to Dr. M.'s.

I stared at Dr. M.'s fireplace sulkily for the first fifteen minutes.

"Do you think the prayers could be getting in the way?" she asked gently.

"No," I muttered. I wanted to yell *Yes!* But I didn't dare. I would already have to add *I'm sorry if it sounded like I was complaining, please forgive me if it sounded like I was complaining* in multiples of five on the way home.

"Obsessive-compulsive disorder is a disease," Dr. M. said quietly. "It's like two wires in the brain are disconnected. I know you want to fix it by yourself, but sometimes it's impossible without a little help. It would be like me asking you to grow two inches taller by next week. You think you could do that?"

I had been unwilling to accept her diagnosis a year ago but this time I was so tired that I didn't protest. I wanted her to tell me more about these loose wires. I imagined these frayed ends floating in my tangled brain, the circuit that I could never close no matter how many times I said *off, off, off* or *Amen, Amen, Amen*. I was mys-tified by how effortlessly she separated my prayers from His all-encompassing love or disappointment. For those brief moments, I just listened to her interpret my repetitions as a clinical condition, an illness as pristine as the flu. I even allowed her to talk about going on a class of medications that had been known to help people with OCD.

"I'm not going to stop praying, though," I warned her, loud enough for Him to hear definitively.

"You don't have to. This will just help alleviate some of the anxiety surrounding it," she said. "Remember, Abby, you can stop at any time and I will help you through it."

I wished she would tell me I *had* to go on medication, so I wouldn't feel so hideous and profane, but she just sat there, waiting for my decision. I chewed off three hangnails and made two more before nodding limply.

"Now, I can't prescribe anything, but I know a very nice man. . . ."

Dr. F.'s office was in a high-rise off Central Avenue, just past the pet cemetery with the windmill in the middle. Dr. F. had a ton of legal pads. On one he wrote down all the things I needed to pick up. On another he noted the songs I still had to sing and how many times I washed my hands per day. On a third he wrote the length of my prayers. He gave me a prescription for a tricyclic antidepressant called Anafranil. He said to be patient, call him if I had any questions, and he'd see me in two weeks.

I did have a question—who was going to die first and how fiery and gruesome would it be? I heard countless sirens shrieking past while Mom backed out of the parking lot and I promised Him over and over again that I would still pray and I was sorrier than ever and this was only going to make me less nervous and more truly pious. Mom saw me whispering furiously and patted my knee.

"You're okay, Chicken."

She meant well, but her interruption meant I had to start over. I heard her suck in her breath as she waited for me to say *I hope you get there in time* fifty times. I knew she wouldn't exhale until I was done. Then she took me for ice cream and when she ordered Pralines and Cream on a sugar cone, I did too because I just wanted to be as sure and unbroken as she was.

All summer she drove me back and forth between the two doctors because I was too unnerved to drive on my own. Every time we got in the car she made sure we had some new distraction. She even let me change the radio station—something I'd never dared to do when in the car with either of my parents. Most of the time, if I landed on something other than classical, she said, *Ugh, all those drums.* But if I could find Joan Baez or James Taylor she hummed along and made her own *ba da ba daaaaa*'s soft and low.

We also rated all the store window displays. Mom thought it was hilarious that there was one shop called Mr. Shower Door.

"I mean, do they even need the mister part?" she said with a laugh.

"It is pretty insulting to all the female shower doors out there," I chimed in.

"Yeah—I bet Mrs. Shower Door is working hard too!"

When ambulances passed, Mom grew quiet and I knew she was counting *I hope you get there in time*'s with me. If I tried to go beyond fifty she'd pipe up with "C'mon, that's enough!" or "You're done, Chicken!" accompanied by a hefty thwap on the knee. Her voice would have a prickly exasperation to it, so I'd stop because I didn't want to upset her more. Whether she really was annoyed or not I'll never know, but in those moments her potential frustration eclipsed His. I was so grateful for her flustered chirrups as I reached fifty, for the evidence of her protecting love.

While Dr. F.'s capsules steeped inside me, I often felt like a burn victim wearing new skin, the air grazing at my limbs. Each step on our slate path felt precarious. I didn't know whether I'd be struck down or if everyone I loved would be picked off one by one. Mom watched my every move, pulling me into her chest and wiping the sweat and fear from my forehead. I was detoxing from an all-encompassing and all-seeing narcotic. I was terrified when she left the room. I said my prayers once a day each morning. I said them diligently, cautiously. I asked for forgiveness for trying the meds and said I hoped it didn't make Him mad. Mom timed me and gradually I cut back, shaving off five minutes, then ten, then twenty. Each time when I came out of my room she said "Good girl!" like I had done hard work. Then she promised me again that He wanted me to live a full life and not be stuck in a locked closet all day.

Mom and I were inseparable again. We shopped weekly at Filene's and took long walks by the water. At night we sat on the back porch eating canned salmon and fresh tomatoes from the farm stand. We climbed on her bed and did the crossword puzzle; we traded books and painted each other's toenails and spent Saturday afternoons in the drugstore blasting each other with sticky scents. We went to the pool at odd hours so I wouldn't run into too many people my age. Whenever we saw Mom's friends they told us how much we looked alike. We were both pleased. It was true. I didn't wear blush regularly or tie silk scarves around my neck, but we had matching sets of skinny legs and a slight kangaroo paunch. Our eyes were the same color blue. I watched her sometimes when she was sleeping by the side of the pool, her jaw slack, her breath serene. I definitely had her long nose and knobby fingers. She knew everything about me, and she promised me that my secrets were safe. She was not only my mother, she was my best friend. *Forever and ever no matter what.*

There was no one but us. Betsy was settled with her boyfriend in Pennsylvania; Jon was out in California at law school. Even our dog, Sandy, was gone, but Mom said she had lived a good life and besides, this way she could go to Connecticut for the weekend without boarding Sandy in a kennel. Mom's renovations were done. Jon's room was now officially an office with a computer and matching printer. Mom had started typing up some of her stories. Before she had kids she was an editor at Random House and she'd published a few children's books of her own. She had piles of loose-leaf paper with frayed edges and journals bound together with rubber bands that had been stashed away for years. She showed me a short story she'd been working on called "The Red Chiffon Number."

"I think you'll recognize some of the characters," she said with an awkward smile. It was about the red dress she wore the night my father proposed to her. The narrator was a young woman named Jan, new to high heels and living on her own in Manhattan, squirreling away her loose change to make sure she had the right dress for this date which she hoped was *the night*. I was charmed but also embarrassed to read about my mother being this girlish and fluttery—so adoring and unsure of herself. The story had a sensuous ending, where the red chiffon number came off. I read it through multiple times before handing it back timidly and murmuring, "Mom, it's amazing."

"Oh, come on, I don't know about that. But my friend Eleanor has a writing group that I'm thinking of joining so I wanted to have something together."

"Oh you should! You should!" I'd never been the one giving *her* advice before. We were both uncertain about the role reversal and she cut me off with an abrupt "Okay, well, come here. The whole point of that was to give you this. I think you'll fit into it better now that you have some boobs."

The chiffon was cool against my skin and wrapped around my torso in the tenderest cinch. Inside the wisps of red and rose I felt the silk lining caressing my spine. My mother zipped me up and we both stared into the mirror.

"Wow."

"Yeah."

She pulled my hair into a pile on top of my head and couldn't resist adding *Just a dab, I promise* of rose to my cheeks. She put small rhinestone droplets into my ears and then stepped back and sighed.

"I remember . . . mmmm," she said, her eyes getting puddly, and I didn't know whether to hug her or look away.

Before I headed back to Chicago for school, we passed Mr. Shower Door one last time. Dr. F. took out the lists he'd made at the beginning of the summer and studied them.

"First let me ask you, how do *you* think it's going?" he said.

"I dunno. Okay, I guess."

"Do you notice any differences?"

"Not really. I mean, maybe my prayers are shorter, but I don't know what else."

He started reading off his legal pads and making notes as I answered.

"Do you still pick up glass and paper clips?"

"I'm only allowed five a day."

"How about the songs you have to repeat?"

"We don't have a dog to walk, so no."

"How much time would you say you spend washing your hands?"

"That's definitely down."

"And prayers?"

"About twenty-five minutes."

"Hey! Sounds pretty good to me." He smiled.

"Thanks," I said quietly, not sure if it was a compliment or if he was boasting about his own work. I was nervous and wary of all his check marks and cross-outs. I wasn't convinced going on Anafranil was a wise or devout move. I loved being able to walk by staples and safety pins. I could sit down at a meal without hiding in the bathroom to pray and wash for ten minutes beforehand. But I was still frightened. Though no one had died this summer, I had the sense that G-d was not pleased with my decision to medicate. Our connection felt strained, and I wanted to reassure Him that in no way did I think faith was a disease. I just didn't know *how* to tell Him this. I was only allowed to talk to Him twenty-five minutes a day and there were a lot of sick people to pray for. I didn't know how to ask Him what was right and healthy. There was no room in our relationship for spontaneity or casual conversation. So I swallowed my pills each night and recited the Kaddish each morning. And I sincerely hoped He felt my undying love and respect as I finished *Thank You, Amen, Thank You, Amen, Thank You, Amen, Thank You, Amen, Thank You, Amen.*

Summer had always been the scariest time of year. The cicadas marshalled in exploding brains, unremitting cancer, and blowouts. This summer had been the longest and most fearsome of all. I felt more and more naked each day. It was a time of infinite and infinitesimal change at which I couldn't look too closely without incurring another tragedy. Mom and I gazed out the window and laughed at shower doors instead. We played dress-up and sprayed imitation colognes. This was the summer of growing two inches taller, or quieter, or at least closer.

we've replaced it with folgers

. . . .

The first thing I did when I got back to school was sign up for a full course load, the university choir, and a group of well-meaning yet ineffectual idealists called Students for Peace. We had a lot of bake sales for people starving in India and meandering meetings about how to be more organized. But it gave me someplace to go on weekends. I needed to keep myself busy so I wouldn't think about all the prayers I wasn't saying. I was rooming with Marie and I told her that I would need a half hour in the morning for prayers but I probably wouldn't make it home at night for our Bible chats. She said that was okay. She'd broken up with her youth-group boyfriend over the summer and was thinking of exploring new faiths on campus.

That fall I was also cast in a play about two French sisters who get hired as maids, flirt with incest, and eventually murder their mistresses. I'd been in a ten-minute play the year before in which I had to fake a prolonged heart attack, but only a handful of the girls from my dorm had shown up for the two performances. The French play would be my first foray onto the main stage and even the auditions felt exhilarating. The characters were riotously sexual and secretive and I delivered my lines ferociously. I adored being onstage because I could inhabit an entirely new life. I didn't have a past to bury or a future to run from. I was French and primal and impenitent. Performing filled my body and mind with a new focus; it stemmed my stream of unmanageable thoughts and gave me new words to memorize that weren't prayers and couldn't save or kill anyone.

During the first rehearsal we read through the play and then sat down with our date books to confirm schedules.

"Oh, wait. That second weekend of shows. That's Passover, right?" asked Ruthie, the girl who played one of the mistresses I was supposed to bludgeon.

"I don't know, is it?" answered the director.

"Yeah, it is," I moaned, finding the date in my book. I blinked at the small italic letters *Passover begins at sundown,* feeling the weight of their elegant curls. Passover was one of the biggest Jewish holidays. Mom was planning a lavish Seder and had offered to fly me home. And beyond her, above her, surrounding us all and shepherding me home, hovered Him. No play could be more important than His ordained celebration. I didn't say anything for the rest of the rehearsal, but when I got back to my dorm room I called Mom to plead woefully.

"It's on the main stage! Why is Passover so early this year?"

Mom said it wasn't the end of the world and that there would be plenty more plays and plenty more Passovers in my life.

"But what should I do?" I begged her.

"It's up to you, Chicken."

It wasn't up to me. I read my script one more time. I wanted to live in those words. I wondered mournfully who would replace me if I bowed out. Maybe they would put a note in the program saying that I was originally cast as the younger maid, but due to unforeseeable and all-seeing circumstances, I wasn't able to perform. This was the deprivation I deserved, though. If I was to be a true servant of G-d's there would be many tests like this, I reasoned. It was my responsibility and honor to accept these challenges. Mom was right. There would be other chances to get back onstage. Especially if I revered G-d and followed His calendar. Abraham had been willing to sacrifice his son for Him. The least I could do was relinquish a play about incest and murder.

It actually felt rewarding to tuck the script in the bottom of my desk drawer. My chest rose with self-importance as I called the director and told her I couldn't be in the play. I'd be home with my family recounting the Jews' exodus from Egypt. Then I had Mom book me a flight.

I ran into Ruthie by the theater bulletin board the following week. She told me I was a better Jew than she was.

"Nah." I shrugged, secretly pleased. "I'm sure you're a great Jew."

"You're great onstage, too," she said with a certainty that made me blush. "Seriously, you're perfect for that part. Have you done a lot of theater?" I was unnerved and drawn to her at the same time—her ice blue eyes, her glowing red cheeks. She had a splash of freckles thrown across the bridge of her nose and the clearest skin I'd ever seen. It was her first big play too and she told me her parents would be upset about it because she was supposed to be immersed in her studies, but she was determined to do the play anyway. As we talked, we figured out that she had been my math TA for the past semester. Ruthie was a month younger than me, but she had already placed out of all the math courses offered for undergraduates and was on the fast track to a PhD. I told her she was smarter than I'd ever be. She shook her head forcefully, her brown wavy hair falling in front of her face. She leaned in closer to me. I felt a rush of giddy expectancy as she held my wrist fast.

"Listen. I have an idea. Are you going to Off-Off tryouts next week?"

Off-Off Campus was the university improvisation-sketch troupe. Each year they chose seven students to write and perform original revues. Ruthie said we had to try out together, that we'd make incredible scene partners. She knew for a fact that Off-Off needed smart funny women and she said we were the smartest funniest women out there.

"I've never done improv," I admitted flatly.

"Doesn't matter," she promised. "We've got this. You in?" I agreed, ecstatic that we were already a *we*. The next week, when we were both on the cast list, her cheeks flushed even redder and she declared us unstoppable.

Ruthie was right. We *were* unstoppable. Indissoluble. Joined at the hip night and day. We loved the same actors, authors, colors, flavors, music. We howled wildly to Deee-Lite and Talking Heads. We traded shirts that were almost the identical shade of blue. We stayed up late in her room making up dance routines and writing sketches for the next Off-Off show. We came up with an entire musical about *Oedipus* and Ruthie said I was the only one who could pull off an innocent yet beguiling Jocasta. We set the story in the antebellum South so we needed straw hats and bandanas, but that was no problem, because Ruthie's family had been in Hyde Park since they emigrated from Russia in the late seventies. Her parents lived just around the corner and they had plenty of old clothes we could scrounge through for costumes.

When I spent time at her house, I was astounded by the way her family spoke to one another so bluntly, often storming and sparring. I had never experienced this kind of open conflict in my house. Ruthie had disagreements with her parents, even intense fights, and it didn't mean she loved them any less. Mere moments after ranting at one another, Ruthie's dad offered up a dirty joke or her mom brought out fresh-baked desserts. Nobody in her family ever died.

Ruthie's mom made incredible home-cooked meals for us—crispy chicken and Russian beet salad and warm challahs. I even ate the stuff that smelled funny because I wanted Ruthie's family to like me. They were all equally gifted, but of course Ruthie was the most exceptional of all—a math genius, a performer, a writer. She showed me her poems and short stories—the most chilling and profound words I'd ever read. In return, I told her my history of loss. Aunt Simone being flown in an emergency helicopter, the drone of cicadas and the amazing amount of smoked fish and cold cuts, a stepfather who arrived with gifts and left in a pear-shaped coffin. Ruthie held my hands in hers as I spoke. Her eyes pooled with my sorrow and she wept openly for me.

Ruthie and I began having late-night writing sessions together. Not for Off-Off, but for our dark and forbidden thoughts. She told me to write down everything, anything, just—*Do not lift the pen until you are done, now go!* She timed us with her stopwatch and her pen immediately propelled across the page. When Ruthie wrote, her breath grew labored and she bowed into her notebook. Wherever we wrote—a dorm room, a café booth, a deserted stairwell—it felt like the most intimate setting because I could feel her stripping away all pretense, chiseling through to the ugliest truths. When Ruthie's stopwatch went off, we read our pieces out loud. The rule was, neither of us could edit, interrupt, or comment. No excuses or self-deprecating preambles, either. Just the unarmed sound of our voices.

Being with Ruthie was intoxicating. I adored her as I had Ellyn years ago, imitating her handwriting and speech patterns. I wanted to *be* her. I was in awe of how deeply she felt everything, how quickly she could drop from full-bellied laughter to tears. Ruthie was raw, uncensored, and unafraid. Most amazingly, she admired me too, which made our friendship infinitely greater than anything I'd forced Ellyn into years ago. I didn't need to tell Ruthie she was my best friend forever and ever—it was implicit in everything we did. I still roomed with Marie and I saw other girls from the dorm but most of my time was spent with Ruthie. I lay awake at night and tried to imagine what she was dreaming or how I could make her laugh the next day. People asked were we twins? Lovers? This question always made us laugh because there was no sexual attraction and Ruthie knew I'd never even kissed a boy. I had the same boisterous laugh as Ruthie did now, because I'd adopted hers. One day I hoped to be able to cry like her too.

Ruthie was a voracious crier, which inspired and intimidated me. I'd never encountered someone who honored her angst, who lived in it and explored it. I began to see how dry I had been for so many years. My lips and skin were always chapped and irritated, my eyes blinked anxiously when I felt overwhelmed, but never released anything. It was how I'd been brought up. My mother's night table always held at least a half dozen trial-size hand creams at once. She had ointment for her eyelids because they cracked and flaked too. The doctor said she was allergic to her own tears.

Talking with Ruthie made me think about Mom's shushes differently. She was trying to blow away my incantations and repetitions to disentangle me, but also because she needed some peace and quiet. She didn't know what to do with my mind's incessant chatter, the *litany of the dead,* as she called it. She had two late husbands to mourn and a life to start over and no space to breathe. She was occupied with cleaning out closets and packing sweaters with fresh mothballs.

I could tell Ruthie anything and she always held my hand as I delved into the scariest parts. Ruthie was the only person other than my mother and Dr. M. who knew the Finast story. She listened to the whole thing and I could feel her tears even though I was too embarrassed to look at her. I told her about the people I'd killed on the way to Dr. M.'s and showed her my prescription. Afterward, whenever we were on the street together and she saw me pick up a paper clip or nail, she gently pried it loose.

"I've got it," she'd say. She told me how brave and talented I was. She said I was magnetic onstage—praise that I'd never heard before. I'd shake my head and say, "No, *you* are." But I lived for her approval. Ruthie was my best friend and my long-lost sister and in many ways she was my mother now too, though I would never let myself acknowledge it. Mom was slowly and stealthily being unseated.

It reminded me of that old commercial for Folgers instant coffee where a hidden camera was placed in a four-star restaurant and the announcer spoke furtively into the microphone: *We are here at (insert name of four-star restaurant), where we've secretly replaced the fine coffee they usually serve with Folgers Crystals. Let's see if anyone can tell the difference!* And then everyone at the tables was so happy with their coffee—they oohed and aahed and said *This tastes even better than I remembered!*

I loved that commercial when I was younger because it made me feel I was in on a delicious secret and because it was such a simple trick. Replacing Mom with Ruthie was equally simple and so seamless that I never saw it happening. Or else I instinctively chose to ignore what I was doing. I still spoke to Mom on the phone at least two to three times a week, often just as she was falling asleep at night. She didn't like the fact that I was out so late all the time.

"But it's an hour earlier here," I explained repeatedly. "And Ruthie and I were working on a new scene for the show."

"It's the walk home I'm talking about. You're not the most observant sometimes and it's not well lit."

"It's okay, Mom. I promise."

"Is it? I worry." I knew she was concerned about not only the poorly lit streets but also my all-consuming relationship with Ruthie and the theater. Mom often told me that it was great to be creative and she was all for me trying new activities, but I should be careful not to get too caught up in one thing.

"You're just so good at math and science. I'd hate to see that all fall down the tubes." The conversation usually ended with her asking if I was wearing enough blush. I lied and said yes, but she saw right through me. "You could be so pretty if you just had a little more color on your face," she lamented.

Ruthie didn't fuss over herself with makeup and I had decided that neither would I. Ruthie wore one style of jeans and used one type of pen and I was captivated by the order and transparency of her decisions. I yearned to be that close to my truth.

I still spoke to Him every morning for a half hour, and I went to Hillel once in a while, but less and less because Off-Off shows were on Friday nights and we were already in previews. On the walk over to the theater I repeated a new prayer for us to *please have a good show a great show the best show EVER.* I wanted G-d to be okay with my new love of the theater even if it wasn't as holy as a rabbinical career and I could do more serviceable good if I fed orphans or found a cure for cancer. I felt so unhindered and buoyant under those stage lights. I hoped in some way I was channeling my father and Aunt Simone, tap-dancing and skedap-bopping on top of the clouds. When I prayed for *a good show a great show the best show EVER,* I yearned for them to hear me too.

What I never prayed for, never hoped or wished for, was Tristan. Tristan was in my Greek theater class in the fall of my sophomore year. He wore his shirts inside out and his hair was gnarled in rough curls. I swore to Ruthie that I hated him. We were paired up as scene partners, and he said he could only rehearse after hours at the basement coffee shop where he worked on campus. When I met him there he stole us each a bottle of orange juice from the cooler, explaining that he deserved at least that much because the wages were insulting and the closing shift sucked. Then we hurled passages from *Orestes* at each other as he pushed a dirty mop across the linoleum floor. Tristan was one of the older members of Off-Off. I'd seen him perform—he was just as attractive and arrogant onstage as when he wielded a mop. He told me our previews looked good and I needed to be louder but some of my material was pretty funny. I hated him for the half compliment. I hated myself more for hanging on his every word.

The opening night of our revue *was* the best show EVER. I repeated my prayer ten times instead of five for good measure before the curtain went up. Our cast was strong. Our transitions were smooth. Ruthie's scene got a raucous round of applause and I felt sharp and strident, especially during the improv set. *Oedipus* brought down the house. Ruthie and I bayed at the moon and floated all the way to the cast party. We grabbed Boone's Country Kwenchers and headed straight to the dance floor, wiggling our hips wildly.

"Tristan is totally checking you out!" she shouted into my ear above the music.

"What? No!" I shimmied harder, trying to shake the goofy grin off my face.

"I'm serious. Look," she urged. He was skulking by the stairs, slugging a beer. I couldn't tell where he was looking, mostly because his scowl made me feel so flushed and distracted.

"Just go say hi." Ruthie nudged me toward him.

"Hey." He nodded.

"Hey."

"Nice show."

"You think?" I could've kicked myself for sounding so eager. Tristan smirked. Then he said he had something he wanted to tell me but he didn't know if he should or not. I said he should.

"All right," he grumbled. "First, come here."

He pulled me toward him and we kissed. It tasted like a bottle of seltzer exploding in my mouth. He took me around a corner and we kissed some more. His tongue snaked into my mouth and I tried to follow his lead but I was concentrating so hard we had to stop so I could catch my breath.

"Can I walk you back to your dorm?" he asked.

"I guess. Just hold on a sec." I giggled. Then I found Ruthie and quickly gave her a play-by-play of what had happened as I put on more ChapStick. She was ecstatic. "Go go go go!" she cheered.

Tristan and I kissed more in the hallway by my door but I explained that he couldn't come in because it was 2 a.m. and I had a roommate. "I had a really fun time though."

"Yeah, me too." He grinned mischievously.

After I closed the door, I sat on my bed and felt my whole body quake with a panicky tremor of pleasure. I tasted his salty tongue on mine and smelled his pine-scented deodorant and heard his deep growly *Mmmmm*'s.

I also heard something closer, like thunder in my bones—His creeping and silent loathing. The true reason I couldn't let Tristan come in. I stayed on that bed for I don't know how long with my back flush against the cold stone wall, knees tucked into my chest. I spoke in a rumble of my own. Stronger than a whisper. Softer than my full voice. As intimate as I knew how to be. There weren't enough words to express the depths of my shame, to give myself over to G-d entirely, body and soul. *I'm so sorry if I've offended You or done something bad. I promise I love You the most forever and always forever and always. Forever and ever and always forever.* I went on begging His forgiveness until I was dazed and wilted. I don't know how I ever got to *Amen.*

I also don't know how I went back to Tristan. I knew I was transgressing, but the medication had chipped away just enough space in my holy armor so I could sneak out and lunge into Tristan's arms. Letting him touch me and enjoying his touch was still base and sinful, so I turned off all the lights when we were entwined. I felt Him watching, and I knew He could strike us both down in an instant, but I couldn't help myself. Being with Tristan made me feel taller, brighter, more exotic and mature, and for the first time I saw myself as desirable. Ruthie said we were the perfect couple and that we would make hilarious babies. Mom was delighted too. I called her after every date. She said he sounded wonderful except for the Irish Catholic part and she couldn't wait to meet him.

"Just remember to wear blush and how are you fixed for Anafranil?"

Tristan got me a job at the campus coffee shop where he worked, so I was busy and caffeinated at least eighteen hours a day. I couldn't sit still or look at the sky too long or I would feel His omnipresent eyes asking me *What do you think you're doing?* I had to keep moving. Each morning as I brushed my hair and stepped into my clogs, I stood at the edge of my mirror so I wouldn't have to face my full reflection. I smoothed on burgundy gloss and quickly turned away from my lips, my neck, my shoulders, which had now been touched. Which were no longer pure.

For months Tristan and I kissed and tumbled, groped and moaned on his futon in the frat house. I was careful never to let him go too far and I made sure I was home by morning so I could say my prayers. I didn't mention Him to him and I certainly didn't mention him to Him, but I knew He saw it all, especially the parts under the covers. I felt as though I was living a double life, only it wasn't as glamorous as the life of a Russian spy or those Bond girls in cat suits who drank martinis. As I walked home from Tristan's early in the morning, I made myself stare at trees so I couldn't see the next pin or screw on the curb. If that didn't work, I sang the *I'm picking up one more thing* song under my breath. It was a little ditty I'd invented over the summer that was supposed to help me when I caught myself circling the block, scavenging for sharp objects. Dr. M. loved it. She said recognizing I was having trouble was about 99 percent of the battle. Which was great, but she'd never told me what to do with that last 1 percent. Often I'd sing all the way home from Tristan's and still have fistfuls of glass and pockets stuffed with twigs and thumbtacks.

I kept my litter piles and my prayers hidden from Tristan. Secrecy was the only way I knew to preserve and honor their sanctity. I wanted to conceal my medication, too, but soon decided that that gave the pills too much reverence, so I showed him the bottle. *It's an anxiety thing,* I said dismissively. He didn't question it. He said a lot of his relatives should be on medication too. On the nights I stayed with him, I waited until I felt his limbs loosen with sleep and then, crouched in front of his minifridge, I swallowed my slick yellow capsules. I tried to snap my neck back quickly the way Mom always did with her vitamins, as if taking these mind-altering chemicals was a normal everyday thing to do. But it wasn't normal and I often jerked my head too fast so I was left with a capsule-shaped scuff mark in my throat that tugged at me for days. Then I lay back down next to Tristan's snoring body and tried to block out everything except the squirrels running through the rafters, pawing at the rotting wood.

I was dating Tristan and letting him touch me in naughty places and it was fun and made me giggly and I washed my hair more, but it was nothing like my love affair with Ruthie. The only times we were apart was when I was praying, kissing, or sleeping. We wrote two more shows together and I was especially pleased with a vampy lounge number that I thought my dad would have loved. Mom came out to see it and afterward she said I had a lot of pizzazz up on stage.

"Chicken, really. I'm so impressed. Of course, I'd love it if you'd stand up a little straighter. . . ."

She met Tristan after the show and told me he was very nice and she could see why I was attracted to someone so charismatic. I told her I was glad she liked him because it was getting pretty serious.

"All right, but don't forget, you can still date other people, Ab."

"No I can't!"

She told me that when she'd first started dating my father she was seeing another man at the same time. I was hurt by the thought of her two-timing my first and only true boyfriend.

"People don't do that anymore, Mom. At least, not me," I said crossly.

It was the first time I can remember challenging her, and we both were stunned.

When sophomore year ended, Ruthie and I rented an apartment together for the summer and I got a job teaching theater at a day camp while she waited tables at the same local café as Tristan. He and I had been rolling under the squirrels for nearly a year and each day I felt more enamored of him, still incredulous that he wanted me. He wanted me a lot. We began having tense discussions about why I wouldn't have sex with him. Ruthie said I should go for it. Mom said having sex could be fun and not to worry, I would always be her little girl. But I wasn't sure. I couldn't ask G-d what to do because I knew He would be sickened by my carnal urges. I already felt permanently stained. Tristan said he respected that I was a virgin and that I wanted it to be special but I was giving him blue balls and it was painful and why wouldn't I just trust him? One night we fought loudly on the street and I screamed, "All right already! Let's just do it!"

Tristan made sure it was romantic, turning on only a thimble-size night-light and blaring his favorite CD of British rock. I lay silently while he put on his condom, listening to his Irish flag snapping against his window in the night breeze. He was very gentle, tracing my neck with kisses, telling me how much he appreciated my concession. I couldn't orgasm, but he said not many women did on the first time. And though it hurt a bit at first, I did feel emboldened. I was a woman now. Afterward Tristan and I lay there and he told me I was incredibly sexy. Then he let me wear his pajama bottoms and we drank stolen bottles of orange juice and watched *The Simpsons*. He assured me next time I would have more fun too.

"Mazel tov!" Mom clapped.

"I'm so happy for you," cried Ruthie.

"And he said next time . . ." I explained.

There wasn't any next time. A week later Tristan and I got dollar milkshakes at the coffee shop and walked slowly to the park. He waited until we were slurping the bottom of our Styrofoam cups before he said that he'd been thinking maybe we should take some time off.

"Time off how?"

"Like, maybe we should break up," he said with a shrug.

Next to us kids were flying overhead on a jungle gym and spinning on tire swings and monkey bars. Below us the earth was splitting apart.

"*No no no no no!*" I pleaded. "Please no?"

But Tristan's mind was made up. He sounded bored as he mumbled *sorry*'s and *hey-it'll-be-okay*'s. He stood up to leave again and again but I kept asking him to please tell me *why*? Was it the sex? Was it the nonsex? Could we be friends and then maybe try again? What about our plans to ride bikes to the lake next Saturday? We could ride bikes without dating, right? What if I collapsed on the way home from the park that night, could I at least use him as an emergency contact? He said yes to that one before leaving me on the sagging bench to burp up warm vanilla shake.

I limped home to the two-bedroom-no-ventilation apartment Ruthie and I had rented. This couldn't be happening. But it had to be. I deserved this punishment because I chose Tristan over Him. I'd known this all along and yet I kept going. I even gave him my virginity. I didn't blame Him for this tragedy. I was disappointed in me too.

Ruthie cried harder than I did over Tristan. That night she sat me down at our three-legged coffee table and said we'd get through this breakup together and it would only make us stronger. She knew that I felt disgraced about having sex and that I felt I'd never have done it if it weren't for the medicine. It made me loose and immoral. I was

144

furious at Dr. F. for giving me a false sense of freedom. I was mad at Dr. M. and Mom too, for convincing me that I'd be better with a magic pill. I was livid with myself for falling for it, for trying to disprove the truth. Ruthie and I talked for hours about how medicine deadened the senses, numbed the soul, muted the voices that needed to shout. I didn't even know if I could trust my heartbreak while medicated. It felt good to throw out the bottle, listening for the soft clink against the bottom of the garbage can. Ruthie held me and said I was the strongest person she knew and she would stand by me until forever.

I called Mom and told her I'd learned my lesson. I was done with boys and I was done with sex and most of all I was done with Anafranil.

Mom drew in a breath and said carefully, "Are you really sure you want to do that, Chicken? I know this feels awful right now, but there are other gefilte fish in the sea. I promise." She reminded me about her high school prom and her peplumed victory.

"You already told me that story," I moaned.

"Yes, but it's still true." I pictured her cradling the telephone on the other end of the line, her nectarine lips fastened together in a pout, trying to figure out how to ease my suffering and humiliation. I wished she could. I wished we could laugh at shower doors and try on dresses. But I was so far away from her.

"Honey, Tristan is one thing. But the medicine . . . you've made such progress. I promise it's going to be okay."

"Sorry, Mom. I just can't."

I also couldn't explain it to her anymore. I just needed to cry and she wouldn't like that, so I hung up. I cried for losing Tristan, for losing my virginity, and for all the oceans of litter I'd left on the street to tear through unsuspecting tires and destroy innocent lives. I cried for how small and ineffectual Mom's voice sounded as she repeated *I promise*. I cried for how sonorous and sad His voice was inside me and the gulf of time and trust I'd created between us. For the insurmountable task I had of earning His pardon again.

Ruthie and I did a lot of crying that summer. Shouting, too. Throwing hairbrushes and ripping up Tristan's old letters. Every day when I got off work at day camp, I waited in the park until it was time to pick up Ruthie from her café shift. We wandered toward Lake

Michigan arm in arm, dissecting the day. When I picked up a bottle cap or wrapper, Ruthie wordlessly pulled it from my palm, zipped it into her knapsack, and squeezed me tightly. Then we sat on the lake-soaked rocks by the water and ate leftover scones from the café and filled up countless pages in our journals with tales of hunting and haunting. We sobbed Diet Pepsi tears and raged at our fathers for being absent (mine) or too demanding and Russian (hers). I prayed for Ruthie's family. I prayed for Mom. I prayed that He could forgive me for straying and that my father could forgive me for having a boyfriend besides him and that everyone who was ailing could *heal completelypainlesslysoon completelypainlesslysoon.*

Without the medication, the exploding brains and burnt-out cars slowly crept back into my line of vision and the streets revealed more treacherous waste each day. But the truth was, they had never left. I'd just been too chemically blinded to see, and each day without medicine was bringing me back to earth.

Ruthie encouraged me to write it all out. She kept clicking that stopwatch so I would have a place to go, a page on which to disintegrate. When I felt corpses chasing me, I laid them all out in my notebook for her. My vision had narrowed and darkened again, and only she understood it. Our nights together, hunkered over our notebooks, skin wet with the lake's mist, were my stillest moments. My *quiet time* was lengthening, my pleas and apologies to the Eternal growing more and more frenzied.

I only saw Mom once that summer, when she bought me a ticket home for a long weekend. I insisted Ruthie come with me. She was my touchstone as Mom had once been, and I needed her by my side. The first night home, Mom invited her best friend, Lynn, for dinner on our porch. Lynn brought a neighbor named Bernard, who told long and drippy stories that made little sense and Ruthie and I pinched each other's thighs and hid behind our napkins to keep from cackling.

Then there was a loud thud. When I looked up, Mom had disappeared. Her chair had snapped in half and she was splayed on the porch slats.

"Mom!"

"Joan?"

"Boy, must be all the cheese I've been eating." Mom laughed it off, but her mouth was crooked with pain.

I watched, stricken with guilt, as Lynn helped her to her feet. I hadn't pushed her over, but I was laughing and I had grabbed Ruthie's hand and not hers and I had stopped kissing the red chiffon dress and writing that Mom was my best friend forever and though I hadn't meant to replace her or hurt her, I knew now that I had. I excused myself to go to the bathroom to say *Please let Mom heal completely painlessly soon completely painlessly soon.* I said it five times and five *thank You, Amen*'s too but even with my eyes clamped shut, the image of Mom lying on the ground danced in front of me. I scraped at my face until I had dime-size patches of raw skin on my chin and forehead.

There was a knock on the door. "Chicken, are you picking again?"

"No."

She met me as I opened the door, sore and exhausted.

"*Why?*" Mom looked so sad. "I thought we were all having so much fun."

"I can't help it," I whined, turning my face away so she couldn't inspect my open wounds. She held me and smoothed my hair.

"You're going to be okay," she crooned. All I could do was nod. I couldn't tell her that she was the one endangered.

The next day, Mom took Ruthie and me shopping and bought us matching purses. She also got me a blue straw hat that was low enough to cover the scab on my forehead. Then she dressed my chin with antiseptic and a Band-Aid and the three of us took a picnic to the park for an outdoor concert. Mom had made us corn and tomato salad, shish kebob, and fresh gazpacho.

"Mrs. Sher, thank you for being so good to me," said Ruthie, leaning back on the blanket and drinking in the canopy of evergreens.

"Thank *you* for being so good to my daughter."

"And thank you both for pretending that I'm normal," I gulped. I loved them both so much in that moment I thought I might break. I wanted Mom to know that I didn't mean to supplant or injure her and that she was the greatest mom ever. As she was tucking me into bed later that night, I held on to her neck and whispered urgently, "You're still my best friend no matter what."

"Aw, thanks, honey. And you're mine," said Mom.

"*Forever* and ever." She needed to know this. I needed her to know and G-d to know and Ruthie too. I pulled her in closer to me. I couldn't endure the thought of Mom hurting because of anything I'd done. "I *mean* it," I insisted.

"I love you too, Chicken."

"Ayl me-lech ne-men She-ma . . ."

PEOPLE I'VE KILLED AND HOW LIST
(PART TWO)

12. David (poison and mental anguish)*
14. Countless pedestrians, bicyclists, and motorists in Hyde Park**
17. October

*Thirteen has bad connotations, must avoid it.
**Fifteen difficult because one plus five is six, sixteen obviously bad.

running from october

· ·

Mom would always be my best friend, but Ruthie is the one who took me to Walgreen's.

I was just a few months away from graduating, working toward a BA in humanities, with a concentration in Russian language. For my thesis I was translating *Notes from the Underground* (which had already been done much more adeptly) and adapting it into a three-hour play that I would later put on in a mildewed café. Ruthie was getting her math degree as stipulated by her parents, but it was clear to us both that we would only be happy pursuing acting or writing. Mom slowly accepted this fate for me, though she often warned, "Ab, the theater is full of rejection. I just don't know if you can handle it. You're too *sensitive*."

My prayers continued to hold steady between thirty and forty minutes each morning, and I walked briskly around campus, singing up into the treetops and often shielding my eyes with my hands like blinders so I could keep my dangerous objects pile small. Sometimes it worked and sometimes I couldn't stop the blowout from engulfing my brain. Ruthie and I still met regularly to write it all out, to draw it in the most vivid and violent colors, to wail it in the loudest tears.

I was completely unresolved about my sexuality. Even though I'd made promises to G-d to stay chaste, I often daydreamed about guys in my classes. I went on a few dates, but I wouldn't sleep with anyone and I apologized to Him for each kiss. I belted out my Cement Mixer lyrics so I could be Daddy's little girl, but my body betrayed me with its unwanted desires and then I had to apologize to Dad and to the Heavenly Father again. I felt miserably disconnected above and below my neck. Ruthie said there was nothing wrong with sex and this was our time to have fun and Mom said as long as I wore blush and used protection it was fine and I told them both that I didn't want any boys in my life, but then there was Mark.

Ruthie had her eye on Mark before I did. He was two years younger than us, but Ruthie said he was mature for his age. She'd met him at the university theater and declared him smart and sensitive. Also single. She made sure we all went to the same apartment party after an Off-Off show. There was a big space cleared in the living room and a stereo hammering out a techno beat, but no one was going to be the first to start boogying. The windows were open and the night was misty, all the lightbulbs had been covered with blue cellophane so the empty floor glowed eerily like a lunar landing. Ruthie and I got wine coolers from the hall, leapt into the middle of the room, and launched into one of our dance routines, bumping our butts together and laughing rowdily. Mark was hanging out in the kitchen, and our plan was for Ruthie to get some snacks and casually encounter him by the dip bowl while I waited on the cement porch. Only, when she came back from her mission, she announced categorically, "He likes you more."

"No. What? No."

"He does. I just asked his roommate."

"But I barely know him. That's stupid."

"Ab, it's fine. Do you like him?"

"I don't know. I mean, yeah but . . ."

"So go for it. He totally likes you."

I felt off-balance, though I'd only had a few swigs from my Boone's. The night sky started rotating slowly around me.

"It's okay," Ruthie said again. I couldn't tell if she was saying it to be gracious or if she meant it. Either way, I was eager to find out more about this cute boy. I lurched forward, pushed open the screen door and marched onto the barren dance floor, jerking my hips doggedly as I watched Mark out of the corner of my eye. Pretty soon he and his roommate were dancing too, and then Mark and I were alone on the cement balcony and the real moon was nowhere to be found because the night was so hazy and close. I heard him saying something about growing up on the plains of some Dakota but I didn't know where exactly because I was too busy trying to ignore his soft-looking lips and negotiate a silent supplication for His understanding. I itched from wanting something so badly but not wanting to give it a name, an unutterable pining. We stood on the porch for a long time, our noses just grazing each other, letting the party disappear behind us. Mark said he couldn't wait to spend more time together.

"Me too, me too!" I chirped into his ear. Then I went to the bathroom and ran the water loudly so I could giggle without being heard. And I gave my hands a good scrub, because this was certainly unclean.

The walk home from the party felt incredibly long and awkward. The air was sour from too many kegs tipped over onto the spongy frat lawns. Ruthie wanted to know what had happened and I was more than eager to tell her, but when I did she put on a smile that reached only halfway across her face.

"That's great," she said in a false, bright voice that meant it wasn't great at all.

"Really?" I asked.

"Yeah." She obviously wasn't going to tell me her true feelings.

"Thanks," I whispered shyly, and we hugged, only not so tight.

Mark and I became an item within days. We loved to eat soup and Slurpees and make out until our lips went numb. We went for road trips up and down Lake Shore Drive in his white hatchback, grabbed South Side burritos and jazz at the Checkerboard Lounge, and came back to his apartment to undress each other slowly, adoringly. In the morning I'd scamper back to the apartment I shared with some girls from my dorm, steal into my bedroom, and lock the door so I could pore over my prayer book and update my sick and traveling lists. My heart pulsing wildly, I'd articulate my Shemas as naturally as possible. I hoped if my words were devout enough they could erase my actions. I couldn't let Him smell my fear. I added a new prayer for traffic lights and I kissed my three-speed bike and chanted *thank You* twenty-five times whenever I got to or from Mark's place safely.

Mom was delighted with Mark because he was Jewish, and when I found myself toppling into a spiral of unholy condemnation, I tried to tell myself that Mom and Dad and even Jews in the Bible fooled around. I reminded myself that G-d had to concentrate on global events like Ethiopia and Kosovo and couldn't be worried about trivial things like whom I was French-kissing. I just needed to keep my body separate from the stormy terrain in my head. In my SiRo journal I was careful to never spell out Mark's name completely. If He was reading, I didn't want it to seem as if Mark was that important or that anything we did on his couch was meaningful.

When Mark and I slept together for the first time, it was languid and comforting and full of silent caresses. Nothing like it had been with Tristan. Mark's curtains blocked out the street, the balmy night, and hopefully beyond, coloring his tiny room a deep indigo. We fell asleep naked and spent. I snuck home the next day and locked my door for an hourlong *quiet time*. I took long breaths to steady myself and repeated my sick list three times so He knew I wanted everyone ailing to heal and not get sicker. Also that I was sorry if I had made anyone sick or if I sounded as though I wanted someone to be sick or sicker. The following week, Mark and I had sex again. And again. Each time I added a name to one of my lists or a new psalm from the prayer book. I was sorry for anyone who'd fallen ill or gotten into an accident while I was too busy nestling in Mark's arms. I was sorry for all the pain and war and famine that I ignored so I could tumble under his sheets. I was sorry I was so weak that I had succumbed to these dirty human cravings instead of devoting myself unequivocally to prayer. When I reached the final *Amen,* I'd bound out of my room so I could prattle at one of my roommates instead of starting the repetitions over again.

One morning, instead of getting on my three-speed and taking off, I was convinced by Mark to sleep in, and the next thing I knew it was 9:30 and time for classes and I couldn't get home first to do my prayers. The whole day I waited for the atmosphere to break apart, the call from the dean saying my mother had been consumed in a fatal inferno rising up from the earth's angry core. I ordered coffee in a whisper and kept my hand lowered in class because if I hadn't spoken to G-d first, I shouldn't speak at all. A current of dread trickled through my veins, my lungs couldn't take in enough air as I walked home across the quads.

After that, I tried praying at Mark's a few times. I told him he had to leave me alone for thirty to forty minutes and not ask questions and he didn't. I shoved my back against his door, plugged my ears with my fingers until my brain throbbed, and spoke into the darkness, pretending with all I had that there was nothing unchaste going on. But He and I both knew better. On the days I prayed at Mark's, I was withdrawn and restless and often had to collect a lot more trash. I lived in a constant commotion, trying to race every ambulance and put out every fire. I had to repeat most of the prayers again whenever I got home.

I could breathe much easier when I stuck to my routine. Even without meds and while in a relationship, I had the rituals pretty much under control. I wasn't washing my hands as much; I was down to picking up five things a day; and I kept *quiet time* under forty-five minutes. I also had the ambulance prayer and the Cement Mixer song; healing prayers at accident sites; chants for traveling in planes, trains, and on bicycles; fifty kisses up to the sky near traffic lights and at funeral parlors; and before any performances I hid between the trash cans in the theater's parking lot and sang my *Thank You G-d for making this all possible* song.

I could live with this. I lived *for* this. Through my connective tissue ran a fixed and fierce piety that nobody could take from me. Ruthie had helped me see that we all had secrets and this was mine. I was compelled and honored by my divine undertaking. I'd done some bad things in the past. I continued to give in to hungers like sex and Slurpees, but I was hopeful that praying regularly could put me back on track. And maybe He would keep an extra arm extended to hold me and my loved ones out of harm's way. After all, no one I knew had died in the past four years.

Until October.

Ruthie and I had graduated and moved into an apartment above an all-night diner. After Mark and I started seeing each other regularly, Ruthie and I never discussed her crush on him again, and I was relieved when she began dating someone she'd met at an audition. I couldn't acknowledge to her or myself that I might have wronged her. Our lives were hectic but charged with struggling-artist ambition—we were waiting tables at local cafés and taking improv classes at a theater near us called ImprovOlympic. We started writing another show together—Ruthie's idea, of course. It was a sketch show for just the two of us about mental illnesses. The first scene was about two chefs, and the joke was that she was trying to mix the ingredients but I couldn't stop counting and recounting the tablespoons of baking soda. We hadn't performed it for anyone yet, but I didn't care if we ever did. The only laughter I was listening for was Ruthie's anyway. I still considered her my guru and muse.

Mark was busy because he was still in school so I didn't tell him and I didn't want to tell him and I didn't think I needed to tell him that I missed a period. I didn't say it in prayers either, because it was nothing—it *had* to mean nothing. I did tell Ruthie, because she caught me frozen in front of the mirror and she knew it was something. We called my mom and then we walked to Walgreen's to buy a test. And then another. The pink lines coming into focus, distilling my whole being into one impossible moment.

I couldn't have a child. I barely had the time or money or wherewithal to bathe and feed myself. I stared at the test again. It was as horrifyingly real as the Jeep in the high school parking lot, only now there was a fertilized egg—some would already call it a life—and I was hooked on to it, dangling, flailing, suspended. I would do anything to escape this reality. Ruthie moaned with me as I sat on the toilet staring numbly, my pants around my ankles, which were somehow attached to legs, hips, gut, and deep beneath the rib cage, a frantic valve pumping blood in and out.

Hours later, Mark was screaming, "Why didn't you tell me before you told her?!" and I was screaming, "Why are you screaming at me?!" and Ruthie was screaming, "Please! Don't fight!" I couldn't imagine what The Big Guy was screaming above us.

My mother flew in the day before my *procedure*. She brought me a new blue bathrobe and swaddled me in it, taking me in her arms and purring, *It's okay, Chicken. Of course you're making the right decision. You're too young to have a child.* On her walk from the subway, she'd bought brie and wine from the local grocery store and she worked hard to charm us, to make the night easier. She asked Mark how his studies were going and told Ruthie she loved what she'd done with her hair. As she nibbled cheerfully, she chattered on about the great public transit system here in Chicago.

"It's just so clean and easy to navigate. And all the flowers on the crosswalks! Is that Maggie Daley who arranged that? I'm going to write her a letter!" She offered me a wink that I knew was code for *You're okay* and I wanted to thank her, but all I could muster in return was a bleak grimace.

As we were changing into our nightgowns that night, she said quietly but firmly that I had to stop acting like a ghost. Abortion was one of our rights as women and it was nothing to be ashamed of and nobody had to know about it. She said the good news was that now we knew I was fertile and one day I'd make a great mom, just not today. She told me it was okay if I was done with Chicago and wanted to come home; I'd given it a fair shot. I told her I wasn't sure. I was taking improv classes with Ruthie and we were writing a show together.

"I know you and Ruthie are close, but you don't have to do *everything* she does. Wouldn't you feel better if you were closer to home?"

"I guess. . . ."

Even if I retreated back to Westchester, I would never be her little girl again. No matter how slowly she rubbed my back and how softly she hummed, I understood that she could never wipe away the ruins of what I was doing. We said the Shema together and then Mom suggested we make one of our old lists—this time of people in our neighborhood and in the surrounding towns at home who she knew had had abortions.

"See?" she concluded. "It's not the end of the world."

Her unequivocal acceptance made me even more despondent. I didn't know how or why she was petting and kissing me as I willingly annihilated another potential human. I needed to hide from her, just as I needed to hide from the walls of my room, from the unshaded window, and the endlessly inky sky outside. After Mom turned the lights off, I wanted to beg His forgiveness but I couldn't find the words. I jabbed my fingers into my eye sockets until everything turned a blistering neon. I jabbed harder. Only as soon as I lifted my hands the walls took shape, the window frame coming too quickly into focus, and I was irrevocably present. Even with my mother lying on the futon next to me, snoring evenly, I was certain once again that none of us was safe. I fell asleep wondering who else would die by my hand.

The next morning, Mom, Mark, and I went to the clinic together. The windows of the building weren't windows at all. They were bulletproof and a permanently dirty gray color. In the waiting area there were large terra-cotta pots of straggling tropical plants, with leaves extending like comets across the beige expanse of wall. There were magazines telling you how to make space in your closet. How do you know if he's cheating on you? one asked. Do you suffer from unknown allergies? posed another. These were the questions the rest of the world asked itself. Maybe I would write a follow-up questionnaire: how do you know if you're killing a life? When does a fertilized egg become a human being? How do you live with yourself after you've committed murder? I'd add catchy before and after pictures of me by the plants.

When they called my name I was taken to see a nurse. The first thing she asked was if we used protection.

Yes.

No.

Yes.

I don't know.

I couldn't trust myself to know. I thought we had. But maybe I was wrong. I stammered. The nurse checked off one of her questionnaire boxes and moved on.

When I got back to the waiting room I asked Mom and Mark what the right response was. Mark answered me but I couldn't make sense of his words. Was he saying that there was a hole in the condom or that I was a baby killer? Mom said we probably did use protection, she wasn't there, but either way it didn't work and that was okay, it would be okay.

Then another nurse took me into a room where everything was salmon colored and she told me to keep breathing and then she emptied me out.

Everything was gone. I was gone. If someone were to shine a flashlight into my pupils, they would find nothing behind them except a wasteland of iniquity. I used to mow down pedestrians, poison stepfathers, and molest children, but Sue Simmons never caught up with me. I could tell Mom about it and squeeze my eyes shut while I walked past Walter's and slowly their agonized faces would retreat.

But the imprint of today was not going away. They wheeled me into another pastel room and I lay on a cot with the other bleeding monsters, and now there was no doubt and no sanctuary—this was more real than real. I was a murderer.

That night, Mom took Mark and me to an all-you-can-eat buffet at the Mongolian stir-fry restaurant. I wanted Ruthie to come too, but she was working. Mom was talking about the different kinds of soy sauce and warned us to save room for the great desserts, as if this was some sort of special celebratory meal. I felt bottomless. I placed water chestnuts and prawns in my mouth and waited to hear their soft thud as they dropped out beneath me. Later we watched a movie and Mark wanted to sit next to me, but I wouldn't let him. Mom said maybe I'd be more comfortable in my new bathrobe. Ruthie offered me a glass of water. I told them all to please leave me be and then coiled myself into a corner of the couch so no one could touch my body.

The next morning, Mom flew back home and when we spoke on the phone the closest she came to discussing the abortion was to ask, "How's the tummy?" as if I'd eaten bad yogurt. I responded, "Okay, I guess." And that was it. She sent me more blush in the mail. This had always been her cardinal rule—dress up the darkness until it is forgotten. Buy a brooch and pin your throat shut. But I didn't know what to do with my remorse. It was so much bigger than me and I felt it tracking me—a permanent fog pulling at my skin and winding through my hair, following my every move. I threw out the home pregnancy tests and made Ruthie swear that she would never breathe a word of what I'd done. I told Mark to go away and took a new job in a think tank where nobody knew me or my past. When I wrote about the abortion in my journal, I called it *October,* so it could be confused with a Halloween costume. Each morning when I prayed, I murmured my lists and psalms as quickly as I could. I no longer had a lump of worry lodged in my chest that I could slowly dissolve with lists and psalms. My whole body was clenched in sorrow and helplessness. I apologized for any loose paper clips or offending remarks I might have left behind. I told Him He was Great and All-Powerful and Most Merciful. I couldn't conceive of how to pay retribution.

I started running.

At the think tank I had a stunning new office mate who worked out at lunch and ate only fat-free burritos and M&M's. One day she invited me to the gym with her. I'd always been too clumsy to excel at any sports, but I climbed on the StairMaster next to her and tried to keep pace with its rise and fall. I loved following the numbers as I sped up, the woozy rush I got at the top of each peak. Later, when I showered, I felt an electrifying exhale throughout my entire body. I swore I would be back every lunch hour for the rest of my life.

I also started running into strange beds. I flirted with anyone and everyone. I was reckless with men, especially at work. I wore snug pants, slinky sweaters, and mascara, and batted my newly defined eyelashes at a professor named Phil, who was old enough to be my father. I loved the way he nodded approvingly at me. His office smelled of leather and leaked classical music into the hall. I found out he was twice divorced and drove a Saab 900, the same car my father bought just after he started suffering from his mysterious fevers.

I told Ruthie about getting coffee with Phil and she warned me to be careful. I assured her he just wanted a good friend. But then he invited me over to his apartment for duck à l'orange and white wine. For dessert he wanted me to listen to Schubert on his bed. I ran to the bathroom and tried to find my reflection in the mirror, but the walls were tilting and shuddering.

I'm so sorry. Please forgive me, I sputtered, though I was sure He had long ago stopped entertaining my pitiful apologies. When I came out, I stood in Phil's doorway and stared at his drooping golf socks as I commanded him to please take me home.

"Really? Are you sure?" He smiled sadly.

"Yes."

"How about just a cuddle?"

I knew it was misguided and selfish, but I couldn't help myself. We spooned as Schubert's desolate concerto flooded the room. Phil's arms were warm and steadfast and with my eyes shut I could hear my father's *bippety scap bap* and smell the Tums on his breath. I hoped he could forgive me for what I had become.

Ruthie and I were tighter than ever. Letting go of Mark had sloughed off all the dead space between us. We went to the theater practically every night. Ruthie was onstage a lot and introduced me to incredible teachers and performers in the improv scene. We were both invited to work with an all-female troupe and soon I was performing next to some of my newest heroes and doing interviews in the local papers about the future of women in comedy. Every time I got onstage I felt a surge of both delicious hope and almost crippling stage fright. On the days of performances, I tried to work out harder, so my body would be toned and energized before I arrived at the theater. My preshow prayers got longer as I beseeched Him to keep those I loved safe while I was onstage, and to make me funny, nimble, and authentic, even though I didn't deserve it.

Each morning I gazed at the fire escape outside my bedroom window and chanted one prayer for each rung. I couldn't let my eyes stray to the brick wall in my bedroom because it reminded me of the night I lay next to my mom, bleeding. Then I put on my gym shoes and headed out for a jog. I was running from Him most of all.

Ruthie had always been my counselor, but now she was my refuge and solace, too. We adopted a dog and moved into the bottom floor of a rickety old house. The kitchen linoleum peeled up in big, flaky islands and there was one hole so big we could see all the way to the basement below, but we adored it. We decorated the walls with copies of the *Stillman-Sher Dispatch*—the newspaper that she'd made up about our street. It included interviews with our dog and fake investigative reports about the local dry cleaners—private jokes that were funny only to us, which was how we liked it. Even with the front curtains open, the apartment never got more than a damp mist of light in it. The wood paneling kept it murky like a cocoon. We rarely had guests over. It was our private space and our dirty dishes and no one else could hear us when we stayed up late crying or writing or yowling to angry music.

I loved our new home, as long as Ruthie was there with me. But soon she was on the road touring with the Second City, a job we had both coveted for years. At first it was fun traveling with her vicariously. She called me from each stop and we talked like an old married couple sharing our moments apart. But some nights she was too busy to call and I waited in the house, scared of my own shadow. I tried not to look dejected when she told me she'd be gone for the next week and a half. Even when she was in town she was busy rehearsing, writing, and performing with numerous other groups. Once in a while I asked her when we would be able to put up our half-written cooking show and she said soon.

My own acting career was not exactly soaring. I'd quit my office job so I could audition more, but then I wound up taking part-time work at a music studio to cover rent. I tried to make up my own hectically productive schedule. *Quiet time,* then shower and into workout clothes. I jogged through snowdrifts to work, then sat by the phones wheezing as the sweat thawed into a sour puddle on my chair. I tried to write funny scenes in between calls. I did shows once or twice a month at ImprovOlympic, and one of the teachers told me if I wanted to be heard I had to stop hiding next to the piano. I was cast in a play about a pack of communist ants who overthrow a ship and another about an evil clown in which I was the love interest who happened to be a bearded lady. My mother flew out for that one and sat in a musty café basement for the three-hour circus-tragedy.

When she came to our apartment, Mom told me our home was dank and drafty and "not exactly her favorite." I told her she was overlooking its hidden charms. She said I was spending too much time on prayers and she didn't like that I still had piles of trash lying around and was muttering under my breath when we went by traffic lights.

"You look terrible. Are you sure you're eating and sleeping enough? When are you coming home?" All valid questions that I refused to answer. Her hand circling my back made me feel lost and homesick. She begged me to look up a therapist. She said I shouldn't still be obsessing and maybe I'd consider going back on meds or coming back to New York and pursuing theater closer to home or getting a graduate degree.

"In what, Mom?"

"I don't know. English. Psychology. You can do anything you put your mind to, Chicken. You just have to stop all this ritual business."

My new therapist's name was Paula. She was younger than Dr. M. and had clear olive skin and dark hair that she twirled into a loose bun. The first day I tried to summarize events for her. In one breath I told her about the abortion and how I felt like it was a terrible mistake and I had killed someone innocent and that actually this was kind of a running theme in my life, but anyway, I was much better now that Mark was out of the picture and I had to concentrate on my career. My best friend, Ruthie, was doing really well; she was hilarious and superbrilliant and maybe Paula had seen her onstage already?

Paula said, "Maybe. Can we talk about some of these themes you mentioned?"

I repeated the only thing I was willing to discuss: "Ruthie is my best friend forever and ever."

YOM KIPPUR PRAYER*

The sin we have committed against You by malicious
    gossip,
the sin we have committed against You by sexual
    immorality,
and the sin we have committed against You by glut-
    tony.
The sin we have committed against You by narrow-
    mindedness,
the sin we have committed against You by fraud and
    falsehood,
and the sin we have committed against You by hating
    without cause.
The sin we have committed against You by our arro-
    gance,
the sin we have committed against You by our inso-
    lence,
and the sin we have committed against You by our
    irreverence . . .

For all these sins, O God of mercy, forgive us, pardon
    us, grant us atonement!

*Must rap on my chest with a fist each time I say the word *sin*.

star 69

· ·

The only time I went to synagogue anymore was for Yom Kippur services. Yom Kippur is the holiest of the Jewish holidays and it's traditional to fast from sundown to sundown and spend the day atoning for the past year's sins. After graduation, I'd tried synagogues in Hyde Park, Evanston, and up and down Lake Shore Drive, often sneaking into the back row of folding chairs because it was so crowded. I cherished the chorus of supplication surrounding me and the complete anonymity as we listed our transgressions. No matter where I was, every prayer book said "the sin *we* have committed," which always comforted me. Maybe I wasn't the only one with a foul past. Many congregations pounded their chests as they chanted, and I loved that, too. I made a strong fist and rapped just above my heart, savoring each twinge of pain I could inflict on myself.

I also got an amazing sense of contentment from fasting. By the end of the first night I already felt groggy, light-headed, and thirsty. Every time I tipped with wooziness I reminded myself that I had earned it. When the closing prayer was intoned and the doors opened, I came out into the autumn evening and imagined myself floating just above the pavement, feather-light, slightly shaky but renewed. My tongue would be fuzzy from dehydration, and it scratched as I licked my lips, famished and ignited by my clean soul. Ruthie and I often splurged afterward at our favorite Italian restaurant, ordering big plates of gnocchi and asking for three baskets of warm bread.

Pasta was one of the only things we ate now. Ruthie had a special way of preparing it at home—boiling the noodles and then dumping the marinara sauce right out of the jar so nothing was too hot or too cold. For dessert we had Diet Pepsi and baked potato chips or pretzels. I don't know when we'd weaned our diets down to these three food groups, but I enjoyed their simplicity. Ruthie ate a lot less than I did and even though I was usually still hungry, I tried to match her portions. We ate in the dark too, which gave it a secrecy that I also treasured. For lunches at the music studio, I decided I would allow myself only bread and raisins from the grocery store. Feeling my stomach roil and fold was a lot like knocking on my breastbone as I listed my sins—it was gratifying to focus my brain on these raw sensations. It was the punishment I had been waiting for.

I was in awe of Ruthie's discipline. Her meals grew smaller as she wrote, rehearsed, and jogged every day. She was absurdly prolific, constantly meeting with new writing partners, and she had an agent who booked her for commercial voice-overs. When she performed at Second City, they hung her picture on the wall just inches away from Gilda Radner's and Tina Fey's.

I tagged another mile onto my daily runs. I made new lists: of memories, mistakes, obstacles I wanted to overcome, and people I could trust unconditionally. (That one was the shortest: *G-d, Daddy, Mommy, Ruthie*.) I went to ImprovOlympic and watched shows while I nursed a hard cider in a darkened corner. Drinking was almost a prerequisite to joining the improv community—it was easy to down two or three glasses while watching shows, yearning to be as uninhibited as the performers I was admiring. On weekends I took classes at Second City and walked past the famous faces with my head bowed. I felt weak with inadequacy.

When Ruthie came home from tours I rushed at her. I wanted to know where she had been and how big the audiences were; what it felt like to be awash in their laughter and applause. Ruthie patiently described it all to me. She asked me how I had been and I wanted to have glamorous stories for her too, but I had nothing. I didn't know how to tell her how lonely and miserable I was. I sighed impatiently as she nuzzled the dog, who panted and yipped playfully.

"Yes, I missed you too!" cooed Ruthie. Then she turned to me. "Does she need a walk?"

"Yeah, I guess. I was about to . . ."

"That's okay. I got it."

I watched the two of them pull each other down the porch steps, my lips pressed together in a frown.

"How about missing me?" I muttered feebly. I didn't know how to tell Ruthie I was starting to blame her for my loneliness and misery.

Second City held annual auditions for its touring company. They were by invitation only and they typically asked about five hundred people to try out for three to four prized spots. Ruthie had been hired on her first try. I auditioned twice without even getting a callback. I went back to ImprovOlympic, ordered more ciders, and forced myself to cower in front of the piano when I got onstage. After my third Second City audition, I was put on the short list. I'd never heard of the short list before, but I was ecstatic.

"Thank you so much! Thank you so much! I'm really excited, this is the best, thank you!" I gushed at the producer.

The short list consisted of a dozen names that he kept buried in his desk drawer under his scrap paper and pens for an indefinite period of time. I soon learned that many people sat on the short list for years. As another winter descended, I jogged through the biting wind, blasting tempestuous classical music on my Walkman and crying icy tears. Our neighborhood seemed deserted and seedy now. The house across the street had a fire in their basement and no one was hurt but the whole block smelled like a forgotten campsite and the snowdrifts grew spiny with charred pine needles.

One day, when I was at the music studio, I spied Ruthie through the window. Business was dwindling and there was nobody else in the office most of the time, so I did ab crunches and stared out at the street a lot. I craned my neck so I could follow her in the downtown crowd. She was laughing with a castmate from Second City and in a few short hours she would be onstage in front of hundreds of adoring fans, all clapping and cheering for her, and I shivered as I realized for the first time that I loved her and hated her at once. She didn't know where I worked, but I hid behind the filing cabinet anyway. I couldn't stand how much better she was at everything. She was smarter, faster, funnier, more passionate, more daring. When she was away I sprayed her perfume on my neck and tried on her worn cotton shirts. But I was still the runner-up, the imposter.

As I ran home later that day, I bawled sullenly. I was never going to catch up to her and I was nothing without her. I stamped through the door and screamed at the dog for liking Ruthie better than me. I made a can of fat-free pea soup with pretzels floating in it and washed and dried my dishes so she wouldn't know that I'd eaten. I decided that the next time she cooked, I wouldn't eat any of her pasta. It was the only way I could think of to distance myself from her.

But the next time we were both home, it wasn't Ruthie I found in the kitchen.

His name was Ben. He and Ruthie had been dating for a little while—he toured with Second City too and had long, sad eyes and soft, fair hair.

"Sorry," he mumbled. "Are these yours?" Small, wet crumbs flew out of his thin lips. He pulled my bag of pretzels out from behind his back bashfully, like a child caught pilfering penny candy.

"Yeah, but it's okay."

"And this?" He held up a tub of Philadelphia cream cheese. It was left over from the last time my mom had come into town.

"Whatever. You can have it."

"Ruthie's already asleep and I was just watching some TV. . . ." he started. I didn't dare look at those eyes again. I already felt unexpectedly nervous and something close to tipsy.

"I couldn't sleep either so I thought I'd . . ."

We moved into the living room and he put the snacks down on the table for us to share. That's all we did. We sat on the couch covered in dog hairs and ate pretzel sticks smothered in cream cheese and watched a documentary about Jim Croce and we didn't say anything more except "So sad" and "These are really salty." I tried not to let my gaze wander from Jim Croce, but when they did, the television colored Ben's thinning hair a moon's silver-blue that I could feel shimmering under my skin. The whole night felt infinitely possible, a present about to be opened, an unstruck chord.

It also felt illicit. The next morning when I sat down on the floor for *quiet time,* I repeated each prayer an extra time, especially the ones concerning Ruthie. *Please let Ruthie be completely happy healthy always and her family be completely happy healthy always. Completely happy healthy always. Completely happy healthy always. And please forgive me for all my sins I'm sorry for all my sins.* I didn't speak of my late-night snack to anyone. Not Ruthie, not Mom, not Him. But of course, I didn't need to. The only one I hid my secret affections from was myself.

Much of the next year and a half passed in an indistinct blur. I didn't want to recognize my growing infatuation with Ben and how much it hurt Ruthie. I kept myself terrifically preoccupied—running, praying, counting fat grams, writing, improvising, and most of all, denying my feelings emphatically.

When I spoke to Mom now, we skimmed above the surface of conversation. She told me the local gossip and the answer to the crossword puzzle that she couldn't get for the longest time. I assured her I was getting enough sleep and wearing blush. Both of which were lies.

When Ruthie was home our talks were equally stilted.

"Hey! How was Iowa?"

"You know, same old. What's been going on here?"

"Same old."

My prayers were even getting impersonal and tired-sounding. I asked Him to please forgive me for anything bad I might have done and to please protect everyone in the Middle East, even though I had no idea what was going on there. I couldn't be more specific in any of my conversations because all I wanted to really discuss was when I had last seen Ben or the smell of his ashy breath.

My mother paid for me to go to Paula once a week. I scheduled therapy after a Spin class or at least an hour on the gym machines so I was too out of breath to think about my words. Mostly, I reported the latest rumors in the improv community and moaned about how unjust the casting was.

In the spring of 1999, I was hired as an understudy for the Second City touring company. I was replacing Ruthie, because she'd been promoted to a resident stage, which meant she got to write and perform her own material.

"Ruthie, that's awesome!" I cheered.

"No, Abby, you're awesome!" she replied.

Not long after that, Ruthie got me signed at her commercial agent and I started auditioning for television and radio.

"Ruthie, you're the best," I cooed.

"*You* are," she corrected.

Then Ruthie and Ben broke up.

Ruthie said it was sad but it needed to happen. They were on different pages. I said yeah, that was sad.

"Really? You think so?" she asked.

"Yeah, I mean, I guess so."

"Why?"

"I don't know. It's an end? But also, it's a good end. Or, it could be. I think. Maybe."

I said a special prayer that Ruthie would fall in love *happily healthfully with someone who loves her completely happily healthfully too*. I prayed that *Ruthie's family will be always all completely happy healthy, including her siblings and all of their children*. I prayed to protect myself from the truth, which was this:

Ben was the most beautiful, gentle, humble lost soul I'd ever met. We toured together and every time I was near him I was surer than ever that we belonged together. When I heard his husky voice in the theater hall my breath grew shallow and I teetered with anticipation. Ben had begun dating someone else, but that made no difference to me. Like Will years ago, the fact that he was unattainable only heartened me. It had to be real because it was so difficult. When we were on the road together, our cast stayed up in the hotel room and ate chips and vending machine candy and called in to radio shows. I pretended to fall asleep with the others, but really I was watching Ben smoke packs of Marlboro Reds tipped back in a chair with the TV on mute, slowly letting out a column of smoke, narrow and focused. Ben had perpetual insomnia and I pinched my wrists to stay awake too. Even if he didn't know it, I would not let him be alone. I would wait for him as long as it took and we could grow old and lost together.

Ruthie was eager to talk when I got home from a tour out West.

"How was Wyoming?"

"Oh, you know. Same old. What did I miss here?"

"Nothing. You and Ben seem to be close."

"Our whole cast is close." I felt her eyes on me but was too scared to look at her. "Did you wash the dog?" I asked with feigned interest. "She looks really fluffy."

A year into touring, I had been to Hawaii, Maine, South Carolina, and Seattle. I loved it on the road, especially the nights we closed the local bars after shows and then played cards until sunrise. When I was home I only wanted to wash my clothes and repack my bags for the next trip. And find ways to see Ben.

Ben's insomnia had gotten worse. He told me he'd been up for weeks. His apartment was just a few blocks away from ours and I said he could come by anytime and we could watch TV together. I was in the back room by the garden, so he could just tap on the window without disturbing *anyone else*. Neither of us referred to Ruthie by name.

One night he came over. We didn't need a Morse code—I could feel his silhouette before he even reached the porch steps. I opened the door and he slumped in silently.

We ate pretzels on my bedroom floor and searched for constellations through the web of snow-draped branches outside my window. Then we went outside so Ben could smoke. We were only sharing these sleepless hours, I reasoned, we weren't kissing or even touching so it wasn't wrong.

"Does it smell smoky by the back door?" Ruthie asked the next day.

"What?"

"It smells like smoke. Cigarette smoke."

"Huh."

"Come here. Smell it."

"Actually, I was just putting some laundry in. Can I smell it later?"

I began actively avoiding Ruthie. I made sure she'd left for the theater before I came home in the evenings. I extended my workouts, rode my bike to and from the theater, stayed at Improv-Olympic or the bar across from Second City until I was sure she was asleep. I snuck in through the back door and devoured bowls of pretzels and diet soda until I felt bleary and bloated. In the morning, I raced through *quiet time* and grabbed a PowerBar before heading out to the gym again, hoping to be on the stationary bike before Ruthie awoke.

Sometimes she caught me lacing up my sneakers. "Where are you going?"

"Crazy day. How was the show last night? See you later!" I'd chirp, slamming the door. The hinge was out of its joint and the door flew back open with a loud smack, but I tore off anyway, as if I hadn't heard it.

For a year and a half I prayed daily to the Lord but I was truly obsessed with Ben. Our house was slowly crumbling. The floors creaked under a landslide of untouched bills and naked paper towel tubes. None of our kitchen drawers closed all the way and the walls were stuccoed with slivers of yellowing tape that had lost their posters and their glue. The angry CD that Ruthie and I used to listen to together was stuck in the CD player. The pantry shelves were bare except for loose sticks of dry spaghetti, and the dog left trails of kibble that we crushed underfoot. The phone cradle had been missing for months and the only way to hang it up was by banging the receiver onto the floor.

Ben called exactly once for me in that year and a half. I remember because I snatched the phone with the hope that it was him, then skidded into my bedroom, shutting the door, and stayed in there for hours. We talked about the farm next to the house where he grew up and the color of corn in August and the other side of the globe where it was already morning and mostly we talked about nothing at all. By the time I opened my door I was sure Ruthie was at the theater for the night and I was looking forward to biking to the gym and daydreaming about rolling farmlands. Only Ruthie hadn't left. She was right in front of me.

"Who was that?"

"What? Oh, just . . . Matt." I shrugged.

"Matt?" Her eyes flashed like the hottest part of a flame. "Really?" she asked slowly, her voice low and exact. She was giving me one more chance to tell the truth.

"Yes," I said, stalking past her. "Going for a walk," I mumbled, hooking the dog's leash on with a stern yank and stumbling with her down the front steps.

I walked quickly, explaining to the dog that no it wasn't good to lie but really I was only lying because one phone call didn't need to be an issue. See, Ben and I weren't doing anything wrong, we were just friends and Ruthie was the one who broke up with him and that was almost seven months ago now and didn't that mean it was over? I knew I should ask for forgiveness, but I didn't know whom to start with. I doubted He wanted to hear another lame confession and I didn't think the dog was even listening and really if I said sorry to Ruthie that would mean I was doing something to feel sorry about and I wasn't. I looped around the block again, growing more and more indignant and agitated. I didn't know why but this dog had never liked me. I tugged her hard so the leash caught just under the saggy part of her chin and she yelped a little.

Maybe if I sang the Heaven song or "My Heart Belongs to Daddy," that might soften my lungs, which were quickly seizing with cold and worry. But how many times would I have to sing it and could it ever erase my blemished soul? I picked up a frozen gum wrapper and two twigs, but I knew the whole time it was a fruitless effort. My crimes had taken a new form now—heartless and depraved in their duplicity. I was killing everyone in every car and anyone whose name I'd left off my sick lists, and most of all I was betraying my best friend. *I'm sorry* I moaned at the plastic Santa stuffed into the burned-out basement window. I didn't believe in Santa Claus, but maybe he had some pull with G-d just because he was a vaguely religious figure.

When I got back inside, Ruthie was holding the phone, crying.

"It's not even that you lied," she sobbed.

"I didn't—"

"Abby, I pressed star sixty-nine. Ben answered because he thought it was you."

"But that's because . . ." I whined.

She waited for me to dwindle into silence before whispering, "What's sad is that I didn't trust you. That I don't trust you. Anymore."

I marched off, barricading my bedroom door with my plastic daisy night table. Then I sat on top of it and wrote in my journal. In code, to erase any evidence of my wrongs:

Dear SiRo, have to look for another apartment. Spider thinks I like Van Morrison which is not fair because she broke up with him and that was almost a year ago and plus we are just friends I think. I love you Mom. I love you Dad. I love you most of all, G-d forever and ever.

The next week I told Ruthie that maybe we should consider finding separate spaces once our lease was up. Ruthie swallowed hard
but didn't say anything. I explained very carefully and dispassion-
ately that my late father got horribly claustrophobic in elevators and
I must have inherited that gene because I was feeling closed in and
I thought it would be best for both of us to have more air. I did not
add that I wanted Ben to be able to call and spend sleepless nights on
my back porch whenever he felt like it.

"When did you start feeling this way?" she asked softly.

"I don't know. A while ago," I announced glibly.

Ruthie and I were breaking up. Divvying up tampons, socks, the
unmailed letters we wrote together to our parents, our bodies, our
lost innocence. We had been in this dilapidated house for three years.
We had been a duo for nearly a decade. I was taking the Brita filter and
the TV. Ruthie was taking the couch and the dog, who leapt around
us barking at our piles of anger, our forgotten library books. When
Ruthie was at the theater I emptied my sock drawer, pulling out the
envelope I'd labeled *Just for ME*. There were about thirty slips of paper
in there—little memos I'd written to myself over the past year—*Got
an audition for Crest voice-over today!* or *Jogged three miles in twenty-five minutes!* or my favorite, *B said my scene was the funniest in the show tonight!*
Small victories that I hadn't wanted to share with Ruthie anymore. As
her career skyrocketed and I dove headlong toward Ben, secrecy was
still my best weapon to combat ugly feelings like jealousy and desire.

The day before the moving vans came, Ruthie handed me a copy
of a scene I'd worked on for Second City that never made it into a
show. It was about a couple on a date and at the top I'd typed, *Cast:
Abby and Ben*.

"It's good," Ruthie said unconvincingly.

"Nobody likes it."

"It's strong. You might think about trimming it down a bit."

"Yeah, it's boring," I reached toward the garbage with it.

"The Dave Matthews line was pretty funny," she added.

"Really?"

Her opinion still meant so much to me, even though I was too
bound up with envy and guilt to say so. I wanted to tell her that she

173

would always be funnier than me, but when I looked up from the script she had already gone back into her room. It was years later before she told me how much that scene wounded her. She and Ben had seen Dave Matthews in concert together. I remember her coming home smelling like smoke and sweat and the first jitters of adoration. We had sat at this same kitchen table and talked about this fair-haired boy who was so lost and so beautiful. Back when the table still had legs to hold it up.

I moved into an airy two-bedroom with a distant cousin of mine. She'd never heard of *quiet time* or Second City and she hung a four- by five-foot painting of a golf course on the wall of our living room. This was good, I told myself. This was right. We had a back porch with hanging plants and plastic lawn furniture. My cousin cooked thick stews and sweet rum cakes and ate them unabashedly in full daylight. I unpacked my litter and my journals and called my mom to tell her we'd arrived safely and there was room for her on the couch.

"Good job, Chicken," said Mom. "You know I like Ruthie just as much as you do, but you need to do your own thing. That relationship was getting to be too much. Now, how are you fixed for nightgowns and blush?"

I didn't see Ruthie for months after we split. Most days we rehearsed in the same building, but we managed to avoid each other. I prayed for her daily, though. I asked for her dreams to come true. For her heart and her mind to be forever fulfilled. My prayers still took about a half hour, and I was grateful that I could tell my cousin not to disturb me and then disappear in my new closet. Every time I recited the Shema I felt steadier. Every time I listed the ailing, I could push Ruthie's sorrowful eyes further out of my mind. Prayers liberated me from all accountability or blame.

I was on the road a lot over the next year. It was challenging to fit in prayers and running while we traveled, but most days I was thrilled by the touring life—especially stepping into a new auditorium and feeling its promise. And any chance I got to immerse myself in conversation with Ben—he dated a few women during this time but I still considered our platonic relationship more significant.

The next Yom Kippur I can remember I spent with him. Ben wasn't Jewish and he didn't come to synagogue with me, but I was thinking about him while I beat my chest. Before the holiday began, I biked over to his apartment toting a bag of dripping Chinese food and gorged on moo goo gai pan and vegetable lo mein with his roommate until my eyes watered. Chinese food was the one treat I allowed myself on special occasions, and I had stayed at the gym an extra twenty minutes that day in anticipation. I wanted Ben to join us, but he said he wasn't hungry. The more time we'd spent together, the more I'd heard this refrain.

"Okay, but you promise me you'll eat it later?" I asked.

"Promise."

The sky was cool and cloudless as I pedaled hastily to the synagogue to lose myself among the multitude of sinners. Heads were already bowed and the rabbi and cantor were in their special High Holiday robes, a cleansing white. It was my favorite time of year—a chance to clear out my body and mind and renounce the past year's misdeeds. All the songs sounded like dirges as we bid farewell to our sinful pasts.

For transgressions against God, the Day of Atonement atones; but for transgressions of one human being against another, the Day of Atonement does not atone until they have made peace with one another.
(Mishnah Yoma, second century CE)

It seemed to me I'd never really heard this prayer until that night. I'd recited it for years and years, many times next to Ruthie. Much of the Yom Kippur liturgy was repeated four or five times over the course of the holiday. On this night, I saw the words for the first time. With each reiteration they appeared starker and more accusing on the prayer book pages. I said the prayer louder and louder, enunciating each word meticulously so everyone around me could hear. Hoping, wherever she was, Ruthie could hear. Needing, wherever He was, for Him to hear. Rapping on my chest to prove my contrition.

THINGS MY MOTHER HAS SWALLOWED
IN HER ALMOST SIXTY-EIGHT YEARS
OF LIVING LIST*

Seventy-six black olives in one sitting

Caviar from Petrossian (fancy Russian restaurant
where they change your silverware before you even
begin eating)

Pieces of the sky falling on 9/11

Countless pounds of smelts, schmaltz, onion rye,
chopped liver, herring, gefilte fish (Jewfood)

Frog legs

Reindeer meat

Bad shrimp on a barge with her new and unacceptable
boyfriend, Carl

The parts of the Kaddish she was crying too hard to
speak

A gallon of barium to show what's going on inside her

* Easier to skip numbering.

THINGS I HAVE SWALLOWED
IN MY ALMOST TWENTY-EIGHT YEARS
OF LIVING LIST

Formula

Apple juice

Vinegar straight out of the bottle

Gaines-Burgers dog food (on a dare)

Mom's homemade egg creams

Dad's omelets

A paper clip (stupid story—had to check my poo for a
week to make sure it came out)

A year's supply of Anafranil (cumulative)

About five cases of pinot grigio (over a two-year
period)

Countless gallons of coffee

My words when I was too scared or sad or mad or
alone

the force of gravity
. . . .

Ben was an intensely private person. Being in his apartment alone
with him made me jumpy, even if it was only to help him with spring
cleaning.

It was a few months after Ruthie and I had split, and outside the
first spring shoots were peeking out of the earth, but Ben's living
room was still wintry and dim. The furniture smelled of cigarettes
and corn chips. His microwave was crusted with dried nacho explo-
sions. We tackled the kitchen first.

"I'm so sorry. You sure you want to do this?"

"I love cleaning!" I squealed, scrubbing and soaking, spraying
windows and counters. We moved on to his bedroom. It was small
and held only a mattress, a bookcase, and two cinder blocks holding
up a stereo and a pile of CDs and cassettes.

"Not much we can do, huh?" he said apologetically, his pale lips
forming a half-smile. His insomnia was constant now and I told
him that maybe if he rearranged his bed and let in more air he'd
feel better.

"How about this?" I dragged the mattress over to rest against one
of the sliding closet doors. "Then you could look up at the trees?
Hey! And who's that?"

There was an oil painting on the wall. Three shadowed profiles,
the last one wearing a wide hat with a feather in it.

"Me, my little brother Seth, and Rembrandt."

His brother Seth had painted it. Just before committing suicide.
I stared at the feather as Ben relived that night, his voice muted but
steady. Ben had been there. Ben was still there. He said there was

dried blood between the bathroom tiles that couldn't be loosened eight years later and Seth was still gone. Every day, gone all over again. Ben's face grew long and vacant as he spoke. When he stopped, the story felt unfinished. I yearned to comfort him, to touch his dry, smoky skin.

Ben and I slowly merged through our burdened silences. We stayed up countless nights over the next year; him bent over an ashtray chain-smoking and me trying to figure out what he was thinking. He told me that I should stay away from him because his thoughts were too tortured and vicious. I told him I wasn't scared. I fantasized about stroking his laden shoulders and cradling him in my arms until his nightmares receded.

Forever passed before he asked if he could kiss me and of course he could and of course this was the earth becoming one with the stars and a new universe full of uncharted cosmos. We didn't undress, only hovered over each other's bodies. I hadn't had sex in the six years since the *October,* and I was still fearful and ashamed of my desires. I was only too grateful to lie beside him. Then Ben read to me from a used book on my shelf and I wasn't listening to the words, I was just hearing his throaty whisper and knowing this was the most romantic and perfect night of my life ever.

The morning after Ben kissed me, I left to go on tour again. (Without him—Ben had recently been promoted to a resident stage.) I would be gone on a three-week gig through the snowcapped mountains of Utah and North Dakota. As our plane lifted off, I whispered the Shema into my hands ten times. Ten times didn't feel like enough. Neither did twenty. I twitched with excitement and unease about the night before. As we ascended into the clouds, I knew I was coming closer to G-d, that the skies were expanding in all directions. I feared His Almighty disapproval of me and the lovesick grin on my face. I added five more Shemas to prove my devotion to Him always. Then I quickly struck up a meaningless conversation with the woman sitting next to me so I could declare prayer time officially over.

I wanted to tell her about Ben's soulful, sad eyes and the downy hair on the back of his neck. The blue arc of his cap brim as he leaned in to kiss me. I wanted to play and replay everything he'd told me, even the parts of unspeakable sorrow. Especially those. It was more than love. It was destiny. Finding my way into Ben's arms was like finally coming home. I didn't actually say any of this out loud. Talking about it would have ruined its sacredness.

There were delays flying into Colorado Springs. Up to eight inches of snow. Black ice on the highways and roads. Once we did land, it was ten o'clock at night and we had at least two more hours of driving to get to the hotel. The cast split up into two rental cars and headed out. Someone in my car wanted to listen to Radiohead. The stage manager insisted on a CD of pan flutes and jungle mating calls. We were taking an ad hoc vote when the whole world stopped.

Just ahead of us, an SUV had spun out. The vehicle's windows were all open and the air was hollow and sore with blood and rust. It was every blowout I'd ever imagined—metal and rubber, flesh and bone twisted together in endless carnage. Only this time it was real. We were watching it happen just a few feet in front of us. This family of four being pulled in a swirl of lights—red, white, yellow, into the night, howling. This was not one of my fantasies of a prom night or a lone trucker. This was not make-believe and it didn't matter if it was a shard of glass or a candy wrapper or anything else that came before this moment. This was a human life. Cut off.

We were stopped for hours, watching the Jaws of Life cleave the car in half and the paramedics carry out the mother and children. The father they left in the car with his face lifted up to the half of sunroof that was left. His face perfectly clear and luminous in a breach of car and sky and beyond. Hardening as his whole life seeped out of his skin. I'd never seen death this distinctly before. There was blood drying in a small creek down his temple. There was a sunglasses case clipped to his rearview mirror. There was a solemnity to his nose, a horrific tangibility to his crumpled ski jacket, his unmoving chest. There was an undeniable end to him. This man who was moments before a father, was now a corpse.

I hope you get there in time. I hope you get there in time. I hope you get there in time. I hope you get there in time. I hope you get there in time.

I repeated it even though I had already so obviously failed him.

For the remainder of our drive I held on to that sudden, impenetrable face of death. I can't recall whether we listened to Radiohead or mating calls. I was too busy listening to my heart thumping madly; too busy trying to figure out how I was involved in this tragedy. I knew I hadn't been there to physically plant that ice or loosen an errant tire; nonetheless I was culpable. I was not pure of thought or action. The first thing I had to do was come clean about my stolen kisses from the night before.

When we got to the hotel it was some predawn hour of the morning and even with the extra hour in Chicago I would be waking Ruthie up, but I called her anyway.

"Hey, Roo."

"Hello?" We'd seen each other backstage once or twice since we'd moved out, but we hadn't talked in months.

"Hi, it's Ab. I'm actually on ski tour, but I just wanted to tell you something. It's not really even something yet, but I didn't want you to hear it from someone else and then think it was something when it's really not or it could be but it's not unless it's okay with you."

I told her Ben and I had sort of gotten together. Not really together. Just a few kisses.

"I thought you guys kissed a while ago," she said bluntly.

"No! We didn't, I swear! I mean, not until last night! But how are you I feel like I haven't talked to you in forever I read the reviews of your show and I really want to see it congratulations!" I yammered.

"Thanks." Her voice gave away no emotion whatsoever. I told her I'd heard about the role she got in an upcoming film, that she was serious about her new boyfriend, that she'd adopted another dog. The improv community was incestuous enough that I could learn just about anything about anyone if I asked the right people. She listened to me ramble until I stalled out. Then I asked again, "But how are you?"

"Good, you?" she countered.

"Good. I mean, it's really icy here and we saw an accident tonight but yeah, I just wanted to tell you about . . . Ben and see if . . . ."

She waited.

"If it's okay."

"It's . . . whatever. Ab, thanks for calling. I should get going. It's late."

"Yeah."

It wasn't the absolution I'd been seeking, but I felt somewhat relieved. Only, I still couldn't erase that lifeless man from my vision. I whimpered helplessly for his children, who were now fatherless. I had no explanation for them, either. They didn't deserve this fate. I missed my mother horribly. I'd been calling home less and less and now I needed to hear her and make sure she was all right and that I hadn't somehow hurt her too. I needed her to know that even if I kissed Ben I still loved her more than anyone.

"Helloooo?" she slurred.

"Mom! It's me!"

"Everythinokee?"

"Yeah, sorry I'm calling so late, the roads are really slick but we're here safe and I just wanted to tell you that I love you. And actually I have some news about that boy Ben remember I told you about him? But it's okay, I'll call you in the morning."

"Mmmmyeah."

I sank to the floor weak from worry, the phone in my lap. I took off my hat and coat, but I was too scared to get into bed and close my eyes. I could still see only that frozen face and its ribbon of dried blood. I dialed Ben's number. His roommate said he hadn't come back from the theater yet. I waited another hour on the floor until he called back.

"I miss you," I admitted bashfully.

"I miss you too, Abigail." He sighed. He insisted on calling me by my full name, which only reminded me more of my father. I trembled with longing for both of them.

"Can I tell you something?" I moaned.

"Please."

I told him about the man I'd watched die that night. I retraced his face in the halo of floodlights and the whole night stopping around him. I described how his last breath was so close I could almost touch it. How I wondered whether he would be cremated or buried. How I mourned for those poor children, who thought they were going on a vacation but would now have to stand and listen to pebbles landing on their father's coffin. Ben said he was so sorry I had seen that. He assured me the children would be okay and he wished he could be there to kiss me good night and read me a bedtime story.

He almost sounded like my father as he said it. He promised to stay on the phone with me until I was ready to sleep and he did, as we held each other and the dead man between us, just listening to each other breathe.

For the rest of the tour, I saw that man's upturned face when I slept and when I woke; he haunted me every time we were on the road and sometimes even when I was onstage. I couldn't say why he affected me so—the blowout was too grand to come from a forgotten paper clip and I had witnesses to account for my whereabouts before the actual collision. But I knew this devastation somehow stemmed from my new lust for Ben and the way I had seized him from Ruthie. I knew this specter was mine to carry with me for the rest of my life. Even today its colors and edges are imprinted on the backs of my eyelids.

Ben and I flung ourselves into an all-consuming intimacy. Within months of kissing for the first time, we found a one-bedroom apartment with a porch overlooking an alley and space behind our desk in our living room/study/dining room where I could do my prayers in the morning. I loved our place. Mostly because it was just big enough to fit all of our belongings. The dancing Santas, cackling witches, and giggling valentines that Ben's Nana sent us. His piles of mix tapes and my rubber tree and the silhouette of Rembrandt above all our books. I painted the big room the color of faint daybreak and the bathroom a bright lemon-lime called Zippedy do da! Even the man at the paint store squinted when I pointed to the swatch, but I was determined to clean the tiles regularly and make it the cheeriest place in our new home.

We also had a narrow kitchen with black-and-white-checkered flooring and enough room for us to stand side by side at the sink. But we never did. Something was very wrong with the kitchen, said Ben. I agreed with him. I didn't let myself see that something was very wrong with Ben. Ben was a recovering bulimic who hated food and hated himself even more for needing it. He was a commanding presence onstage, but in the confines of our home his eyes grew vacuous and his shoulders sloped forward into a sickle. He was weak and exhausted from not eating all day. All week. Ben had been starving himself for years. He had learned to live this way after his brother died. It was why I had caught him sneaking a bag of pretzels that night we watched Jim Croce while Ruthie slept. This was Ben. Fueling himself only with cigarettes and coffee fumes. His unanswered hunger was the mortar holding together his sagging skeleton; resolving inside his graying skin.

Ben promised me that he wouldn't make himself sick. In return, I kept our shelves pristine, so he wouldn't be tempted to binge. The refrigerator contained only Diet Pepsi and baking soda for freshness, and the pantry was filled with boxes of lightbulbs and recycled newspapers. We lived next to a twenty-four-hour supermarket. Ben stopped there on his way home from the theater at midnight and bought only the things that he would eat that night—the menu was always the same—pita bread, low-fat cheese, sliced turkey, tortilla chips, and salad dressing. I would hear him come in through our back gate, plastic bags rustling, and try not to pounce too eagerly. Our routine had few variations:

"Hi, hon, how was the show?"

"Good." He'd lay out a pita and the first slice of cheese.

"Good crowd?"

"Yeah." He added two pieces of turkey, one more slice of cheese.

"I got a newspaper so we can do the crossword."

"Cool." Glass. Soda. Salad dressing in a small pool on the side of the plate, topped with chips. I'd follow him into the living room, where we settled on the couch. Then he'd eye his food suspiciously.

"What am I doing?" he'd spit disgustedly. "This is too much. I don't need this."

He'd turn his body away from me so I couldn't watch him devour his meal. I only wanted to kiss him, pet him, touch his clenched jaw, and ease the food down his throat. But I knew without asking that he couldn't share his pain with me. It had no narrative—no beginning, middle, and end as his brother had had. It was Ben's burden to bear and he guarded it just like he guarded his crowded plate, with his turtle-shell back hunched over the coffee table.

Each night I waited for the crinkle of his grocery bags in the dark. Sometimes I fake-slept in the hopes that he would eat more slowly, more calmly. Often I couldn't stand waiting and I walked over to the supermarket and met him in the pita aisle. I was careful not to comment or offer suggestions while he shopped—silence was the only way to secure his trust. I just trailed next to him while he filled our basket. There was a retarded cashier named Vicki, who worked the night shift and obviously adored Ben too.

"Good evening there, Victoria," he would greet her respectfully, doffing his Red Sox cap while she scurried to put away her microwave baked potato and wipe her mouth. Her smile would erupt like a firecracker when she turned back toward him.

I tried to talk to her too, but we didn't connect in the same way. I wanted to tell her that I got it. That I was in awe of him too. That I felt honored to walk home with him through the abandoned parking lot, to lay my slices of turkey on a matching plate and carry it to the coffee table. I soon adopted his nightly regimen but I sat on the floor while he was on the couch. We ate watching reruns of Regis and Kelly without saying a word. I felt blessed just to share his space, to hear his jaw slowly grate, his teeth chomp. *I'm here! I'm here!* I cried inside, willing myself to look only at the television. This was also part of our unspoken pact. I would not turn in his direction for the entirety of the meal. Even when he gagged from eating too fast (which happened a lot) and I wanted to run to him as he crouched over the toilet bowl. I was petrified of the sound of someone vomiting, even before my father threw up in the snow. But now all I could do was listen as Ben coughed up his paltry meal. I waited patiently until he settled back down before lightly touching my hand to his back.

"S'okay," he croaked, squeezing my knee.

"I know it," I answered. Our meals were more affectionate than any of our sexual contact. We rarely had intercourse anyway—we were both too famished and exhausted by the time we met at the end of the day. I told Ben I adored him and would do anything to make him feel better. He said he didn't deserve someone as beautiful and loving as me.

A month after we moved in together, Ben was about to go onstage one night when, as he described it, the ground came toward him. One of the producers called to tell me *Ben fainted, he's headed to the emergency room, they're not sure what it is, but he wanted us to call you, he says he'll be home soon and not to worry.* I ran out of the apartment, hailed a cab, and told the driver, "Take me to the hospital! It's an emergency! Please!"

The doctors ran tests on his eyes, ears, thyroid, cranium. They did MRIs and CAT scans, took blood from his chalky fingers and poked for new veins. All the tests came back negative—there was nothing identifiably wrong with him. But he was dizzy, nauseous, unsteady. The ground kept reaching toward him. When he came home, his mother and I hounded him to make more appointments, get more opinions. On the days he was too lopsided to stand up, I lay with him on the couch and kissed his swampy neck. I told him I would be there with him until the earth righted itself again. Until the end of time if it took that long.

Weeks passed. Months. A year. Ben's illness-with-no-name grew worse. He found getting out of bed difficult and his eyes had grown rheumy. He went through another battery of tests at Lehigh Clinic: MS, brain tumor, vertigo. They all showed up negative. He quit his job at the theater and when he had the strength he walked the streets with a pack of cigarettes and a paperback book.

Every day was a blowout now, a self-replicating catastrophe with Ben in the middle, the world spinning red and white, cement and sky around him. I was thinking only of him as I biked from the theater to the gym to our cavernous apartment. My path was narrow and sure. My whole being focused and purposeful.

I can see now it was also the most vibrant I'd ever felt. Caring for Ben was what I had been born to do. In some veiled corner of my mind, I actually got a thrill each time Ben woke up too dizzy to move. My spine lengthened with pride as I consulted with his mom on the phone or friends took me aside to ask what was really going on. I found myself stepping over litter to get home faster; sometimes I even sped past an ambulance on my bike without chanting for its swift arrival. I was too concentrated on the accident that was on our couch. I was the one person that Ben wanted to see at his sickbed and I was sure I was the only one who could and would save him. The similarities between Ben and my father became more stunningly transparent every day—they had both gone to Syracuse, both bemoaned their receding hairlines, both loved spicy foods, and even danced a similarly soft two-step. Only this time, I would not let him die.

My morning prayers took on new meaning and motivation. I even mentioned Ben by name as I prayed for his health—the first time I had ever introduced one of my love interests to G-d. I added more prayers so He knew that I was thinking about the welfare of all those in need, not just Ben. I prayed for at least a half hour in the morning behind our desk, I recited mantras on the rowing machine and Stair-Master, and I kissed my bike one hundred times as I locked it up, thanking G-d for getting me home safely soundly happily healthfully. I hung up a mezuzah on our door and kissed that one hundred times too. My preshow prayers lasted fifteen minutes and I did them wherever we toured, locked in a storeroom or closet, if necessary folding myself into the stage curtains.

At the stroke of midnight each night, Ben and I met at the grocery store, then walked home and prepared for our meal on opposite sides of the coffee table. We layered our cold cuts hurriedly, both grunting with hunger. I'd gotten better at skipping lunch. I was too busy praying, exercising, and rehearsing with a rapt ferocity. We'd lost about a dozen pounds between us since meeting, and I was so humbled and grateful to know this famished determination with him. It was all I'd ever wanted. To be small and mighty. To know there was one person beside me who loved and needed me and was gasping for air. And I had the chance to rescue him. I loved him so much; I knew I could pull him out. I felt stronger than whatever force of gravity was tipping him upside down.

After our repast I'd excuse myself and recite the Shema and a short benediction in our checkered kitchen.

Thank You for the moon. Thank You for this kitchen. Thank You for this night and thank You for Ben. Please heal him completely painlessly soon. The grocery store security lights trickled through the metal bars on our windows and I kept track of my place in my prayers by stepping on a single black or white square for each repetition. Then I'd tiptoe into the bedroom and curl myself around a pillow. Ben was usually on the couch, watching TV. He found sleep only in fits and starts, while I snored deeply, my belly swollen with bread and cold cuts, dreaming of our life together. Our backyard with an inflatable pool and Ben dancing around our split-level ranch house singing *ya dada dida doobi da!*

My mother would never say it when we talked, but I could tell she was not happy with my new living arrangements. When I called home she started the conversation with "Oh! Well, if it isn't my long-lost daughter! I thought you'd never surface! I was just about to send the hounds to sniff you out!"

She asked what was new and how Ben was but she rarely waited for my answers. "I feel like a broken record, but when are you coming home?" was usually her next line.

"I'll see how much tickets are," I promised, though I never priced them. I was still touring and I couldn't imagine leaving Ben anymore in his time of need.

After a full year of inconclusive tests, Ben decided to take a break from doctors and clinics. I told him I fully supported him in that decision. It was also the summer that my mother went on a barge trip through France with her new boyfriend, Carl. When she came back she reported that it was beautiful but she had hives all over her body and a stomachache from eating too much shrimp. Two weeks later, the hives were gone but she was still in pain. Mom's doctor wanted her to drink a gallon of barium to see what was going on inside her intestines. I asked Ben if it was okay if I went home to be with her. My brother had settled with his new wife in Canada and my sister was studying overseas. Ben said he would be horribly lonely without me but yes, of course I should go.

"I'll be thinking of you and your mother the entire time you're gone," he said.

"She's fine. It's just a little stomachache," I told him. I was trying to reassure myself as much as him.

I'd been promoted to a resident stage at Second City and had only four days in New York before I started writing my first show. When I flew in, the house felt peculiarly small to me, like a grade-school classroom I'd outgrown. In my closet hung my Bat Mitzvah dress along with my ice-skating costume and some of Mom's old pants. On my bed she had laid out two nightgowns that came just past my knees. I didn't tell her that I'd long since stopped wearing night-gowns. Instead I said that I couldn't wait for her to come out to Chicago and see my next show, that now I would get insurance through the actor's union and I could get her choice seats at the theater and complimentary pretzels and cocktails. We were sitting in the hospital waiting room and I knew I was blathering, but I needed a distraction so I wouldn't watch her as she gulped and gagged on her jug of radioactive paste. While the technician took pictures of her insides, I wrote lists of everything we'd swallowed in our lifetimes. The doctor said he'd call her if anything looked funny.

"I don't think he's going to find anything in there," Mom announced on the way home. "Carl says it's probably from the shrimp we had and I think he's right. Did I tell you he's coming up for dinner?"

I went for a jog by the water. I concentrated on pulling my knees up and I counted out my laps around the church fountain. I decided if Mom wasn't going to worry about her stomach then neither would I. When I got back to the house, Carl met me at the door.

Or really, his lip did. He had a puffy lower lip that drooped in a permanent sulk. He also had a lazy eye that was stuck pointing at our umbrella stand. The other zoomed in on me.

"Six-letter word for *chaos* or *utter confusion*," he said.

"Hi, I'm Abby."

"I know. At least that's why I opened the door. Any ideas? Six-letter word for *chaos*? Hey, Joan, how about *mayhem*?"

"Mayhem!" Mom cried, rushing to his side with the Sunday *New York Times* crossword puzzle in her hand. She held it flat while Carl scrawled his fat, misshapen letters and they both smiled for me. This was dating over the age of sixty-five, I thought.

Carl not only did the Sunday crossword in pen, he also worked part-time as a psychiatrist, volunteered four mornings a week at a nursing home, and most recently had taken up the clarinet. He opened his black case, twisted the instrument into alignment, and treated us to all of the major scales in rapid succession. My mother applauded gleefully when he was done.

"Just picked it up for the first time two months ago. But I'm an avid learner. Don't do anything halfway," he explained. Then he winked at Mom. With his good eye.

I wanted to report to Ben how pompous and pouty Carl was, but I knew Ben would still be walking the streets at this hour.

"Dinner's almost ready! I just need my two helpers to shuck the corn and we're set!" called Mom. I poured myself a glass of wine. Then another. My drinking had steadily escalated since I'd been with

Ben. He'd taught me how to soften the thorny edges of hunger that way. Carl was still singing his scales while we sat down to eat. He told me about his upcoming birthday. He was turning *the big seven-oh*. The whole family was flying in from different parts of the country. Did I think it was inappropriate for him to ask that people bring their own dishes? he asked. Catering could get really expensive in large quantities. What about if everyone more than two hundred miles away brought cold dishes and then people closer brought hot ones?

"I said we could order Chinese—" Mom started playfully.

"Joan!" Carl snapped. "I'm telling a story."

Even with the wine loosening my limbs, I felt his words prick my skin with annoyance. He continued to prattle on for the entire meal. Whenever my mother tried to add to the conversation, he found something wrong with her choice of words. When she mentioned a movie they saw, he told her she was mispronouncing the director's name. She recalled a restaurant they tried and loved. Carl said the meat was tough. The worst exchange was about the color of Mom's new crop of hydrangeas. My mother had always kept an exquisite garden, winding paths of tulips and azaleas, bleeding hearts, and pachysandra. The hydrangeas were her pièce de résistance—they were a piercing azure color with glimpses of violet in the middle. Carl quizzed us to see whether we knew why some hydrangeas were blue and others were pink. Mom said the acid in the soil turned them blue.

"Wrong!" cried Carl triumphantly. "The more acidic the soil, the more pink the flowers are."

"Gee, I could've sworn it was the other way around," Mom said meekly.

"Nope! Pink!" he yipped.

"Oh, but I thought—"

"Pink!" he roared. "Pink pink pink! Don't believe me? Look it up! Abby, do you have good reference materials in the house? How do we settle this? Joan, why don't you believe me?"

Three days later, I made my mother and Carl drop me off at the airport early. Mom's barium test had shown no obstructions and the doctors concluded that it was probably a virus of some sort. I was sure the real cause of the affliction was Carl. I sat on the toilet in the departure terminal pressing the flusher over and over again to drown out my storm of tears. When I got home I told Ben that my mother was gone, that Carl had somehow kidnapped my best friend in the entire world forever and ever and brainwashed her. She let him sit in my seat at the table and do the crossword puzzle in permanent ink. It wasn't even that he was droopy and lazy-eyed and not my father. It was that he acted like a big mopey baby and he picked on her and she timorously accepted it. Ben said I needed to tell her my feelings. But I couldn't communicate anything to my mother except unequivocal devotion.

I called and told her I'd arrived in Chicago safely, that I had a lovely time, and that the nightgowns she'd given me were exactly what I needed.

"Oh good, honey. I love when you visit, though it's always too short," she said. "Of course, I don't think you're eating enough. You look a little gaunt. You really could be a beautiful girl—much prettier than I was at your age. Are you talking to Paula about how much you eat?"

"Yes, Mom." We said the Shema together. Wished each other pleasant dreams. Then I hung up and sobbed for us both.

I did talk to Paula about eating. I told her that sometimes I was so scared of consuming too much that I felt frenzied and breathless. That I didn't think I was working out enough to really gain muscle tone. Paula said that if I ate smaller meals throughout the day maybe I'd feel more satiated. Also, that when I felt anxious I should try imagining myself flying. My fears were the clouds and I was rising above them, ascending weightlessly into the stratosphere. I loved the image, but it did present another worry, which I couldn't name for her or even for myself—above the clouds was G-d and I didn't know how He felt about me anymore. I was more confused than ever about my faith. Sometimes my prayers felt long and sluggish and I couldn't wait to finish and get to the gym. I spoke about prayers vaguely with Paula.

"I really like praying, but sometimes it gets long. I guess I should promise you for next week that I'll cut my prayers back to a half hour again."

"That sounds good," she replied. "What do you pray for?"

"Oh, you know, just saying thank you and hoping that sick people will get better."

Discussing my faith was not only impossible but also highly irreverent. Instead of shortening, my lists got longer. I prayed for Mom to be *completely happy healthy*. I prayed for Ben to heal *completely painlessly soon*. I prayed for my body to be lean and small and dedicated each breath to His service. The morning the World Trade Center was attacked, I didn't find out about it until hours later because I was behind the desk in our living room, struggling to continue my recitations as the phone rang again and again, interrupting my pleas.

Over the next year and a half, Ben's condition did improve slightly, but mostly he just got used to the unsteadiness. We were in a cast together at Second City and also wrote a show for the two of us at ImprovOlympic where we danced together blindfolded. It was a sort of tribute to the way Ben felt every day as his feet touched the shifting earth. Our friends were grateful to see him onstage again. He'd always been a remarkable performer, his wit pure and honest. After the performances, we stayed at one of our local bars until two and three in the morning, lilting home tipsily to gorge ourselves on sodden pitas. Sometimes I had to head home before him shamefacedly because I was so hungry I thought I would throw up. I'd feel his ash-soaked kiss good night hours later. I wanted to be happy for him and his newfound strength, but on these nights in particular, I was frightened and slightly hurt. I hated eating by myself. I hated the way the hunger gripped at me and the amount of food I consumed without his staying presence next to me. I hated the thought that if he got better he wouldn't need me anymore.

But soon enough his swoons came back and he was supporting himself on the back of a chair again. We had just renewed our lease and I had painted the kitchen pink to celebrate our second year of cohabitation. This is where I found him one night, under the dappled light of the alley, staring at his deflated bag of groceries.

"Yay! You're home before me!"

"Yuh," he grunted.

"You okay?"

"Yup."

"You're . . ."

"Just a bad day."

"You want to call that doctor? The one my mom knows from Boston? I think he specializes in—"

"No, thanks. Just . . . let's just leave it."

I don't know what compelled me to press him further. Maybe because I'd had a good show that night and felt particularly confident. Maybe because the return of his illness emboldened me in many ways. Maybe because I'd seen what it was like to grow old and date slobbery clarinetists and what Ben and I had was real and I knew I could, I had to be the one to mend him.

"Ben"—I touched his hand—"I will do anything to help you get better, but if you don't help yourself, I don't think I can watch you do this for always or for so much, for . . . indefinitely." I took a deep breath. I wasn't sure where I was going with this. "Just, I want you to be better and I—"

Ben didn't need me to finish. "Yeah," he said frostily. "Then I guess you should go."

I took back my words in five thousand different ways. I meant *just a little bit.* I meant *you take your time and we'll work through this together.* I meant *we are such an incredible team and together we can heal you, I promise I will heal you.* But Ben was skin, bones, and a fixed idea. As I pleaded with him to reconsider his eyes glazed over and he sat staring at the wall while I ranted and flailed.

I threw myself out the back door and wandered the streets, pounding my feet into the sidewalk. Crushed and angry and so terribly hungry, because it was past midnight, past our mealtime, past everything. I wept all the tears I couldn't find when my father died. Each of my limbs felt dislocated. I tore at my skin and begged the night to be a dream. At one point I was dimly aware of an ambulance going by, flashing its urgency into the sky. But I couldn't even stop crying to whisper *Get there in time. Please.*

MANTRAS FOR EXERCISE*

I am thin. I am beautiful. I shine onstage. I have sparks behind my eyes.

I am healing. I am learning. Please let everyone ailing heal completely painlessly soon. Please let Ben heal completely painlessly soon.

I am strong. I am thin. Please let me be selfless. Please let me look beyond my own nose. Please let me take smaller bites and get fuller faster.

*One for each row on machine or every three steps when jogging.

77 percent lung capacity

I adored performing at Second City. I was onstage every night and the pace was so frantic that I was often rehearsing and writing new material right up until the audience filed in. I was living the dream Ruthie and I had mapped out years ago. Each moment under the stage lights was charmed; each scene was a new reality into which I could escape. I leapt into leopard nightgowns and cat-eye glasses. I strutted out in ridiculous accents, jumpsuits, and teased Afro wigs, feeling intrepid and sexy. I hollered out my songs and shimmied my hips and screamed until my gut shook. Best of all, for two hours every day I impersonated a hundred different people who were not me. I didn't have to think about whether I was blasphemous or overweight. The audience couldn't see the scabs where I'd picked my face or the patches of chapped skin from washing my hands too much. They saw me only as I wanted to be seen—fearless and loud and alive. I hurled myself into each new character, only too willing to lose my identity for those brief fragments of time.

I adored performing at Second City, but I was miserable each time I stepped off the stage.

"This was supposed to be so great! Why isn't it so great?!" I often wailed at my mother over the phone. I had to call from the hot dog stand below my new apartment. After Ben told me I shouldn't wait around for him, I'd moved into a dilapidated building with a woman I knew from the Second City box office. The phone company said our address didn't exist and refused to install service for over a month. The first day we moved in, there was a grease fire below us and our floorboards started smoking. Since then I'd caught a small army of cockroaches each night. I couldn't bear to kill them so I trapped them under juice glasses for my roommate's boyfriend to take care of in the morning. I counted the days, hours, and minutes since I'd last seen Ben and sobbed passionately in tantrums that left me blurry.

"I don't understand. Why is everything so haaaaard?" Mom was the only person with whom I fully shared my bog of self-pity.

"Sssssh, Chicken, it'll be okay. You can't take everything so seriously."

"No it won't!" I snapped. "Don't just say it will be okay when you don't know!" I was furious with her for making what I considered the end of the world sound so mundane.

My mother sighed. She offered to come out to Chicago so we could go shopping and visit some museums. She asked if my commercial agent could look into getting an exterminator. She wanted it to be easier for me and I did appreciate her efforts, but often when we talked I could hear Carl in the background massacring the piano while screeching out a Barbra Streisand medley, which only proved that true love was dead. Mom and I always ended the conversation with me making empty promises to eat more and wear blush.

There were few people besides her that I trusted. I had a good friend from the theater named Megan, but she rarely exercised, ate cookies and cakes, and still managed to stay menacingly petite. From where I stood, all my female friends were skinnier or brighter, more talented and definitely happier than me. I joined a monthly writing group that I loved, but I had to be careful because the host always served breakfast and each meeting I had to come up with a new, polite way of saying I wasn't hungry. I refused to eat near anybody. I was constantly famished and if I sat down I feared I would devour everything in front of me including the paper napkins. I tried not to be home at the same time as my roommate. She was sweet and pert and the chair and footstool she'd contributed to the living room were small enough to be dollhouse furniture.

If I couldn't be with Ben, then I didn't want to be with anyone. I spent most of my time outside the theater at the twenty-four-hour gym by my apartment. The lights were bright, the rooms smelled like Tiger Balm, and the incessant techno beat that they piped in was almost as loud as the noise inside my head. I ran, kicked, sparred, and crunched until my muscles spasmed. I was up to thirty-two minutes on the bike, followed by thirty-eight on the StairMaster and eighteen (a special number in Hebrew meaning *chai* or *life*) on the rowing machine. I also crammed in a few classes each week—yoga, Spin, step 'n' tone. I chanted my mantras while I was working out—one mantra for each machine.

I wanted to be thinner than Ben. I wanted to be sicker than Ben. I wanted to channel him and bring him back to me through our common starvation. I checked outside the apartment door each morning, but no matter how long I waited, Ben didn't show up with flowers and a dancing Santa. I'd imagined our reunion so many different ways:

He is outside my door with white tulips and tearstained poetry.

He leaves the Santa and a note that says *The world spins harder without you.*

He watches me perform and then follows me all the way home, hiding behind garbage cans at all the traffic lights so he can surprise me at the very end. I take him inside and we listen to Rufus Wainwright together on repeat and weep for all the people we've lost and promise we won't lose each other ever again.

For almost two years I waited for his stooped shadow. I whittled my body down to a hundred and fifteen pounds of cramped muscle and protruding ribs, living on breakfast bars and coffee, cereal, pretzels, and soup. And wine. I could have as much wine as I wanted.

As soon as my show was over each night, I made a beeline for the theater's back bar and asked the bartender to pour me a tumbler of pinot grigio. Sometimes I even ordered the wine during the second half of the show so it would be waiting for me after I took a bow. Wine did what I'd been praying, running, writing, begging for all day. It loosened the clawing in my stomach and unscrambled the knots in my brain. I soon made a new ritual of going to the pub across the street with the cast for a nightcap. I ordered glasses in quick succession, making sure that the buzz never had time to subside. My limit was usually three glasses—I didn't want to become truly incoherent or nauseous. When I found myself eyeing the catsup bottles ravenously, I knew it was time to start home.

I weaved my way up Wells Street either on foot or teetering slowly on my bicycle. Then I made a left onto Lincoln. Everything I knew was on Lincoln Avenue. My first landmark was the hospital where they took Ben that fateful night the earth tipped him over. Then the first professional theater where I'd done an internship after graduation. The funeral parlor and the church that said His name so I could blow kisses and whisper *thank You* twenty-five times. Paula's office, which I still visited but not as often. The Dianetics center with its immense plate-glass windows and a looped video of L. Ron Hubbard promising to restart your life while a volcano vomited around him. I was grateful that they left his prerecorded homily on all night so I had someone to greet on the way home. I envied his sure-footed path, his assertive faith, his ability to resurrect himself over and over again.

When I got home I thanked G-d for bringing me there safely. I kissed my bike one hundred times and my mezuzah two hundred and fifty times and sang my new *thank You for this home* song. I put together my big meal of the day, which was now fat-free broth with vegetables, egg whites, and fiber cereal on the bottom. Then I sat on the floor in the living room with my bowl, my two-liter of diet root beer, the crossword puzzle, and a stash of juice glasses to trap the roaches. The sun was close to rising as I said my night prayers. Without the checkerboard tile of my old apartment, I marked each repetition by stepping in patches of skim-milk light from the streetlamps. *Thank You for this day. Thank You for the walk home. Thank You for this new day about to begin and please help me eat less and slower next time.*

Prayers were the one thing keeping my life in order. They were a lone certainty in the first and last moments of every day. It was comforting to think that I was needed here to pray for people's well-being and safe travels—that someone might need me. Ben was gone, Ruthie was gone, Mom was still immersed in Carl, and I was only too grateful to seclude myself with G-d, my most constant companion. I begged Him to help me be the tiniest one in the room. To be lithe and light and to take smaller bites so I got fuller faster.

There was an undeniable selfishness to my prayers now. I asked for Mom, Ben, Ruthie, and even Carl to be happy healthy always and for peace in Iraq, but I then followed it up with another plea to make me skinnier. My whole being was constricting to the size and shape of my reflection. As I counted out the Shemas I mourned how chubby my fingers looked. I added more mantras as I rowed and pedaled, but still I couldn't catch up to where or who I wanted to be.

There was irrepressible self-righteousness, too. One day as I was biking to the gym I almost ran over a clump of little girls with their mommies coming out of the grocery store. I scowled at their pig-tails and heart-shaped sunglasses, the way their bellies jiggled as they skipped and tripped while waving oatmeal cookies high in the air. I wanted to shake them. I despised them for being so small. For saun-tering by, navels first, full from their sugary treats and loving their shadows on the sidewalk. For being little enough to eat cookies and milk and climb onto their daddies' laps and say good night when it was time for bed. I would never be that little again.

I got off my bike and forced my way through the pack. Then stomped into the street, cursing at the bus that was tying up the crosswalk. I was just snapping my bike lock shut when my mother called.

"Hey, Mom, I'm really busy, can I call you later?"

"I guess so." Her voice was thin and subdued.

"What's up?"

She told me that a dear family friend had died. He was young, only a few years older than me, and had been diagnosed with cystic fibrosis as a child. He'd exceeded all his doctor's gloomy forecasts and played hockey year-round. The last time I'd seen him was three years earlier, after his double lung transplant. I was on tour and he took me on a cruise through Washington, D.C., in his Mazda Miata convertible, laughing into the wind. I could still see his impish smile as we ordered diner coffee and he told me about how he'd soared from 30 to 77 percent lung capacity. And now he was gone.

"So, I know you probably can't make it out for the funeral, but I just thought you'd want to know," Mom said.

"Of course, of course."

My first thought was that I hadn't had him on my sick list in months and there was no way to help him now. I had cut back on my sick and travel lists to make room for more skinny mantras. I would have to add a prayer for his grieving family tomorrow.

"Do you want to talk about it? Or, you said you have to be some-where," Mom continued.

"I do."

My second thought was that she had just stolen eight minutes out of my workout and there was no way to get that time back and I had probably just gained back at least a pound standing here on the side-walk, doing nothing.

this wasn't supposed to happen

. . . .

The Christmas party at Second City was a good place to get hammered. The tumblers of wine were free and both stages were throbbing with strobe lights and people dancing. I was only slightly tipsy when Jay Lynch sat down next to me at the bar.

"Hey there, darlin'. You look nice," he said.

"Thanks, you're not bad yourself."

I knew Jay as the cute guy with red hair that my cast mate Kate had a crush on. He worked as a stage manager for one of the touring companies and walked with an odd sort of shuffle.

"Can I get you something?" he asked. The constellation of freckles on his face twinkled playfully as he grinned. He even had a freckle on his lower lip.

"Sure, if you're treating." I handed him my tumbler and pointed to the wine chilling under the beer taps. It had been two years of mourning Ben and telling myself I would never love again. Jay's eyes were the color of worn denim and they were disarmingly kind as he said, "I've seen you around but we've never really talked. So, hi."

As he reached for our drinks he put his hand lightly on the small of my back, just where my mother used to soothe me with slow circles when I couldn't fall asleep. I felt a wash of heat and pulled my tumbler back quickly to hide my face.

"So, hi," I said back.

We were standing on the Dianetics corner on Lincoln Avenue three weeks later when Jay kissed me for the first time.

"This wasn't supposed to happen," I murmured into his neck. I couldn't figure out what I was doing. And I certainly couldn't figure out Jay. His patient eyes, his strong shoulders, but most of all, the ease of him. He listened to rap and wore his baseball cap backward. For the past three weeks he'd wooed me with stories of his family gathered at his Granny's for Christmas. He said his hero was his father, who had let him sit up front in the Arnold's bread truck when he was five and help deliver loaves of rye to supermarkets before sunrise. His calm unnerved me. I asked him whether he drank whole milk and he said only if there were Oreos nearby. And that freckled smile kept returning.

It was about five degrees as we kissed on that blustery corner, but I told him I couldn't invite him up to my apartment.

"That's fine," he said. "I can dream about this moment all night."

When I got inside, I kissed my mezuzah five hundred times, sang my *thank You for this home* song three times, and whispered, *Please forgive me if I've done something bad.*

The next night when I came home from the theater, there was a note from my roommate: *Call Jay Lynch! Doesn't matter how late! Woo hoo! PS—taco pie in the fridge.* I made my soup slowly and settled in front of the TV. Turned on Regis and Kelly and pulled out the crossword puzzle before dialing Jay's number.

"Hey!"

"Hey."

"I'm glad you called. How was your day?"

"Good. The audience was really slow tonight. Tuesday-night coma."

"How was the rest of your day?" he asked.

"Huh?"

He wanted to talk about who I was outside of the theater. Another aspect of him I was thoroughly baffled and slightly irritated by. Getting to know him would be much easier if I could be a character donning giant sunglasses or a leopard nightgown. But Jay had already seen all my characters. He was interested in *me*. What it was like growing up in Westchester (he was from Long Island), why I came to Chicago, what I'd do with a million dollars.

"Probably get my mom a house in La Jolla and put the rest in savings. She's my best friend in the whole world." I tried to answer quickly, then covered the receiver with my palm so I could sneak in mouthfuls of food without him hearing me swallow. Now he was telling me how much he admired his sister and how his favorite memory was of when he was four and running naked through the sprinkler with his cousins.

"Mmm hmm," I responded, only mildly amused. I was all for sprinklers and close-knit families, but I couldn't allow myself to be taken in by anyone who was this comfortable in his own skin.

"So why don't you tell me something about you that I *won't* like?" I challenged.

"You won't like?" he repeated, warily.

"Yeah. The ugly stuff." A kiss was one thing but I needed to know he was tormented in some way before I committed to staying on the phone any longer. Jay spoke slowly.

"I have a really bad temper sometimes." He sighed. "I swung at this guy a couple of years ago who looked like he was going to mug me." I smiled, imagining the poorly lit street and uncertainty.

"I get angry too," I mumbled. "I punched this girl in college because she wanted all the girls to play basketball in bikini tops."

Jay laughed. "I made some really stupid choices in high school. A lot of drugs."

"I was on medication once for a mental thing."

"Spent a night in jail."

"Almost had a thing with someone my father's age."

"Stole a car with some guys in college."

"Gave my stepdad the silent treatment the day he died."

We stayed on the phone until the receiver slipped with sweat and I could hear my roommate's morning alarm buzzing.

"So when can I see you again?" he asked sleepily.

"I don't have much time to go out. Monday's my only night off and usually I like to do an improv show that night too."

"Next week you're skipping it to go out with me," said Jay.

We met outside the movie theater. I hadn't been on a real date since Phil the professor almost seven years ago. I'd bought tie-dyed jeans at a resale shop and worked out an extra half hour to prepare for tonight. Jay was obviously an old pro at dating. His face looked flushed from scrubbing, his hair was gently tousled. I couldn't follow the plot of the movie we saw because our knees kept inching closer together and I didn't want him to think I was doing it on purpose but I also didn't want to squirm away. When we stepped outside into the night, Jay pulled out his cell phone. I rolled my eyes. Ben had been adamantly opposed to cell phones and I'd adopted his distaste for them as well. I'd found a concrete reason to hate this guy.

When he turned back to me I said coyly, "Oh, was it an important call? You can stay on if you want." I was ready for his look of shame; instead he smiled, freckles lined up neatly.

"Nothing's more important. Just telling the restaurant we'd be a few minutes late."

It wasn't quite midnight, but I was starving. I'd known Jay was set on taking me to dinner so in addition to my longer workout I'd kept my day's intake to half a protein bar and a banana. I ordered wine before we sat down and made sure the waiter stayed close by for seconds. I drank quickly, greedily. By the time they brought our food everything on the table looked hazy.

"Let's splittabottle!" I slurred, so I wouldn't regret the thick olive oil and stuffed mushrooms, the linguini with shaved Parmesan and roasted cherry tomatoes that I was soon shoveling into my mouth. On the cab ride home a tinselly snow fell from the sky. It was incredibly romantic but I had a sneaking suspicion Jay had orchestrated that on his cell phone too while I was in the bathroom. I let him come upstairs anyway. Ordered him into my apartment and told him to go straight to the kitchen and I would join him in a second. I closed the door, sang my song, and counted out my kisses on my bike and mezuzah. After Jay and I messed around in my bed—which I thoroughly enjoyed but restricted to the top of my covers—I waited for his breath to drop into an easy snore before I tiptoed out into the living room to recite my night prayers. Then I snuck into the hall and repeated the ones for my bike and mezuzah again, just so He knew I was His above all and this red-haired boy was merely a distraction.

The following Monday Jay showed up with a spray of orchids and a book. We went to a French restaurant and I got so drunk I ate a full head and a half of roasted garlic. The whole night I was sick, sweating sweet-sour stains into his sheets, turning his Pink Floyd T-shirt a foggy brown. Jay brought me cool glasses of water and said I was the best kind of crazy he knew. I didn't know whom to hate more—him for pulling a Nurse Nightingale routine or me for letting him. When morning came he was bright-eyed and panting like a dog, buoyant about the new day. He said we could stay in bed forever, or maybe go to another movie, or just walk by the lake and get eggs at the diner.

"Sorry, I have to go," I said.

"You don't have to be at the theater until seven, right?"

"Yes, but I have a lot to do."

"Really? Because I thought now that you're not rehearsing you had days free and maybe . . . ?"

"No. I have to get home."

"At least let me make you breakfast?"

"Just toast. And first you need to find me a closet where I can say a few prayers."

"How 'bout you stay right here and I'll shut the door?" he said, kissing me lightly on the forehead. No explanation needed.

My lips were scratchy and crooked from kissing as I started repeating the Shema. I didn't know whether I should apologize for my actions or just pretend it hadn't happened. G-d knew what I was doing whether I admitted it or not. I felt deceitful saying sorry while I was crouched in Jay's closet wearing his soccer shorts, when I knew I wanted to kiss him again.

Thank You for whatever that was, I prayed. Then I started tremulously on my lists. When I opened the door, forty minutes later, Jay had made us coffee and a mountain of toast. He didn't ask any questions and I didn't supply any answers and I didn't know whether to laugh or cry because he looked so pleased to see me. I slurped down a cup of coffee and said I'd have to take my toast to go. The rest of the day I spent on the stationary bike, peeling through fake peaks and valleys, dripping garlicky puddles, and gritting my teeth. I stopped home long enough to shower and do my *quiet time* prayers again before the show.

After my postshow tumbler of wine, I called Mom.

"I don't know. I like him. Did I tell you he has red hair?"

"You did," said Mom. "Just take it slow, Ab. Hey, did I tell you about your sister's new beau? I think she's really happy. She looks great too. Carl's taking us both to the theater tonight."

"That's good." I tried not to sound hurt. I was almost thirty years old and I still needed Mom's approval even for guys she'd never met. It smarted when she spoke of my sister so lovingly. Betsy had moved back to New York two years earlier, and she and Mom had grown much closer. They always seemed to be going to concerts and dinner parties together.

"You could join us if you came home once in a while."

"Mom, it's not like that. We have shows six nights a week."

"I know. I know. But still . . ."

The unfinished sentences were becoming all too familiar in our conversations. The less I called home, the less we had to say to each other. And the number of topics we couldn't discuss had multiplied. Mom had learned not to bring up my eating or my blush because I would just sigh impatiently. I didn't ask about Carl because I didn't want to think of his fat lip touching hers. Just hearing his clarinet yowl put me on edge. More often than not Mom and I fell off into silence.

"All right, Chicken, I should get going."

"Yeah, me too."

"I know you don't want me to ask, but are you eating better now?"

"Yes."

"I bet you're not. . . ."

"Maybe you'll come out for my next show opening?"

"Maybe . . ."

"So I really want you to meet Jay. I want to know what you think."

"Just take it easy. And you can date more than one guy at a time, you know. When I was your age . . ."

I wasn't going to date anyone else, but I decided Mom was right. Jay could not be more than a brief diversion. I wouldn't let him. Even when he showed up backstage to kiss me. Even when he wrote me cards and rap songs and especially when he left a bundle of hyacinths wrapped in tissue paper at the box office. The purple petals were so bright that I felt dizzy gazing at them. He took me camping in the Michigan dunes and we made love on our slippery sleeping bags, then watched the campfire dance and ate marshmallows until our lips were glued in sticky creases. Even when he waited for me to jog around the campgrounds and then say my prayers under a tree. Even when we drove back into the city wearing matching bandanas, smelling like sweat and soot, trailing a swarm of sand bugs and grit behind us.

I laughed and drew him doodles, drank and undressed with him in the loose detachment of a Monday night, but I kept telling myself this was as far as I would go. I couldn't get lost in someone who wore hair gel and called his mother regularly. If I fell into his unhurried gait, if I ate toast with butter at a well-lit table like he did, I could easily lose my edge and wind up doughy and dull. He showed up five minutes early for everything and even when he was disappointed, his freckles stayed intact. He was too stable and solid and if I was going to allow myself to be with a man I needed him to be as tortured and starved as I was. Or at least Jewish. Or taller. Each day I invented a different reason why Jay was wrong for me. Most of all I couldn't take Jay seriously because he was nothing like my father. He wasn't a performer. He had no interest in wearing a business suit and walking up from the train station with a worn briefcase either. He'd never heard of Cole Porter. He was in perfect health.

About three months after Jay and I began dating, I realized that whatever my intentions were, I was falling for him.

He had just left for a tour through Colorado. The same Second City tour where I had seen the blowout years before. There was a note waiting for me when I came home from the theater.

Call Jay's cell! Doesn't matter how late!

When he picked up his voice was rattling.

"Thanks for calling," he gasped. "I miss you."

He told me he had deep piercing pains clawing through his abdomen. He put down the phone to vomit and couldn't say more than a sentence without moaning. The next day, his chest burned, cutting off his breath. *Make sure to call!* the new note said. His teeth were chattering. He sounded like he was being crushed between two boulders.

"What is this?" he whimpered.

"Whatever it is, I'm here with you. I'm holding you. I'm stroking you. I'm breathing you," I cooed. I didn't care that I sounded like a weak imitation of telephone sex. I was stirred by his groans. I sang him the Irish lullaby he'd taught me the first time we lay naked together.

He went to a hospital for tests and antibiotics. The doctors there said it was probably a strain of pneumonia. Ordered him to rest and drink a lot of liquids. But by the fifth day, he couldn't even make it to the phone.

"Abby, we're getting him on a plane tonight," one of the girls in his touring company said. "I don't want to scare you but it's bad. If the air pressure is too much for his lungs to handle, then . . . I don't know." They were going to take him straight to the same emergency room on Lincoln Ave. where Ben was taken. The irony wasn't lost on me. Before the show that night I mentioned Jay by name in my prayers for the first time. I asked for him to please heal. My traveling prayer had new force and focus, knowing that he was being flown home, maybe not in a helicopter like Aunt Simone, but the potential for him to explode was still there. I wanted to wink at G-d and thank Him too. Now I knew why I was with Jay. *Thank You for the chance to save him.*

I felt the lust and heat of danger as I performed onstage that night, waiting for Jay to descend from the sky. I skipped the improv set and jogged to the hospital, my strides long and sure. This was how I knew love to be. Uncertain. Perilous. If Jay died I would explain carefully to his parents that I had tried not to get involved with him and that their son had an amazing heart. I would also buy Arnold's Jewish rye for the rest of my life.

The doctors on Lincoln Ave. decided Jay had a severe case of pneumonia. He was put on bedrest and given a stronger dose of meds—painkillers for his engorged lungs that were pressing on all his other organs. Then he was released. As we waited for a cab he leaned into me, shivering, and told me I was his girl.

Once again, I was in my element. Taking care of Jay gave me clarity and determination. I did not leave his side for days, even to go to the gym. I snuck into his roommate's room after he'd left for work and found a new hiding spot for my prayers. I held Jay so close that I was soon coughing too, which delighted me. Then I called in sick to the theater and made sure his sheets were dry as the fever drained out of him. When he was awake I wiped his dry lips with a moist cloth and fed him crackers. I even ate with him—together we consumed ten liters of diet soda and eight cans of minestrone in three days. We pulled off the couch pillows to make a pallet on the living room floor and lay side by side watching music videos. We took a walk two blocks away to the convenience store for more soda and we moved so slowly it was almost an hour round trip. When he was asleep again, I counted out my night repetitions by the row of bricks on the apartment across the alley.

There was no eulogy to write. No phone calls to his parents. Jay was recovering. It took him a week to sit up straight without cringing, two more for his skin to sift through grays and blues before settling into its rosy glow, the glimmer in his eyes reemerging triumphantly.

As spring crept in, we were both alive, growing even. I came over to his place every night after the show with crackers and soda, but he was feeding *me* now, or turning out the lights and pulling me into a slow dance. He woke up in the mornings giddy again. He loved to spend hours with us just looking at each other naked.

One morning that had already turned into an afternoon, I called my mother.

"Mom, he's all better!" I reported victoriously.

"That's nice. This is the one with red hair, right?"

"This is Jay. He was in Colorado. In the hospital. Now he's better. We're making pancakes!"

"So have you been over there the whole time?"

Her words slapped me in the face. She was right. I had completely absorbed myself in Jay's illness and now that he had recovered I had no function, no reason to be with someone red-haired and capable. He didn't need me. This was a colossal misunderstanding. My role was supposed to be that of the caretaker, the superhero. I'd missed workouts for him. I'd even asked G-d to intervene on his behalf. I packed my knapsack and told him I really had to get going.

"Where to?"

"I just have stuff to take care of. And I can't . . . just sit around." I was unlocking my bike, shaking my head, trying not to sound completely asinine. My coffee curdled in my stomach.

I needed to do my prayers at home and then get in a workout and write up some lists and maybe go back to the gym for an afternoon class and I needed some time just kissing my mezuzah. I should get some more high-fiber cereal and call Mom just to make sure she's not mad and let her know she was right, I was wasting my time just hanging out on a couch with a completely happy healthy boy.

"Wait!" Jay said. Vehemently, resolutely.

His eyes were five thousand different colors of blue and blinking fast.

"Wait, please." His voice was softer, but still strong. He took my bike lock from me. "I just have to say something. I just need you to stay here for one minute so I can say something."

"I have to—"

"I know you need to go but I have to say . . . this is scary. I want you to come to my sister's wedding this summer in Spain. I want you to meet my family because . . . I love you. I really love you."

I didn't know what to do with his tears and his truth. He was so still and so stable and I didn't want to want him this much.

"What was the scary part? Saying the word *Spain*?" I chirped.

"Please," he said. "I'm serious."

the incredible shrinking truth

It didn't matter that it was the middle of a summer afternoon, that the square below us was roaring with taxi horns and peddlers eager to hawk their last ripe mangos and bougainvillea. Our curtains were drawn. The lamp on the night table cast only a small umbrella of yellow light. My mother stood next to it and carefully unbuttoned her blouse.

First I saw the familiar crop of freckles and birthmarks radiating across her chest. Warner's wireless brassiere in eggshell, size 36A. I was wearing the same one. In my almost thirty years of life, I had never bought myself a bra. Mom had always either picked up an extra on sale while shopping or passed on her hand-me-downs. Even when they had been tucked into a padded envelope and mailed to me in Chicago, they arrived still molded in the soft scoop of her breast. Carrying the sweet mustiness of her rose talc.

She unbuttoned further. Pulled out the bottom edges from her waistband. Slowly opened the pressed cotton and arched her stomach forward.

"Ta-da!" she sang timidly.

A thick current of twisted pink cut across her torso. Cutting her in half.

"Pretty impressive, huh?"

Mom's spleen was infected. It weighed eight pounds—a little less than I weighed at birth. A few months earlier she'd been diagnosed with a blood disorder, *polycythemia*—too many red blood cells. It wasn't life-threatening, but it was incurable and was most successfully treated with old-fashioned leeching and sometimes a splenectomy. When I told her that I wanted to come home for her operation, she said, "Bah. It's outpatient. Remember how boring the barium was? I'll get Betsy or a friend to drive me there and back and then I'm going to sleep for two days. It wouldn't be any fun." When I called her after the procedure, she sounded disoriented but pleased. Her doctor had let her hold the spleen, which was distended with her unwanted blood. Mom named it Schmendrick, Yiddish for *that guy*. She typically reserved that name for people who gave her a hard time at the checkout counter, or my ex-boyfriends.

Looking at her now, I felt I was the real Schmendrick. Why hadn't I gone home to be with her? I wondered if I'd prayed enough or if I'd been thinking about her at the moment she went under.

"Wow, Mom," I said slowly, reverentially.

"Right?"

"Yeah. Wow. I mean, *wow*."

I moved in closer, viewing her at different angles as if she were a complicated painting. Someone had literally cut her open from side to side. Reached in and pulled out the parts that were no good anymore. She had lost a lot of weight, too. Maybe more than me, I noted jealously. With her new groove of unexposed skin she appeared taller, more logical. Top fitting precisely above bottom. She could pose as a magician's assistant who was in a saw trick gone awry.

"Mom, it's really beautiful."

"Oh, come on." She pursed her lips. "I wouldn't exactly say *beautiful*."

"Well, I think it is," I said again. I could tell she was flattered. I wanted to thank whoever had performed her surgery. The courageous and generous surgeon who had marked her for life. After almost seventy years, my mother finally had a *scar* to prove how much she had been through and survived.

"All right. That's enough. Do not pass go [and] do not collect two hundred dollars." This was my mother's favorite command. (I've added the word *and* in the middle so the *go* and the *d* are separated.) It was her way of saying no more dawdling, there's stuff to do. We brushed our teeth and Mom put on a clean top. She hung up her cotton skirts in the closet and waited for me to do the same before hooking her arm through mine so we could promenade down the hall.

Mom and I were in Barcelona—our first trip overseas together. I'd just finished a string of Second City performances in Amsterdam and the following week I was going to Jay's sister's wedding on the Spanish coast. I'd invited Mom to join me for the week in between for moral support. I was nervous about meeting Jay's family for the first time. I was nervous about my feelings for Jay.

Despite my mother's warnings, I'd tumbled into love for Jay headfirst. He had recovered completely from his pneumonia four months earlier but I couldn't manage to let go of him, no matter how fast I ran, pushed, and pedaled. When we slept together I felt an overwhelming and fundamental calm. And he said he didn't want anything more than to start planning our lifetime together. Days before leaving for Spain, we'd signed a lease on an apartment together. We would be living over a German bar that played "Tiny Dancer" on repeat and we had too many rooms for our five pieces of furniture. The day we moved in we got a ticket on our rented van because we were double-parked while we had sex on our new mattress.

But I still needed Mom to meet him and confirm that this was a relationship worth pursuing. She didn't approve of the fact that Jay wasn't Jewish. She didn't like that I'd dropped another ten pounds since we'd started dating. But I hoped she could be won over by his gentle disposition, his constant optimism, and his affinity for rye bread. He continued to amaze and confuse me. I had no reference point for a companion who was this open and unencumbered. I had fewer and fewer memories of my father as a whole, sturdy man. Every day, Jay told me he loved me. I wanted my mother to tell me it was okay to love him back.

Mom was delighted with the idea of Spain. She used her frequent-flyer miles for a last-minute ticket and declared it the perfect way to celebrate the Schmendrick removal and explore a city that had charmed her forty years ago. She would even pay for our hotel.

"We'll just explore and relaaaaax," she told me.

Only, as we stepped into the tiled lobby arm in arm, it felt more eerily momentous than that. Not that Mom and I hadn't slept in the same bed and studied each other's bodies before. Not that I hadn't been asking for her approval after every show and had her appraise each apartment I'd lived in. Even though our phone conversations had grown more distant, they always involved my asking her for advice or trying to impress her with my accomplishments. But it had been a long time since we'd been alone together. Ten years since the summer I started on Anafranil and we listened to James Taylor and played dress-up with her clothes and waited for me to grow two inches or at least for the world to shrink. That was before I had added more prayers, more kisses, dance moves, and lists. Before I'd fallen in love with Ruthie and Ben and eating with the lights off, living under a cloak of secrecy. Before my mother and I had narrowed to just two hundred pounds combined.

And now, with our matching spindly arms linked, Mom leading us forward into the crush of the late afternoon on the Rambla, I felt anxious and vaguely threatened. As if at any moment one of us could trip on a loose stone and break in two, and all of our blue-couch confessionals would scatter in the streets. The abortion, too. The piles of litter and the blowouts that I'd stowed in pockets deep beneath all these new repetitions and rituals. Mom walked too slowly. Or maybe it was too fast. I struggled to figure out how to keep pace with her, searching for her green sandals on the path.

"What are you doing? Pick up your feet, Chicken!" She jabbed me with her elbow. "Mmm! Do you smell that? I'm starved."

This was the secret closest to my lips now: I wanted to tell her that I wasn't hungry, that I'd rather walk more to build up an appetite. This was the line I'd rehearsed in front of the mirror. But it was so pitifully untrue. The cafés were just unshuttering their windows after siesta and a thick gust of olive oil and ceviche herded us through the crowds. Street vendors shouted and fish flapped their tails wildly on beds of ice. Eating with Mom would be precarious. I knew she was watching. And she knew that I was watching her watch. And I knew that she knew that I knew she was watching.

"Look up!" she ordered. Twisted spires rose in front of us. A stone fountain caught the sun in its misty shower. And above it, the sky yawned in ripe golds and limitless reds. I should have sent up a special prayer of thanks for these colors I'd never seen before, but I wasn't sure how many times to repeat it and if I could sneak it out of the side of my mouth without Mom noticing. I also wondered whether I should include a new prayer for her scar or her bony shoulders, and I hadn't figured out where I was going to pray tomorrow morning with the hotel closet full of her skirts and scarves.

Maybe it hadn't been that long since we'd been close. Maybe we hadn't changed that much. Maybe she felt my breath constrict even before I did as I searched the side streets for a darkened alley where I could hide and whisper my *I'm sorry*'s and *please*'s. My mother had always known how to find me, no matter where I climbed and spun in my cyclones of panic. And she did it again now. Before I could say a word. Before we could be struck down. She swooped in, gripped my arm tighter, and pulled me into a broad open doorway.

"Table for two, *por favor*?" she trilled at the bartender. Her flamboyant *r*'s made us both giggle with relief. The bartender showed us to a table outside in the middle of the busiest sidewalk and set down two glossy menus with a flourish. We pointed to a carafe of white wine and clinked glasses, inebriated from the moment the wine touched our lips. It seeped into my skin, coloring the spires rose. I took another languid sip, imagining my whole body as a porous sponge. If I closed my eyes to half-mast, it didn't matter who was watching. I no longer needed to thank G-d for the endless sky or count how many marinated mushrooms I placed in my mouth. For this first night, I was only too grateful to have my mother in charge of everything once again.

The next morning I staked out a spot on our hotel balcony where I could utter my prayers up to the rooftops.

"Okay, but I'm timing you," Mom warned. "We need to be downstairs by nine." She wanted to make sure we took advantage of the complimentary breakfast.

"I promise." I shut the heavy wooden doors and stepped into the dazzling morning sun. Bedsheets and dishrags of every color danced on laundry lines that were somehow fastened to the sky.

I thanked G-d for these exquisite, simple moments. I asked Him to please keep Mom completely happy healthy always and forever and I thanked Him for Mom's smart doctors. I asked Him to please forgive me for all my sins and transgressions. To help me eat slowly, thoughtfully, in small amounts, and to help me find time to exercise.

Most of all please help me to serve You always. Thank You, Amen. Thank You, Amen. Thank You, Amen.

"So, it's more than a half hour now," Mom said later, while blanketing her misshapen croissant with bright slabs of butter. We were the last ones at breakfast because my prayers had taken longer than expected. The pan of complimentary eggs and sausage was empty.

"Twenty-two minutes," I said firmly. I tried to ignore the way her eyes fixed on me.

"Not by my watch. Anyway, I thought you had it down to fifteen."

Fifteen was her invention. My morning prayers had never taken fifteen minutes. My backstage prayers took fifteen minutes—give or take. But she didn't even know about those. Or the ones I'd said last night after I felt her breath lengthen into sleep. Besides, twenty-two minutes in the morning was a tremendous feat.

"Paula knows," I offered.

Paula had helped me set goals and cut down my *quiet time* to twenty-two minutes. And to stop praying for ambulances. But I hadn't told her that every time I shaved off a minute of prayers I added it to my exercise routine. That the best way to ignore a siren was to jump, lunge, run in place, and count my footfalls until I found a light-headed nothingness where I could escape. Each morning a stab of fear pulled at me when I caught my reflection in the mirror. But I couldn't tell Paula. She was pretty and health conscious and I didn't want her stealing any of my weight-loss ideas. I didn't tell her, or Mom, or even G-d that in many ways I had given up on saving the rest of the world because I couldn't see past my pale and flaccid skin.

"How often are you going to Paula, anyway?" asked Mom as she scooped an errant glob of jam from the edge of her plate into her mouth.

"Once every other week."

"I wonder if she's really doing anything for you," she sniffed. When I made us late for breakfast, Paula had turned into a Schmendrick in Mom's book.

"Mom. It's okay. Please?"

"And that's all you're having? Some dry cornflakes?"

"Just leave me alone, Mom. This is supposed to be my vacation too, okay?" I stared at my palms to avoid her startled look. I knew I was being insolent, but I had no choice. It was almost ten thirty and I hadn't exercised yet. I also hadn't exercised the day before, because I was traveling. My legs felt slack and cumbersome. I needed to move. I needed to jostle my brain and clear through my tangles, and most of all I had to protect myself from my mother's watchful eye.

The morning became a series of hostile negotiations. Next I had to break it to her that I would need to jog for an hour every day we were in Spain.

"And what am I supposed to do during that time?"

"I thought you'd want to take a rest or something. I can go in the afternoon while you take a nap or . . ."

This was an insult. Joanie Sher had never been a napper. She did not nap. Naps were for the old or infirm. They indicated a serious illness or malfunction, and usually whoever took a nap in our house was also wearing the *sick sweater*—an oversize oatmeal-colored cardigan knit by my Aunt Doris and heavy from years of broken fevers and disjointed dreams. I remember my mother being ill exactly once when I was little. I climbed onto her bed and stared at her while she took a sick-nap, weakened by a flu. She would only let me stay in the room if I promised to nap too, but really I was spying on her the whole time. It took her forever to lie still—her eyes fluttering, bits of dream coming out in guttural grunts. Then finally, her body sinking into the sheets, her fingers tapping out Debussy on the covers.

"You can't take a break from running? Just for a few days?" she said, biting into a triangle of soft cheese. I didn't answer her.

"So, I guess I'm going to sit up in the room and wait for you, then."

"It'll be quick, I promise."

"Right. That's what you said about this morning." She shook her head as she savored the last clump of butter on her knife and stirred another creamer into her coffee. I scowled into my coffee cup. I resented her for being so cavalier with her food and her requests for companionship; for being so unaware of everything I had to get done. Everything I'd worked so hard to hide from her. I wanted to tell her she was in no position to be judging me—driving herself between me and my prayers or my workout. She was the one with an unsteady stride and a gaping hole in her stomach, after all. I was absurdly healthy in comparison. I took a last sip of coffee and put down my cup definitively. According to Paula, I was not responsible for my mother's feelings.

I never told my mother that therapy had also been helping me to recognize myself as a separate entity. Paula had carefully suggested that my intensely close relationship with Mom was unique and supportive but also had proven a bit stifling at times. That I could be Mom's best friend forever and ever and also have opinions of my own without dishonoring or hurting her. I took in a deep breath and announced my first such decision: I would spend an hour jogging and my mother would do whatever she could to amuse herself. Mom raised her eyebrows and dabbed her frown with her napkin.

"If that's really what you want to do . . ." she said, clearly displeased. But, I noted with relief, she did not break in two.

Our days in Spain were full of exploring. We wandered through Gaudí's maze of swollen windows and psychedelic turrets. Smelled flower petals the size of our faces and roamed beaches gilded with the finest sand. Mom conceded to a brief siesta the first day after lunch. The other days she strolled and bought bright tiles and picture frames for souvenirs while I attempted to jog the cobblestone streets, weaving and stumbling through the crowds. There was no space to navigate and I couldn't go fast enough to break a sweat. I huffed impatiently on the heels of sultry Spanish women. Their high-hipped skirts and small crescent-shaped calves. The shift of their thighs and lure of their bare necks. I wanted to chase them and steal their breath, their laughter and length and possibility. I hated jogging. I always had, I decided. I'd much rather be on a machine where I could ascend programmed peaks and track my calories. I was hardly jogging. I was stalking.

Our nights were sumptuous. Mom and I went to outdoor cafés and ordered tall pitchers of sangria. I drank voraciously and chewed on the soaked orange rinds until my brain softened and my eyes tripped lazily over the menu. Each morning I prayed to eat less. Each night I drank until my mind was cloudy enough that I could gorge with abandon. We feasted on toast points with roasted peppers and tapenade; fresh fish dripping with pesto and glistening capers. On our left, a cathedral rose majestically. On our right, a bronzed man named Pascal who wanted to play *anyting for dees beautiful ladees, sistairs, yes?* We giggled at his manicured moustache and his seductively plucked guitar.

We licked basil-dusted plates and sucked on olive pits until well past midnight. Mom told me she once ate seventy-six black olives in a single sitting while she was reading *Sense and Sensibility*. I'd heard this story before, but I loved the way her voice unwound after she'd had a glass or two. Then she told me about the last time she was in Spain with Dad. She held his name on her tongue before swallowing.

"Daddy's the one who gave me those olives. It was a big can of black ones, because he knew I loved them so much." She fell under his spell again. "I still can't believe he *picked me.*" She sighed. I'd never heard her that wistful or effusive about my father and I wanted to weep for them both.

She began to unearth stories that came from somewhere profoundly new. At first cautiously, tentatively, while she crumbled cheese over her grilled eggplant. But soon she was spilling a precious history into the wine-soaked night. Her words were unedited, unrefined, rolling out in grainy gray footage that had been stowed away long ago. I was astonished by her openness. She told me how scared and mad and sad and confused she was when she couldn't get pregnant. Her doctor had told her they should look into adopting instead. *We didn't want to blame each other, but we just couldn't understand what was wrong. It was mortifying. Daddy was so upset.* Hearing her call my father *Daddy* made her seem smaller, more alone. The tests. The interminable waiting. The adoption agency had hundreds of hoops to jump through. The doubting. Of herself, of them as parents, of the whole process. Then, the disbelief. Bringing Jon home in his yellow bunting and wanting to hold him forever and also having a powerful urge to run away in fear. His eyes opening, giving her entire existence new shape and meaning. A few years later cradling Betsy, her face the most exquisite color of porcelain. *I'd never seen anything so beautiful. She looked like a perfect little doll. You've seen pictures.*

I had seen pictures. The characters were all familiar, the chronology matched up; but I'd never heard it articulated like this before. Her words felt cherished and fragile, as if they had been buried deep, on just this side of extinction. I felt the weight of their infant limbs, the soft swell of their hiccups. She invited me into her past and I saw her exposed in a way she'd never allowed before. I didn't know my mother could even acknowledge emotions like these. I drank in her words noiselessly, careful not to interrupt her.

"And of course you know the rest," she said with a coquettish grin. At age thirty-nine, she began throwing up. The doctor told her he'd made a mistake. She was pregnant! She and Daddy were ecstatic. I jutted out my chin proudly as she described me emerging, miraculously unfolding like a flower. I blinked back at her with infant blue-green eyes, the *only* eyes in the universe that would ever match hers. We raised our glasses again to rejoice in our identical eyes, our scrawny legs, the flurry of chocolate-chip birthmarks that extended across both our bellies. We laughed at the empty tables around us. We hadn't even ordered dessert or liqueur yet!

But with the first bite of flan, her voice hollowed again. She told me about the desolate days of her life after Daddy died. *I didn't know what to do. Aunt Bernie and Aunt Doris did all that cooking.* She felt pressured by her friends to start dating, to move on. The stale banter at singles events. The exterminator who invited her to a dance for tall people. None of her married friends would invite her to dinner parties because they thought an odd number at the table would be awkward. Her friend Penny's husband went on a business trip and Penny called my mother to say *I guess I know how you feel now, Joanie. I'm miserable without him.* And Mom wanted Penny dead too. *I mean really. How insensitive. She had no idea!* My mother's voice took on a wounded timbre. She was finally unleashing the hurt that had been fomenting inside her for almost twenty years.

Every night, a new café. Every sip, the sky grew wider; there were no limits to what we could say. The protective sheath I'd constructed around me so vigilantly began disintegrating. The hours of crunching and lifting couldn't make me strong enough to resist this tidal wave of intimacy. The lists I'd made (with Paula's help) of how I was different and distinct from my mother drifted away. Sometimes

I wanted to climb across the table and bury myself in her bosom. It had been ten years since we were alone together and I missed her so much.

I told her that I felt lost. That I thought something was wrong with me. That I couldn't walk down the street without watching women's bodies and I hated them for walking so slowly and being so thin. That I wanted to hurt them and I wanted to hurt myself even more. I voiced anger and fear and unknowing that I'd never found words for before. I tried to confess hurriedly so neither of us could catch up to their meaning, particularly the part about hurting myself. I reeled through my mounting insecurities about my career. I told Mom about the freedom and command I felt under the stage lights. How much colder it was in the dressing rooms, where I didn't fit in and I was always sure it was just a matter of moments until I was fired. I wallowed in memories of Ben, how much I wanted it to work with him even though I knew all the arguments against it, the logical rights and wrongs. I told her about the ominous edge to his voice when he couldn't find his legs and the way he disappeared right in front of me. I admitted that I loved his illness almost as much as his potential to heal.

"You never . . ." Mom began, and then she stopped herself. Our unspoken pact was to exhume, not to fix each other. Instead, she put her hand over mine and described a Schmendrick of hers who scared her with his temper. *He never did anything. But I didn't like where it was going.* Her words were clipped. She talked about the end of her relationship with Carl, who told her he thought polycythemia was an exaggeration and accused her of making herself sick. I wanted to scream *I hated him! He was so cruel to you!* But again, we lapsed into respectful silence.

I sheepishly turned the discussion to Jay.

"He's fun and he's healthy, Mom. He eats meat and butter and potatoes and root beer. I never thought I'd fall for someone with red hair! I really want you to meet him."

Jay's sister, Jess, had rented a farmhouse in the Spanish countryside for the week leading up to her wedding. Family and friends were flying in to start the celebration early. Weeks ago, Jess had sent both Mom and me invitations to a big barbecue on Saturday. I thought it'd be fun for us to go and I assumed that Mom had already said yes. But I could tell from her unsmiling face that she hadn't.

"It's just, we don't have that much time here, Chicken," she explained. She picked up an olive pit and inspected it. She seemed distinctly uninterested in Jay. She had stood by while I plummeted into impassioned and ultimately destructive relationships with Ruthie and Ben—she had no interest in watching me get thinner or hurt again. When I told her Jay was unburdened she shrugged distrustfully. She hadn't accorded him Schmendrick status—she appreciated an avid traveler and liked that he paid for dinner when we went out. But with her abrupt aloofness, I could feel the spell of our intimacy vanishing. She recrossed her legs and blew her nose distractedly—signs that she was done with this part of the conversation. She expected this young man to be a diversion, not a lingering presence—not on her vacation, at least.

"Right, right. But I thought if we went out there together. Took a picnic . . . ?"

"We'll see," she said, draining her glass.

"What?"

"We'll *see*," she repeated, impatient now, raising her hand for the check.

"But I thought . . ."

I stopped. I didn't know what to think. I didn't know how to explain my feelings at this moment to her or myself. I was bewildered and hurt that we could share so much with each other and yet she didn't want to share in the experience of meeting Jay's family. We had traveled so far into our truths and then jolted to a stop. And with her tacit distrust I began to doubt myself, too. We sat, looking at each other, a two-way mirror of unyielding eyes.

"Shall we, then?" said Mom, folding up her credit card slip. Our dinner was over. She reapplied her lipstick as she did after every meal in a restaurant. I thanked her graciously for the delicious food. I meant it, too—I was grateful for all that she had given me. For sharing with me this starry night surrounded by magnificent cathedrals. For nourishing me and exposing her scars. For birthing me.

But I still wish I had found a way to stay at that table and finish our conversation. To say: *Wait! No. I'm not done. We are not done. We need to stay here and say everything. Why do you get to decide where we go and what we do, how I should live and how I should love? How can you end this conversation, this night, this whole week, on* We'll see?

When we returned to the hotel, a message from Jay awaited me. I called him back. He was hoarse from tag football and fits of laughter with his family. He told me that down the road from the farm there was a winery and each day they filled plastic milk jugs with wine and cava for $2 a gallon. He couldn't wait until I arrived.

"And your mom, too. Everyone really wants to meet her." He lowered his voice. "I miss you soooooo much." I pressed the receiver more closely to my cheek. The phone was on Mom's side of the bed, but she pretended not to hear our conversation as she pored over a brochure for Barcelona's Turistic bus line.

"So, the trains run every few hours," said Jay. "If you come out a day early, we could hike this great-looking trail Saturday morning. What do you say?"

I knew my mother would never agree to go early, if at all.

"I can't wait to hold you," he added.

"Can I call you back?"

Mom winked at me as I hung up and acted as though she hadn't heard anything. "So. Sounds like we *have* to go up here and see this Fundació Joan Miró. It's supposed to be bee-yootiful." Her legs were tucked inside the pink nightgown that she had worn since I was a child. Her toes wiggled excitedly.

"Or else we could do the open market and then this route up to Palau Reial. But I know we both like museums and we haven't done those yet."

We didn't both like museums. She liked museums. She also liked book clubs devoted entirely to Jane Austen, and liverwurst on toasted pumpernickel, and she had always wanted to study genetic engineering. Which was why, for all four years of college, when it was time for me to pick the next semester's classes, she called to ask, "So, did you get into that genetic engineering class you wanted to take?"

And I answered, "No, I'll try next term. I have a pretty full load of courses right now."

I never said, "No. I don't want to take genetic engineering. You do." Just as I didn't tell her now that museums made me bored and cranky. I stood there, waiting for Mom to finish the brochure, brooding about the hike and jugs of wine that she would never accept.

"Yeah. Miró's place even has a garden. I'm pretty sure that's where Daddy took me. You'll love it."

I took a deep breath through my nose. "But Mom? About the barbecue . . . ? If we went out maybe even the day before . . ."

A shadow of hurt flickered across her face and settled into her jaw. "What? Why?"

"They really want to meet you. Jay and his mom and sister."

Her whole face screwed into a frown. "You're going to see them Sunday anyway," she said resentfully.

"Right, well, if we took the train out together Friday, and then we could stay over, or not. And then you could have Saturday to do some stuff on your own, and—or else I can come back here with you . . . or Saturday, we could both come back."

I was making myself dizzy listing the options. But my mother saw it perfectly clearly.

"You can go," she said coolly.

"I'd only go if you want to go, Mom."

"Well, it would mean cutting our week short."

"But we'd be there together."

"Not really."

"Yes really."

"Forget it. You do whatever you want." She took off her reading glasses and reached toward the lamp to turn it out.

"No, Mom, wait—"

When she turned back to me, her eyes were glittering with tears. Her bottom lip hung miserably and she swiped at her nose with a crumpled tissue. She was so volatile and contained at the same time; I thought she might snap in half.

"Mom, please. What are you thinking?"

She did calculations with days and nights, dollars and euros and figured out that to go to the farmhouse early meant we would be losing more than $400, not to mention forty-eight hours in Europe together. She said it was more than just the money too. It was about time for the two of us. Abby and Joanie. Girls about town. Time we would never be able to replace, she reproved menacingly. Then she descended into fiery self-pity.

"If I had known I was going to be a *burden*—"

"No! Mom, you're not a burden! All right! I won't go. We won't go. I'm sorry."

It was too late. Her hurt widened and encircled me. Her shoulders were hunched forward and she shook her head fitfully. "No. Don't let me stop you. You go. Have a good time."

I had never seen her so brittle, so feeble.

"No. Neither of us will go. Okay? Mom?"

She didn't answer. Just stared defiantly at the pile of trial-size soaps stacked on the dresser. The thin light from the lamp jaundiced her face and beneath her threadbare nightgown I could see her small puckered nipples. I was dumbfounded at the trajectory of the night. We'd gone from the most expansive trust to this vacuum of time and space. Everything had hardened and shrunk to this one unspeakable truth:

She was not *my best girlfriend forever and ever always*. She was not superhuman. She was my mother. And maybe this was all she had ever been, though I wanted so much for her to be more. For her to be everything. She couldn't have checked every newspaper or listened to every Sue Simmons report. She said she had, but it was not possible. She was wrong about needing a practical blazer and painted cheeks in order to succeed and she didn't know any more than I did whether the abortion was the right choice.

She was just this pink, shallow figure, shaped like a question mark and refusing to look me in the eye.

She turned out the lamp and we lay on opposite edges of the bed, strangers in the dark. Lovers who had said everything but good-bye. The space between us burned like peroxide on a fresh scrape. There was a tenderness to our hurt that I had never felt—that I almost couldn't fathom. A heartbreak that rendered everything broken.

I felt her roll away from me and heard myself sigh. I wanted to tell her that I never liked genetic engineering. That we'd had one conversation about it long ago and I said it *might* be cool to know more about it and then she *assumed*.

Instead I whispered *I'm sorry* again. And then, a little louder, "I'm going to say the Shema, Mom."

She remained silent.

"Is that okay?"

"Psssure."

Ayl me-lech ne-men She-ma . . .

I couldn't tell if she was listening. I wondered if she ever had. I realized that night that I'd been praying not only *for* my mother but *to* my mother all those years. I invented her omniscience, her infallibility, out of mere yearning for it to be true. I'd worshipped her fervently as the Grand Magician's assistant. But now I saw she was nothing but another mess of flesh and bone—she took up less space in the bed than I did.

We spent the rest of the week together as she wished. Each day stepping onto the cobblestones more hesitantly. Each night letting the silence sustain us. I spoke to G-d instead of her. I prayed that she would be *completely happy healthy always and forever and thank You for all of Mom's smart doctors may they be completely happy healthy too.*

APPROVED EVENING ACTIVITIES
FOR HIGHLAND PARK RECOVERY
PROGRAM LIST

Knitting

Crochet

Drawing

Cutting out pictures from magazines (scissors must be
approved with guardian)

Painting finger- and toenails

Listening to music

Reading

Renting movies

Use phone tree!

No caffeine, alcohol, gum, sugar substitutes

No cutting, pounding, scratching

No looking in mirror

three-fingered promise

Schedule for February 29, 2004: (Yay! We get an extra day of Feb.!!)

7 a.m.: coffee, *quiet time,* bike to gym

9 a.m.: fifty-two mins step (mountain path), eighteen mins elliptical trainer, twenty-two mins rowing, three sets each on abs machine, shoulder pulls, pec, and hip extenders

11 a.m.: shower

11:30 a.m.: coffee and banana at café. Make performance goal list, writing goal list, after Second City list, empowerment list. Finish two more scenes for *Saturday Night Live* submission packet

2 p.m.: eat LUNA bar, work on new ideas list

4 p.m.: bikram yoga class

5:30 p.m.: get groceries—LUNA bar box, hummus, fiber cereal, slimming tea, raisins, fat-free cheese, gum

6:30 p.m.: back to café—coffee, gum, (no banana). Make list of places to send short stories, list of new scenes to write. Work on short stories/new scenes

8:30 p.m.: drop off groceries at home, shower

9 p.m.: go to bar with Jay and Megan—only allowed three pinot grigios and one bowl of pretzels*

midnight: (at home) broth, cereal, fat-free cheese, carrot sticks— ONE serving

*Agh! had four glasses of wine and two servings of cereal—but last day of freedom and Jay says it's okay.

Schedule for March 1, 2004:

> 6:30 a.m.: coffee, *quiet time*
> 7:30 a.m.: in car, ready to go
> 8:30 a.m.: fill out intake forms
> 9 a.m.: ?????

The first and second day they let you get used to everything. The lavender walls, the fluorescent lighting, the calendar that says *Take a Leap of Faith!* It's supposed to be your choice, your recovery, after all. But by the third day, they want you to commit. You have to eat everything on your plate at all three meals. That includes the last sip of warm milk and the butter on your dinner roll. Everything.

It was my third day at Highland Park Hospital Center for Eating Disorders, an outpatient program forty-five minutes away from my apartment with Jay, my all-night gym, my life. On my thirtieth birthday, I was expecting a surprise party. I'd outlined in my notebook where Jay could attach the streamers and hide the cake. I'd left open my e-mail account so he could go through my addresses and invite my writing group to pop out from behind the bookcase yelling *Hooray!* and *You're too skinny to be thirty!* Instead I came home from the gym to find him sobbing on the couch. He'd been on the phone all day with Mom, Paula, Megan, insurance companies, doctors, even Ruthie, telling them something had to be done before I wasted away. Paula and Megan helped him find Highland Park, the place where I would spend nine hours a day, five days a week, learning how to feed myself again.

He also bought me a piano bench and promised that one day he'd give me the ivory keys to go with it. But first I had to stop starving, cutting, and pounding myself.

Starving had taken on new ferocity since my first date with Jay. I had long since forbidden him to take us out to dinners, and except for Spain, I only allowed myself one meal a day. When we moved into our rambling apartment, I filled the pantry with rows of high-fiber cereal and hid the diuretic teas I'd been drinking to tide me over until midnight. In our living room, Jay began building set pieces for his touring company—my favorite was an octagonal time machine that spun on metal wheels and made all our clothes smell like sawdust. I longed to travel back in time. As Jay and I fell deeper in love, I winnowed myself down to the same weight I'd been in junior high.

He kept telling me to slow down, that he loved me and I was gorgeous and thin already, but I couldn't hear him. I wanted to be the leanest, most driven woman he'd ever encountered. I wanted to *deserve* his praise and affection. I'd always adhered to a reward system—my mother commended us when we brought home a good report card, her *I love you*'s were carefully meted out for piano recitals or after a tearful confessional. Many of my closest relationships followed this pattern too—I gave Tristan my virginity to ensure his love, I was constantly showing Ruthie my writing, longing to warrant her laughter. My love of the theater revolved around this kind of affirmation. I was happiest onstage because each night I had to earn the audience's affection.

When Jay and I first began seeing each other, I was performing for three hundred and fifty people a night. I didn't require his constant approval and attention. But as my hunger-fueled workouts grew longer, even performing lost its luster. I couldn't concentrate onstage and I complained indignantly that everyone else I knew was getting picked up for TV and film opportunities and I would be forgotten. I wanted to be whisked off to *Saturday Night Live* on Lorne Michaels's shoulders. Or else carted off on a stretcher after blacking out in a step 'n' tone class. Neither was happening. Soon after Jay and I moved in together and the trip to Spain, I quit Second City to "do my own thing."

My last performance there was one of the best nights of my life. After our regular show I performed my favorite scenes out of those I'd written over the course of my five years with the theater. My mother and sister flew in and sat in the VIP seats with Jay sipping cocktails. Friends read small tributes and the cast gave me a whipped-cream pie to the face (a long-standing Second City tradition). I played a recorded farewell to the audience as I gazed out at the crowd, too stunned, euphoric, and petrified to cry.

"Doing my own thing" became more Spin classes, more teas and sugarless gum, and the occasional laxative as I sent out writing packets to TV shows and waited months to be formally rejected from every one of them. Jay and I began to fight bitterly, especially when he wanted us to lie on the couch together or when he tried to caress or feed me. I was disgusted with my body—its lumps and bulges and insatiability. I told him to stop trying to drag me down and make me into his fat housewife. I waited until he was asleep to fill my bowl with broth topped with fiber cereal and nonfat cheese. I woke up each day hungrier and angrier, spitting at him all my fears of never being small enough, or funny enough, or just enough. Whenever Jay told me I was more than enough I only distrusted him more.

Cutting began in L.A. a few months after I left Second City. My agent got me a spot in a two-night revue there, and I announced to Jay that I would most likely move there whether or not I landed a job. Jay joined me for five wretched weeks in California, where I met a handful of directors to see if they wanted the next waif-thin superstar. They didn't. I worked out four hours a day and chewed sugarless gum until my teeth were stained a slick wintergreen. Jay spent his days begging me to stop, and plotting ways to curtail our trip and get me back to Chicago for help. We met only over the glow of the TV or when I forced him out to bars, and when we made love I tried to calculate how many calories I was burning.

One night we went to a dinner party in Hollywood. Lilly, the hostess, was an old family friend of Jay's, and moments after meeting her I was sure they would have an affair. I was furious that Lilly was so much skinnier than me and drinking wine and eating creamy cheeses and laughing, so instead of trying to crush her in my palm I went into her bathroom and made three neat slices with a nail clipper on my left biceps. I had read about cutting in a book about depressed teens and had always been curious. I couldn't fit through her bathroom window and I was desperate to escape this night, this hunger, this boiling fury inside me.

My first incisions were timid and only pinched at the skin. But once I broke through that outer layer with a definitive snip, I felt its delicious sting ripping through my whole body. I gazed lovingly at the delicate lines of blood as they bloomed to the surface, my whole arm drawing together sharply like an intense sunburn. I stroked my cuts admiringly and felt the rest of my body disappear under their violent beauty. Then I pulled down my shirtsleeve, walked back out into the living room with a big sloppy smile, and danced like Snoopy for the rest of the night. Celebrating my newfound freedom.

After Lilly's, my confidence returned. It grew in bright red streaks up my arms and torso. I loved it. Cutting was fuller and brighter and louder and cooler than I ever dreamed and it soothed me like nothing else could. Each day I snipped off new lines of skin on my upper arms and belly. These were the places I hated most on my body. One day I hoped to carve my hatred through all the loose skin until I hit bone. Maybe I could be my own magician and slice myself in two. The first clip was always magnificently startling. A small blood ruby emerging, sparkling. I clipped another piece next to it, connecting them in a thin line. Then another just above the first. And a third. Three seemed a brave enough number. A smile leaked from my lips as I watched the blood fill in. My skin felt raw and radiant, all the nerve endings charging toward this one spot, aligning into these perfect stripes. It was the most present I'd felt in so long. I didn't feel hunger here. I didn't feel lost or stuck or angry or fearful or fat or even alone. Cutting was my most powerful secret yet. The only one I shared it with was G-d.

Until Jay caught my elbow in his hand one night as we were getting into bed. Usually I wore at least two layers of clothing to bed—long johns, sweats, T-shirts—while he lay coolly, bare belly exposed. But we were still in L.A. and I had pulled on a tank top absentmindedly. The palm trees and sunglasses had thrown me off my game.

"What is that?" Jay's face was hard. His tone severe.

"What's what?"

"That."

He pulled my arm closer.

"Oh, that. I scratched myself. On a branch," I added, wriggling my arm free. His eyes were red and fixed, his nostrils flaring.

"Okay, okay. I did it," I mumbled.

"What?! Why?!" His fear and shock leapt at me. His reaction was the precise reason why I'd hidden my body from him as I undressed. Also the precise reason I'd forgotten and put on a tank top that night. It didn't take a genius, or more than one day of rehab, to see how starving and cutting were my cries for attention, that I wanted Jay to see my cuts and marvel at my prowess.

"Don't do that again. Promise? Promise!!" I promised him, knowing full well that I wouldn't keep it. Sometimes I came out of the shower bloodied and showed him right away so I could see his face turn every shade of helpless. He made me vow again and I immediately lapsed. The thrill was too great. The pain too dazzling and vivid to resist. I inscribed my frustration into my skin each time I stepped into the shower, kissing my new cuts as I toweled off. I adored these markings. Telling my story and my hurt definitively, in bold red hieroglyphics. Engraving permanently my path toward destruction.

None of this, of course, made sense to Jay when he saw the bright notches in my arm, and then I got more *what*'s and *why*'s. His lips and tears stung my open wounds while I winced. When we got back from L.A. he hid all the nail clippers and scissors in our apartment.

Pounding my head with my fists began soon after our return to Chicago. It wasn't as effective an outlet and it left no scars, but a girl with no nail clippers had to do what a girl with no nail clippers had to do. And a good pound did provide some relief. Powerful blows to the back of my skull, counting them out in groups of five, ten, twenty-five, fifty. If I could get in two hundred and fifty in one sitting, then I usually achieved a respectable buzz and my knuckles and scalp were sore to the touch. A few times I knocked hard enough to color everything in my vision a ripe chartreuse, or gave myself a riveting headache for the rest of the day. It became taxing to walk a straight line and I often jabbed at my unseen wounds during workouts. Their dull pain delighted me. But pounding soon became endangered too when Jay heard me in the bathroom and started raging, "What's going on in there?! Answer me! What are you doing?!"

I didn't want to laugh at him, even though I was pleased to hear his concern. If I closed my eyes, his roars were almost as loud as three hundred and fifty people clapping for me.

I bowed—bloodied, bruised, and triumphant. Until all that was connecting us was his fear and my scars, and instead of a thirtieth birthday party I got a trip to the hospital.

* * *

I spent my first two days at Highland Park in a fog, staring at the plates of coffee cake and egg salad, scoops of ice cream and peanut butter, listening to talks about finding my inner child, unveiling my confused past. On the third day I had to decide whether I was going to stay.

"Don't do it," said Allie, one of the other patients. I watched her stab a piece of congealed cheese on her pizza and push it around with her plastic fork.

"Please don't play with your food," Mary Ellen instructed. Mary Ellen was our meal monitor for today. Her gray mane of hair clung to her face like lint from a clothes dryer. She had the beginnings of a matching gray moustache.

Allie continued as if Mary Ellen wasn't there. "They tell you that you have to finish, but if you don't, what can they do? They put you on the second floor in the too-crazy-to-deal-with section and then you can eat or not eat or whatever."

"All right. Thank you, Allie, that's enough." Mary Ellen sighed, leaning between the two of us. But Allie wasn't done.

"Plus, you don't have to go to all these stupid groups all the time and they check up on you for like the first twenty-four hours and then the rest of the time you can just sleep. That's what I did."

I trusted Allie. I even revered her. She had the coveted honor of hitting rock bottom, multiple times. She knew what it smelled like inside an ambulance and how stiff they made the restraints while they pumped your stomach. This was her fifth recovery program. She'd already been in AA, NA, and two private detox centers. She said the rules at Highland Park were ridiculous and that everyone in charge just wanted us to be fat like them. I thought she was stunningly beautiful. She had coal-colored eyes and soft, bluish skin. Her dull brown hair hung over her face and her wrists were bandaged from her last bout of self-mutilation. Her teeth were thin and yellowed. She wore big sweatshirts that concealed her rail-thin frame and was perpetually on suicide watch.

The only problem with Allie was that she was half my age. She hadn't taken the PSATs yet, had no idea what Reaganomics were, and she'd never heard of Ollie North. That morning, as we watched a special on Karen Carpenter, she laughed incredulously. *They made CDs that big?!* Her parents were the ones who had put her here.

Her mom signed the papers and her dad promised her a kitten if she behaved. Allie had never filled out a lease, or let go of an acting career, or had a red-haired broad-shouldered boyfriend break a lamp and punch himself to prove that he hurt too. Screaming, *How does that feel? Huh?! You're killing both of us!*

"Listen, you don't have to do what I say." Allie looked at me and swallowed her pizza crust with a shrug. "I'm just telling you what I did. On my third day, I didn't finish dinner and it was nice to just get away." I wanted to ask her whether there were single rooms on the second floor and did the checking up for the first twenty-four hours mean there was no place for prayers? But Mary Ellen broke in again.

"Why don't we talk about something else, huh?" Her flaky lip-sticked smile was centimeters from my face, as if we were best buddies at a slumber party. "So, I hear you're from New York! That must be crazy fun! Did you live in the Manhattan part?"

"No, actually I grew up a little north of the city in upstate New York."

"Oooh wow. And what do they call that?"

"Upstate New York."

"Hmm! So that's different from New York City?"

"Yes."

"What's different about it?"

"It's upstate."

Allie brought an imaginary gun to the side of her head and pulled the trigger. Then she gulped down the rest of her apple juice.

"Can I go have a cigarette?" she barked. "I'm done."

"Me too!" said Emma—eighteen, recovering bulimic, also on suicide watch.

"And me!" Carrie—thirteen, recovering preteen, caught mixing laxatives and wine coolers.

Mary Ellen inspected their cafeteria trays. Lifting up napkins and wrappers to check for hidden pieces of chicken fat. Running a finger along the ridges of a cream cheese container.

"It's all gone," snapped Allie, grabbing her tray.

"Okeydoke, but be back in time for drama therapy or else Dottie will get angry, you know."

The girls raced out of the room. I heard the swish of the elevator doors. The hum of the refrigerator that took up half the room. The clock radio announced only three more songs for Hot 97's lunchtime marathon.

"Done," sighed Lisa—twenty-two, recovering anorexic, suicidal and bipolar. It was only the second word I'd heard her utter all day. The first was *Done* after she finished breakfast. Her skin was the color of driftwood and her eyes looked as vacant as stencils. She'd knitted two scarves and a baby bonnet in the three days I'd been here.

"So am I," said Suzanne—twenty-five, recovering bulimic, victim of rape and incest. Her Cleopatra eyeliner had been slashed on in violent strokes today. She was working on *taking her power back*. "Promise," she added, holding up three chapped fingers for Mary Ellen, the signal that meant she would not use those or any fingers to help her throw up. Lisa and Suzanne wandered silently toward the lounge.

I was the only one left. Just me, Mary Ellen, and a plate of sweating chicken, string beans, and a pile of mashed potatoes. Half a bottle of orange juice and two oatmeal cookies. I was starving, but I was also too ashamed to admit it.

"So, upstate New York, huh?" she tried again.

"Listen, Mary Ellen, I don't feel much like talking right now."

"Okeydoke, just trying to make it easier."

Allie was right. All the counselors here were fat and stupid. I hated Mary Ellen and every one of her frizzy gray tentacles. I hated Dr. Seabalt, who breathed through his giant nose and snacked on yogurt cups while he wrote my prescription for Anafranil. I hated Melissa for her sympathetic nods and Loni for being a vociferous Republican and Dottie for making me reenact a typical meal from my childhood with stuffed animals on stools playing my mother and father. Proving that pounding and cutting and starving had all begun long before Jay or Second City or even Ruthie and Ben. Maybe with my father's fading picture digging into my skin and giving me that first sweet taste of release. Or my anxious shredding under the dinner table. It didn't matter where it had begun. It had led me to here and now and I had seven minutes to figure out where it would lead me next.

I hated Hot 97 lunchtime marathons and the nurses in Daffy Duck scrubs who rode the elevator and turned away from our overloaded cafeteria trays, trying to give us space and time and *unequivo-cal nonjudgmental permission to heal*. I hated this window with its bare branches and steel sky.

Yesterday Loni had spied through that same window and caught me doing jumping jacks in the parking lot. I had to make my own three-fingered promise that I wouldn't exercise on the premises any-more. I hated promises and fingers and the newspaper for saying that it was March. March was supposed to bring spring and green parades and the end of pilot casting season. Plenty of people from the theater who were skinnier than me were being hired for sitcoms and sketch shows while I sat here in this unfunny scene. I hated Jay for his sur-prise birthday intervention and for all his freckled tears. I hated him even more for making me get in the car no later than 7:30 this morn-ing, for driving 80 miles per hour with one hand clamped to my knee. For bringing me here a half hour early and telling me I was so brave and he was so in love with me.

Last song of the hour! We have Maroon Five! Man, these guys really know how to rock it 97-style!

I hated myself most of all, for shoving the chicken, the beans, potatoes and cookies into my mouth. For forgetting about the pat of butter and then scooping that into my mouth too, chasing it with the OJ, wiping my lips, and even smiling for Mary Ellen before that rockin' song was over.

Highland Park was an outpatient program, so I stayed there for all of my meals, Monday through Friday, but on nights and weekends, I went back to my apartment with Jay and listened to "Tiny Dancer" through the floorboards. On Saturdays and Sundays, he cooked me the prescribed menu from the hospital. I wasn't allowed in the kitchen while he cooked because I moved the ingredients around and asked him why he used so much butter, pacing anxiously behind him.

"Please, Ab. Just trust me?" he'd say pleadingly, leading me to the other side of the apartment. *Trust* was the first word they taught us at Highland Park. The first day of the program, Mom called me every few hours. When I didn't answer, she called Jay. She wanted to know what she could do. Should she fly out there? Could she send me a care package? Not food, she promised. She was reading the purple book for family members of anorexics. Did Jay have that book? Could she send that? Could I really get the help I needed in an out-patient program or should I be somewhere full-time? She knew I was too thin. She tried to tell me but I wouldn't listen. Why wouldn't I listen? *Can you get her to listen, Jay?*

Melissa-with-the-too-patient-nod wanted to arrange a conference call with Mom and me so we could answer some of these questions together. During the call, Mom hummed nervously on the other end of the line. I could feel her head shaking, the phone shaking, the hundreds of miles of wires shaking between us. She asked Melissa to please repeat things slowly so she could take notes.

"Abby said she just wants to listen, but can I ask you a question, Joan?" Melissa said.

"Of course!" Mom panted eagerly.

"Well, I've asked Abby a lot about your home life and I wonder if you can think of any interactions or influences that might have contributed to her anorexia?"

I felt bad for Mom. Alone in her blue pin-striped kitchen with her piece of dry-cleaner cardboard for taking notes. Or maybe she was at my father's desk scribbling on the back of a bank statement. I hoped she had a cup of mint tea and maybe a Girl Scout cookie nearby. I had trouble picturing her, especially the expression on her face. She was probably having an equally hard time picturing me. After our trip to Spain we'd taken a break from each other. When we spoke it was to exchange pleasantries and ask about each other's health and to reveal absolutely nothing.

"Well, I always tried to encourage her to eat three meals a day." Mom's voice sounded tinny. "She ate everything as a child. All three kids did, except Jon was allergic to shellfish, but if we were eating fish I cooked him a lamb chop or something. I guess Abby was never much into liver or mayonnaise, right, Chicken? Oops, okay, you're just listening, sorry. I don't know, let me think . . . she started cutting out meat when she got into high school and I worried then. She's always been anemic. So was I as a child. She gets kidney trouble from her father's side. Did you talk about that yet? Okay. Sorry. But I do worry about that. I mean, I've been saying anorexia for a while now—years, really, but she didn't want to talk about it and, you know, I was trying to respect her wishes but then maybe I should've done more? Or, at least something. I'm not sure. Was that what you asked . . . ?"

Her voice petered out. I could tell she had more to say. I heard her pen scratching. Maybe writing a list of better answers or addenda.

"Abby?" asked Melissa.

"Yeah?"

"Do you want to say anything?"

Mostly I wanted to say please take me home and we can say the Shema and you can rub my back and in the morning we'll have runny omelets and toasted challah. But I also wanted to say why did you give birth to me if I had to grow this old and this confused and inherit this sickening paunch and sagging breasts? It's your fault that I look like this and think like this and walk, talk, am like this. I wanted to add I'm sorry, I thought you were G-d's right hand for so long and it took me almost thirty years to hit puberty and to disagree with you. I wanted to subtract the part about my body being her fault; though I couldn't help feeling it was true.

Instead, I said, "Mom I love you and I want to tell you as much as I can, but a lot of the time while I'm here I think I just need to process this for myself."

"I respect that, sweetie," she murmured. I could almost feel her hand rubbing circles along my spine.

Melissa did some annoyingly slow talking about being patient and the journey of recovery for anorexics being built on pillars of patience. I dug my fingernails into my thighs when she wasn't looking. I was still very ambivalent about being there and I was hungrier and angrier every day.

I also felt that labeling me an anorexic was too simplistic and shallow. It was about as accurate as calling someone preppy or a nerd. Anorexia had a doctor-approved definition with common symptoms and side effects and its treatment felt insultingly straightforward and banal. The doctors prescribed us each a medication within the first day. We had weekly weigh-ins, daily activity lists, hourly rap sessions. In each session I told them it wasn't about the food, that I still hadn't hit rock bottom and I'd always been obsessive.

To which Melissa said it's never about the food but I had to have faith and start feeding myself again or I wouldn't be able to get to what lay beneath it.

The second word they loved to dissect at Highland Park was *faith*.

"Faith is a bitch. It's all I've got," ranted Dottie. "I've been in nine different recovery programs. Been sobah for thirty-two yeahs, and every day I get on my knees and tell G-d it's up to Him. I have to work the steps and the most important one is letting my Highah Powa take care of the rest. But it's really fuckin' hahd and sometimes I want to tell Him *Fuck it! Not today!*" I liked Dottie the most, even though I couldn't understand how she could say His name and curse in the same breath like they were buddies sharing a pint or a game of pool in one of her native British pubs. I admired and envied her chumminess with the Ruler of the Universe.

"Faith is trusting that your body will know when it's full. I eat when I'm hungry and stop when I'm not. Everybody's body comes equipped with a *full* button. You'll see, when you start eating healthfully, you'll feel hungry and full too!" chirped Mary Ellen.

"Fatty," snarled Allie under her breath.

"Faith is closing your eyes in the bathroom so you don't have to see yourself in the mirror," whispered Suzanne, with three fingers raised.

"Faith is not listening to those voices," muttered Lisa.

Faith is jumping and the net is there to catch you! said the lamb on our daily calendar.

"Faith is a kitten," said Allie. "What? You want me to have some sort of vision?" she scoffed.

I bit my lips and doodled during these chats. I couldn't discuss faith with these people. My beliefs couldn't be culled and condensed into anything translatable or definable. Describing my faith felt like trying to name the colors in the moon or the taste of spaghetti. It was unique and infinite and impossible to express in one language. I knew this—I believed in G-d and I sang and listed and recited to Him because I wanted Him to be in charge. Because I needed Him to be in charge.

I would talk about cutting and pounding, list-making, litter piles, and even my abortion. But I refused to put *quiet time* or any of my prayers on my list of unresolved issues. I felt heretical even considering my prayers as another ritual or symptom of disease. I thought about those crossed wires that Dr. M. had described years ago. Prayers were more like an unfinished circuit that left a gaping hole. Its edges were barbed and slippery and I had to tiptoe cautiously around it—a misstep could be the end for anyone I loved.

Yet, in spite of my unrelenting piety, on some hidden level, I knew that my prayers were obsessive, because I felt compelled to pray with the same urgency that I felt compelled to bike and run and pick up trash. Each time I prayed I had to promise myself that it was okay if I said something wrong or mispronounced someone's name because I would be praying again in just a few hours and hopefully He knew that I meant "heal" not "hell." Maybe my recitations weren't the safest or most spiritual path, maybe they were based on fear and foreboding, but for almost twenty years they were also the one way I knew how to find space and quiet. G-d was the only One who truly knew me, and I would never betray our sacred bond.

Even when I kept my mouth shut for the entire nine hours of my day at the clinic, I was still exhausted when I left. Especially on the nights when I swore to Lisa that I wouldn't hurt myself. Lisa and I had started making pinky swears my second week into the program. I would refrain from cutting and pounding and she would refrain from swallowing her bottle of codeine. Our pacts made me responsible for her welfare, which I would never jeopardize, but I missed the bruises and scars with a longing that razed me. I missed the quiet release, the palpable surrender to the cold metal on my skin.

Some nights, even with Lisa's skeletal pinky as my motivation, it was too hard to restrain myself. I had begun to drive myself to and from Highland Park, and before I turned on the engine, I planted fifty pounds to the head—a manageable number that left no visible scars. It wasn't just the physical shock I missed; it was the buzzing solace they offered. The more I ate at the clinic, the more destructive angers and jealousies oozed through my veins like poison gas. Urges to bite and hit and steal and scream clawed at me. If I could take this assault and battery on myself then maybe I could save others from harm. I could walk outside after a solid pounding, awash with relief, and march by a whole pile of staples, screws, and paper clips.

I had also started connecting cutting and pounding with G-d. The secrecy of these beatings made them sanctified. He saw me doing these things and I hoped that they could count as part of the punishment I deserved. Just like when I rapped my chest on Yom Kippur, I wanted Him to know that I recognized my sins and was beseeching His infinite mercy. By hurting myself I was hoping to prove my piety and direct all my evil intentions inward. I had never believed in a vengeful G-d. I believed in a vengeful me.

"What did you do that's so bad?" asked Melissa.

"Why are you so mad at yourself?" Mary Ellen sighed.

Dottie made me reenact a conversation with my aborted child. Instead of a stuffed animal, she sat on the stool herself with wide sorrowful eyes and balding head and I ached in my throat, my chest, my eyes, my mind as I begged for her forgiveness. Before I drove home that night, I pounded until the windshield was quivering.

A month into the program, I had a vision. It was a Sunday night and I was at home, lying on the futon in our back room. My head was on Jay's knee and he was stroking my hair, trying to lull me into sleep. We'd just finished lemon chicken and rice pilaf, string beans with butter, and three slices of Swiss cheese. It was delicious and salty and warm and terrifying.

"They're just so mad at me!" I wailed into his shirt.

"Who? Who?" he demanded. I was in therapy nine hours a day. When I got home I could rarely explain where I was in my head or my heart. I usually collapsed in front of the TV and moaned and Jay didn't ask me to replay anything.

"The monsters," I whimpered.

It was the first and last time that I've ever been able to put faces on the tumult inside. They are needy and greedy. Puke-green and gray blobs with dripping fangs, pointy whiskers, and long curly fingernails. They crawl and pounce, drooling, leering.

"Where are they?! I'll kill them! Tell them I'll kick them in the balls and kill them!"

"You can't. No one can." I only wanted to pound or cut them out. "Please let me make just one scratch. Just this once. *Please*," I begged. But Jay wrapped his body around me more closely, his mouth inside my ear, whispering from his gut, "Tell them I'll fuckin' rip their heads off and kill them."

"They don't care what you say." I trembled and writhed as the monsters snickered and undulated. All I could do was lie there as Jay held me down. He had me squeeze his arm as hard as I could, wringing out my insides. I wailed and grunted for what felt like forever, scrabbling against these ghouls.

Dr. M. had once told me that our monsters never die, they just change. The bogeyman who scared me as a toddler became my aunt's exploding brain, which in turn changed into a blowout and a dead man's face tipped through an open sunroof. Those fanged blobs were my newest incarnation. I think all of those monsters were a gift. Cutting and pounding, too. They frightened both me and Jay, but they were finite, tangible demons. They had faces and colors, scar tissue that I can still locate and touch today. They made my suffering real. They were this wide and this tall and this deep and this long.

A new avenue of my faith opened before me that night. Faith was staying in that terror when I wanted to run and tear, spit, snip, and pound in a thousand different directions. Faith was waiting for the monsters to slowly retreat, it was lying under the thick blanket of lemon chicken, Jay's tensed body, and the frozen Chicago spring that still wouldn't thaw, it was watching a rerun of *Law & Order* and weeping because Jerry Orbach was dead and my father was dead and my career was dead and the person I thought I could be onstage and in the mirror was dead and I had to learn how to start over.

After I'd been in the program for a month, my mother visited for a long weekend. We went to the movies and out to dinner and she was very careful not to comment on what I ate or what I looked like. On Monday morning she came with me to the hospital. It was first grade and back-to-school night all over again. While she was meeting with Mary Ellen, I gulped my breakfast and rearranged my stack of journals, so eager for my mommy to hear the hum of our refrigerator and smell our pink vinyl chairs.

"Am I interrupting?" she sang cheerfully as she walked into the room. I made the introductions to my fellow patients and she gave meaningful smiles to each girl. The counselors let me go home after lunch so Mom and I could share our last dinner together.

"I promise I'll get all the food groups in!" she told them sweetly. "And thank you so much for looking after my daughter."

We marched out arm in arm, both rosy-cheeked and buoyant. She said Mary Ellen was a little cloying, and she really should do something about her hair, but besides that she seemed to run a tight ship. Melissa was fine. There wasn't enough one-on-one interaction and the carpeting should be replaced. But all in all, Mom was fairly impressed.

"The girls seem very nice too. Actually, I was prepared for them to look a lot sicker than they did."

"What do you mean? Thinner?" I was immediately defensive. I was just beginning to piece together how much of my disorder was inherited or at least conditioned at home. I was just able to see my late-night gorging as an echo of her distracted gagging, my sliced torso as a reflection of hers. Mom could smell my discomfort.

"Thinner . . . or . . . just sicker. It doesn't matter. It was nice to meet them, that's all."

I didn't want to open this up any further either. I didn't want to reenact any hurts with stuffed animals. I just wanted to have my mommy hold me and tell me everything would be all right. But when we got back to the apartment, Mom was shivering and pacing. She put on her blazer and wrapped the afghan around her legs. Her face was flushed and she said, "Yeah. That's the only thing I don't like about Chicago. A, it's so far away and B, it's so darn chilly."

"How about I make us some tea? Or we could go for a walk?" I offered.

"Sounds good, Chicken. But do you mind terribly if I close my eyes for just a few minutes first?" Her stockinged feet hung over the edge of the couch that she had bought for me and Jay. Before she drifted off to sleep she told me I had such a lovely home and she was so impressed with me for all the hard work that I was doing. I wanted to thank her for visiting, but her fingers were already tapping the first chords of Debussy.

A week later I parked in the back of the hospital's lot by the trees so I could sink into their shade while I pounded my head two hundred fifty times. Admittedly, I was backsliding a little, but after my mom returned to New York I felt a creeping loneliness and self-loathing. Her face was blotchy and sad as she said good-bye and I couldn't help thinking that at age thirty I had amounted to nothing.

Before I started pounding, I turned on my cell phone and saw I had a message. My brother's voice, which was odd, because we'd talked only once since I'd been in the program and he had been respectfully distant. Jon was a reporter in Canada with a wife and two kids, and for now we'd silently agreed to just stick to the facts.

Hello there, it's your brother, Jon. Hope you're doing well. All is fine here. So I just wanted to call with an update. I assume you know what happened initially, but I've just spoken with the doctors and here is what I've gleaned. . . .

I didn't know what had happened initially because after Mom left Chicago I called home once and when the machine picked up I assumed she was out at a chamber music concert. I called Jon back and learned from him that she'd been running high fevers ever since her visit with me. A friend took her to the emergency room and she was now at New York Presbyterian. The doctors were doing some tests *and we can't be sure yet or get upset because the first tests are preliminary tests and yes they point to a type of leukemia called acute myelogenous leukemia but in this second round they are using cytogenic analysis and that's really a more detailed reading of the chromosomes that make up the lymphocytes so if it is in fact leukemia there are four different types and they each require a different type of treatment so there is acute myelogenous and also chronic myelogenous. There are also lymphocytic cell types, and these can be either . . .*

I stayed in the parking lot for the rest of eternity listening to Jon read from his notes. When he was done he asked me how I was feeling and I said, "Can I call you back?" and I was already on the highway home with all the windows open blowing me inside out when I realized I'd forgotten to pound my head. I hoped that G-d wasn't mad at me because I knew I should have, but there was no space to pull over now and I needed to watch carefully to make sure every tree and cloud and blade of grass was actually real. Even the newscasters on NPR sounded fuzzy and unclear. The whole world had gone numb.

I turned off at my exit, but I didn't want to go home. I didn't want to smell the fried onions from the bar below us or touch the lacquered wood of our door. I wasn't ready to say my mother's illness was true.

I circled our block three, four, five more times. Pulled into a drugstore parking lot and found a space between two mounds of hardened April snow. Inside, I wandered through the vitamin aisle—rows of brown bottles promising to give me stronger nails, looser stools, firmer skin. Closed my eyes as I passed the laxatives and slimming teas. Faith was sometimes just turning away. The pharmacist was measuring out small blue tablets through his plastic funnel.

"Are you here to drop off or to pick up?"

"No," I said. "Just looking."

I walked by the shelves of makeup, hair dyes, creams, gels, and pomades. I opened jars and sprayed toilet water and pulled lipstick testers across my palm. I searched through the magazine racks and bins of individually wrapped candy. Growing up, we were allowed to have candy only on Halloween, and we each spread out our booty on the kitchen table so Mom and Dad could look at it. Dad said he'd give us a month's salary for one of my miniature Nestlé's Crunch bars. Mom said, *Rogerrrr,* and then she asked us *How much for the Junior Mints?*

I moved past the bouncy balls and jump ropes. Marshmallow chickens and rabbits and plastic eggs, because somewhere soon or past it was Easter. I stopped in front of the children's art supplies. Construction paper, crayons and markers, glitter glues and glow-in-the-dark paints. I pulled it all into my hands until my arms sagged with the weight of my bounty.

When I got back to the apartment, Jay wasn't home yet. Or maybe he was and I just didn't see him.

I sat down, emptying the crayons out in front of me in a vague semicircle. I didn't have a plan. I'd never been an artist. At my back-to-school-night Mom and Dad came home and asked why I had nothing hanging up in the classroom. I said I'd been too busy. But the truth was there was only one thing I knew how to make. While everyone else was creating flowers and rainbows and googly-eyed puppies, my pictures all looked disappointingly the same.

I picked out a red crayon and colored in the familiar semicircle at the bottom of the page. Then I drew two smaller rectangles in black and five more above that. My hands moved instinctively, mechanically. I added windowpanes and shutters, a ball of green stealing around the sides for bushes, and a pond of lemon lamplight by my father's desk. A crack in the walkway on the second big step.

I held the paper away from me to see what I'd created. The windows were crooked and the paper was dented where I pressed the crayons too hard. But when I closed my eyes, I was certain I'd drawn a Sunday night.

Dad and I are just pulling into the driveway and it is the harshest kind of cold, even with the moo goo gai pan seeping into my corduroys.

until tuesday

· ·

Jay and I pulled out of our parking space in Chicago on July 1. We'd talked about moving back to the East Coast since we met, a year and a half ago. Mom's diagnosis in April made the decision for us. I announced my impending move to the Highland Park crowd one morning in May, just after breakfast.

"You know you're not done, right?" cautioned Mary Ellen. Allie growled at her halfheartedly. She was supposed to graduate weeks earlier, but just before her last day she'd opened her wrists with a razor blade again. I wanted to stay just to see her sass Mary Ellen again. I also knew without being reminded that I wasn't done—I still had to close my eyes when I passed a mirror so I didn't have to see my distorted reflection. I still could eat only with a hospital monitor or Jay next to me, and I had to promise him each time I went to the bathroom that I wouldn't pound or cut (with only limited success). But my mother was battling cancer and I needed to be by her side. Her recovery was not only more urgent than mine, it was also quantifiable, and mine never would be. There was no question in my mind that taking care of her was my calling. I felt that familiar surge of purpose I'd had with Ben, only this time magnified exponentially. I had prayed for Mom's health and happiness every day since my father died. I was essential to her survival, and my duty bolstered me as I waved farewell.

"Keep up the fight!" Loni raised a fist.

"Remember, it's not up to ya!" cheered Dottie.

"I'll do it if you do it," whispered Lisa as we interlocked pinkies.

In June, Jay and I had flown to New York for my sister's wedding and he found us an apartment in Brooklyn while I got Mom settled at home after two weeks of intense chemo. Then we returned to Chicago and packed up our five pieces of furniture, I threw out all of my size zero clothes, and we swayed one last time to "Tiny Dancer" before taking off in the pale green of a predawn sky. We had toast with real butter and coffee cups resting in our truck's console. We also had a new momentum and trust between us—a fearless candor that I had never known before. Not with my mother, not with Ruthie, never with Ben. I could tell Jay when I was spinning too fast and furiously inside—sometimes he saw my disquiet even before I did. He understood that I wanted to be closer to my mom, though I was torn about how to reintegrate myself into her life, how to figure out the next step in my career, how to eat a meal in public. He promised to be by my side for it all.

"We've done the hard stuff," he told me. "Now it's time to have fun." I was daunted by his stability. Sometimes I couldn't see why or how we worked, and other times I couldn't remember life before him. I didn't tell him, but my biggest fear about returning home was that I still couldn't declare myself in love without my mother's sanction.

As we drove east, we belted out the D'Agostino grocery store jingle through the great states of everywhere-else-that's-not-New-York and tried on sunglasses at every rest stop, pulling into my family's driveway just as the Yankees were edging out the Red Sox in thirteen spectacular innings. Jay banged on the truck's roof, shaking the manicured lawns on my street as we yelled, "We're baaaaaack!"

The following day we planned to go to Brooklyn and unload boxes into our new place. Then we'd drive back to be with Mom for fresh tomatoes and corn on the porch.

But my mother woke up on July 2 feeling "a little *feh.*" She sat on the edge of her bed staring at her fingernails distractedly while my sister and I hovered in her doorway.

"What does that mean, Mom? What kind of *feh?*" asked Betsy.

"You know, just *feh.*" Mom shrugged.

With her head bowed I could see her scalp peeking through her thinning hair. She'd debated getting a wig for Betsy's wedding but I'd convinced her that she didn't need one. Instead we spent hours at the salon watching Carmine the stylist stir her gray wisps into a chic updo. In the stark morning light there was no denying that the chemo had taken a toll on her hair and her skin, which hung loosely off her frail shoulders.

"Leave her alone, Betsy," I commanded.

No matter how many hours of therapy I'd just endured, in that moment I remained unwilling to accept my mother's fragility. I turned away from her stooped figure and browsed through the pile of books, magazines, and lists on Mom's night table. I'd missed her chaotic handwriting and the warm floral scent of hand cream that always tinged her bedroom.

"Hey! You're reading Jane Austen for a change!" I joked.

"*Re*reading," Mom corrected me. "Actually, I have about two hundred pages of *Buddenbrooks* to get through before book club on Tuesday. What are you reading these days?"

"Mom, here." My sister wormed around me and stuck a thermometer in her face.

"Your sister does not suffer fools gladly," said Mom. "Abidab, tell me about the drive while I take my temperature. Where'd you stop? Was there traffic?"

"It was awesome!" I was relieved to hear Jay's voice behind me so I could turn away from Mom's watery gaze. He gave a play-by-play of the final two Yankee innings until Betsy cut him off.

"Mom, you're at 101 again. I'm taking you to the hospital." Betsy had returned from her honeymoon with a soft glow and a stern determination to make Mom well. She'd been Mom's caretaker since the diagnosis—shuttling her to and from every appointment, arranging all of Mom's prescriptions in a wicker basket on the windowsill and her hand creams, ointments, and mouthwashes along the bathroom sink. She had all of Mom's medical contacts plugged into her cell phone. Before her wedding there was not a single day that my sister wasn't by my mother's side. Her vigilance was humbling. And threatening.

As I watched her touch Mom's forehead, I was keenly aware that in my mother's darkest hours, my sister had been there and I hadn't. I was too busy drawing my inner child and eating careful rations of peanut butter. If Dottie were here she'd say *Let go and let G-d.* Her mantra had become one of my newest additions to *quiet time* each morning. I also wrote it at the end of every SiRo entry before kissing His name one hundred times. I just had to learn how to live it.

I pushed the brightest smile I could muster out at Mom.

"How about some coffee?" I offered cheerily.

"Sounds great," answered Mom.

But Betsy was insistent.

"This is not a joke, Mom. Abby, we'll see you later."

"Sssssugar!" Mom cursed grumpily, like she'd just discovered a hole in her favorite pair of socks. "I have an appointment with Dr. Rossman on Tuesday before book club. Why can't we wait until then?" She shuffled around the bedroom, filling her purse with cosmetics, crumpled tissues, and her paperback of *Buddenbrooks*.

Betsy didn't answer except to assemble an outfit for Mom to wear. Mom took me aside on the way out to the car. "Are you eating chicken again? Because I thought for tonight I'd just defrost some breasts to go with the corn and tomatoes."

"I'll eat whatever you make, Mom," I said, hugging her. I was so grateful that she was asking me without judgment and that I could say yes. And I was grateful she was worrying about the chicken because that meant she couldn't be that sick and my sister was obviously overreacting.

Jay and I went to Brooklyn with our belongings. When Betsy called me later that afternoon, she whispered into the phone.

"It's bad. You need to meet me at the hospital as soon as you can, and we have to call Jon."

I was scraping at packing tape that had somehow melted onto the floor of the new apartment, trying very hard to make my sister wrong.

"Hold on, Betsy. Don't call Jon."

"They're keeping her here until her doctors come back from vacation. Everyone's out for the Fourth of July weekend."

"Do they know she has an appointment with Dr. Rossman for Tuesday afternoon? It's already Friday. Why can't they just wait?"

"Just—they can't. She needs to see someone now."

"Well, aren't there any other doctors who can look at her?"

"I don't know. No, I guess. I don't know! All I know is . . . Fine! Don't listen to me! I guess I'm just stupid!"

"Put Mom on the phone, please."

I knew I was being cavalier and condescending. It was easier to label my sister crazy than to digest what she was saying.

"Hi, Chicken," Mom said. "Well, at least I'll get some reading finished. They're not letting me out of here."

"I'm sorry, Mom. You want me to come up tonight, or should I wait until the morning?"

"Tomorrow's fine. Don't worry about me. And let Jay lift the heavy stuff, okay?"

Our apartment smelled of fresh asphalt and disinfectant and there was little space between the boxes. We made just enough room for the mattress and climbed up to our roof to toast the greatest skyline on earth. All we could see was another rooftop and a giant exhaust fan from the restaurant below us, but we knew the Empire State Building was just beyond. We'd finally come home.

"I just wish my sister didn't exaggerate all the time," I said to Jay. "She makes it sound like Mom's dying." I told him Betsy had a penchant for being overly dramatic. She drew out stories for their potential shock value and I remembered her holding me captive on her bed when I was little because of an ant I found. She'd convinced me that under our carpets was actually an entire metropolis of creepy crawlers, teeming and squirming, ready to steal into my nostrils as I slept.

"You know she's just worried," Jay soothed, loosening my fingers as I dug my nails into my thighs. This was another anxious habit I couldn't let go of yet, and I often left soft grooves up and down my limbs. But it was better than cutting. "It's going to be okay," he said. "We could drive up to Westchester right now if you want . . . ?"

"Nah, I'll go tomorrow and you stay here. Maybe start on some painting?"

"I'll even mop if you're nice to me."

"Deal."

"You just missed the doctor," my sister said as I walked into my mother's hospital room the next day. She widened her eyes and nodded toward the hall, trying to get me outside to talk in private. I ignored her and turned to Mom.

"I couldn't understand that man. Terrible enunciation," Mom

complained. "Let's just go. I have an appointment with Dr. Rossman on Tuesday. She'll know what's going on."

Betsy announced she was taking me to the nearby mall for an all-you-can-eat sushi buffet so we could catch up.

"Need anything while we're out, Mom?"

"I could go for some ice cream." She smiled and licked her lips like a schoolgirl waiting for her treat. "Oh, and where'd you put my pocketbook? I wanted to trim my nails."

The mall was empty. I piled my plate high, determined to eat composedly even if my sister was watching. Betsy didn't touch her food. She leaned toward me and took a deep breath.

"Something has gone seriously wrong. Mom's blood is flooded with leukocytes. We have to call Jon and Uncle Murray and the girls. This is serious, Ab. This is it."

"Betsy. First of all, please pass the soy sauce. Second of all, you heard her. Just wait for Dr. Rossman to see what's happening on Tuesday."

"You don't understand. Mom might not make it till Tuesday."

"Stop it! Why are you saying things like that?" I snapped.

"The doctor on call came and took me out in the hall. I'm just telling you what he said."

"Well, can I talk to him too, then? Give me his number." I shoveled a gob of sticky rice with wasabi into my mouth and closed my eyes while my throat caught on fire.

When we got back to the hospital, Mom was taking a nap with *Buddenbrooks* splayed open and her reading glasses tucked neatly between her freshly groomed fingers. I put the caramel sundae we'd bought her in the minifridge and Betsy hung up the photo booth pictures we'd taken on the way out of the food court. Four frames of us being silly and then one of us with honest eyes and close-lipped smiles. Otherwise Mom would say it was a waste of money.

That night, Jay came up on the train and sat by me while I called the doctor at home. He came to the phone out of breath.

"Yeth?" This was why my mother had said she couldn't understand him. He had a horrid lisp.

I told him who I was. I told him I needed to know what he'd said to my sister.

"Don't you two communicate?" was his reply.

"Yes, but I wanted to hear it from . . ."

"Lithen, we need to have all three of the children in one room. You need to get your brother down from Canada tho you can all be on the thame page."

I politely thanked him before hanging up dejectedly and allowing my sister to call Jon. After he arrived, Dr. Lispy took us into the Bad News Room in the back of the nurses' station. It was windowless, airless, and had only enough space for a round table with a tissue box in the middle. Lispy nodded approvingly as if he'd taken us to an extravagant restaurant and procured the best table. He told us he'd made a special trip in on a Sunday just to talk to us. He had a gleaming stethoscope clamped to his gristly neck and I wanted to strangle him with it.

"We're looking at two to three dayth. Your mother ith actively dying," he said, drooling. I wanted to know how he was coming up with this ridiculous prognosis. I was furious and indignant and ready to rip off this man's skin. He couldn't keep his tongue in his mouth and he didn't know how to shave smoothly and most of all he could not be right. *My mother is sitting in her room reading* Buddenbrooks, *which is a complicated and erudite tome, you slack-tongued cow!*

My brother cleared his throat as if he was going to say something. Jon had gone to law school and was now exposing first-class felons on the front page of the *London Free Press,* so maybe he would announce that we were suing Lispy for malpractice or misinformation at least. But he only looked back down at his legal pad and went silent again.

"Do you know what her wisheth are? Did she thign a 'Do Not Rethuthitate'?"

Betsy took a tissue from the table and creased it neatly before bringing it to the inside corners of her eyes. I was livid with her for being such a cliché and at Jon for his juvenile handwriting and pit stains. I wanted a second opinion from someone who could handle the English language. I recrossed my arms and legs, silently fuming at the whole room.

"I'll give you three thome time to think about thingth."

Lispy opened the door and left us at the table. The three of us sat there in the cloud of his stale breath, doing nothing. Or I suppose we did do something.

We agreed not to tell my mother she was dying.

"So . . . how are we going to let her know?" I asked.

"Let her know what?" sobbed Betsy.

"What's going on."

"She knows what's going on."

"Did she say that?"

"No."

"Then how do you know?"

"Because I know her."

"Oh, and I just met her on the street!" I barked.

"Okay," Jon said. "Let's not do this right now."

I would love to say that I marched ceremoniously into my mother's room and threw open the blinds—physically, verbally, metaphorically, heroically. That I stood up on a rolling gurney and roared *Enough is enough! We are not fooling her or honoring her or even respecting her with our silence. She is not just our mother, she is a human being who deserves the chance to say good-bye.*

I didn't scream. I didn't make a fuss. Because it's not right to air your dirty linen in public. Especially in a hospital where people are trying to get better or at least pretending to be okay. Or because I'm a heartless coward. I still haven't decided. I sat there, treading water, wind, fire, ether so I could convince myself that there was nothing to say.

Screaming was reserved for the crazy wing two floors down. I knew because Mom was in White Plains Medical Center—the same fine institution where I'd first met Dr. M. almost nineteen years earlier. The same beds my father had insisted on leaving so he could live his last days valiantly at home. I had forgotten this fact until we were walking back to Mom's room and I found myself tracing the monotonous gray swirls in the wallpaper. I had forgotten that my father was ever in a hospital. That he ever had a failing body. He had become so much greater than these dripping IVs and maddening beeping machines that marked the last moments of mortality.

I wanted to stride into Dr. M.'s office right now and flap my arms wildly, hollering *Why must we have all these secrets?!* I wanted to sit in front of her stack of board games and jigsaw puzzles and lose myself in the simplicity of its up, down, get-out-of-jail, back-to-start rules.

I wanted to close Dr. M.'s door and tell her I could very well be my mother's murderer too.

This was not the OCD talking, this was not some cataclysmic fantasy. This was true. Three weeks earlier, while I was home for Betsy's wedding, I was in charge of flushing out the heparin lock on my mother's central venous catheter—a small tube protruding from her chest through which her chemo and antibiotics were administered.

"You remember what they showed you? Cap off, then swab," Mom instructed me.

The gauze peeled off easily. Her skin was cracked from the chemo but still feather soft. This skin that I knew better than my own, its summer bronze and embarrassed blush, its floating freckles and muted rose scent. The tube was what frightened me the most. No bigger than the width of a dime, but it was an open portal into her chest cavity, her throbbing heart and embattled immune system. Through it her whole being seemed so grossly exposed.

"See? You're doing such a great job! So gentle," she cooed. "I really think you'd be great at this if you wanted to go to nursing school."

She waited until I was back in Chicago taping up boxes to admit that the catheter had become infected soon after I left and had to be removed. "Nothing to worry about," she jumped in before I could respond. "It's not your fault. And please, drive carefully."

I never found out how serious the infection was. Whether it led to her final relapse or whether she was already compromised. I had prayed for her well-being every day for almost two decades, and the thought that I could actually obliterate her with one false swab was too chilling even to contemplate. The only human witness to the crime was my mother, and I never had the courage to bring it up again.

I honestly don't know how or if I discussed the infection with G-d. I included Mom on my sick list and prayed daily for her to heal *completely painlessly soon*. I also pounded my head every time I visited the hospital bathroom. Both rituals relieved me for a bit and then left me with the same barren ringing in my ears. I couldn't bring myself to ask Him for a lifesaving miracle. That would give both Him and me too much responsibility. I had emerged from my faith discussions at Highland Park less fearful, but still unsure of who He was. I didn't believe in pleading to a formidable Supreme Being who could snuff out the defenseless but I also couldn't talk to Him as my best buddy, like Dottie did. Most of all, I didn't know what impact my prayers could have on my mother's final days. When I repeated my familiar *completely painlessly soon* (twenty-five times) it was more the rhythm that I needed to hear than the actual words, a refrain that could endure through all trauma and time.

I walked back into Mom's room after talking with Dr. Lispy and she was actively *not* dying.

"Where were you kids? I can't fix the volume on this thing."

Mom was sitting up, both arms outstretched, pointing the remote control at the silent television screen. "I just wanted to put on some blush and watch the news. I feel like I don't know what's going on in the world."

I played with the volume control next to her pillow and then explained that Betsy and Jon had gone to the house to grab some food.

"You should do that too. Did you eat? I bet you didn't. I know I'm not supposed to harp, so I won't. That was nice of your brother to fly down. Unnecessary, though. What'd the doctor on call say?"

"I don't know," I said lamely. "He's got a disgusting lisp!"

"See? Enunciation is extremely important in all lines of work," noted Mom. "What did he have you in there for anyway?"

"Something . . . with papers or something."

A death is supposed to be a discrete event, with a before and after, or so I thought. But I couldn't comprehend if she was dying, why she was dying, if she was aware of her dying, and if the earth would exist after she died. I don't know why I withheld her condition from her when I felt so strongly that I shouldn't. Whether I was trying to make it easier or more dignified for her, or whether it was purely selfish. The choice to stay silent still feels terrifically cruel and unfair.

I told her to find us something on TV while I straightened up. I rearranged the tissue boxes and emptied her butterscotch candies into the pink plastic throw-up bowl next to her bed so if she had visitors she could offer them something to eat. I wiped down the box of rubber gloves and water bottles, restacked the blankets and magazines.

"Aha! You were hiding this from me, weren't you?" I accused playfully as I pulled out the Sunday crossword. Mom made a little mountain of her knees under the thin cotton blanket like she used to do at home and I pulled up a chair.

She had already filled in much of it, including one of the puns that stretched the length of the page. Usually I wanted to dive in and impress her with my vocabulary, the way I'd memorized the vowelly names Oona Chaplin and Emo Philips. But that day, I didn't want to fill in any more squares, even when I knew the answers. If we finished, we'd have to find some other way to occupy ourselves. To not speak of her dying. When her eyes drifted closed I breathed a sigh of relief and tiptoed into the hall to see what time it was. I wanted to run from room to room resetting all the clocks, so we could try this day again.

Sometime later that afternoon. Jon and Betsy were still not back yet. My mother and I were watching the Wimbledon finals. Roger Federer versus Andy Roddick. Federer was lunging masterfully across the clay.

"Oooh! That Swiss guy. So good," Mom murmured. "Come on. What are you still cleaning over there?" I was restless again, refolding extra linens and putting spare syringes into drawers.

"You're being a little . . . you know," she said. She didn't want to say OCD, but we both knew that's what she meant. Tissue boxes, *off.* Water bottles, *off.* Syringes, *off. Everything is off, off, off.* This was what my disease was best suited for—diverting a crisis. My coping mechanisms were so tedious it almost made me laugh.

"Come, sit here," she coaxed, patting the mattress beside her. "Just look at him go! And so graceful too."

I would've rather smothered us both under a single starched pillow or tied the bedsheets around our necks and swung us from the IV pole than sit next to her, holding on to my secret like a live grenade. As the day faded I thought one of us would explode at any moment.

There is something I need you to know. They say you're dying, Mom, but you can't be, right?

Or maybe she would be the first to open up. *Chicken, there is something I need you to know. I'm going but it will be okay. Just make sure to return my library books and empty the dishwasher before you leave the house.*

But neither of us ventured that close. I did say a few ambiguous phrases such as "Hey, if you want to talk . . ."

Or, "Do you need anything?"

But I slipped them in as her eyelids were fluttering again and I could count on her murmuring, "That's okay, Chicken, I'm fine."

What I didn't count on her saying was this:

"You know, the last time Daddy and I made love was while we were watching Wimbledon."

I was stricken deaf and mute. Blind on all sides. It wasn't proper for a lady to speak of such things. It had to be the meds or the fever talking. Not Joan Miriam Lear Sher. Her honesty uprooted me. I didn't know how to respond. For a brief moment I considered pretending to be asleep.

Eventually, I managed to ask timidly, "Who won?"

Mom patted my hand and chuckled.

"To be honest, we weren't really paying attention."

That was the last conversation I had with my mother. Jay and I had arrived in New York on July 2. By July 7, my mother was gone. In between were five days of endless denial.

As per Lispy's orders, on day three Jon reported to Mom's room with a copy of the DNR papers and a fresh legal pad. They spoke with the door closed for approximately eight minutes. Then he came out and nodded, his eyes glazed, his face the color of turned milk. That was all. We did not ask for details and he didn't offer any. Sometimes I think knowing what was said could give me some consolation. Were there angry tears, bitter offense, woeful acquiescence? But when I ask Jon if he recalls what happened he says he can't remember that meeting at all. He only knows before she died she told him he was a good son.

That same afternoon, we called my mom's sisters. Her closest friends. My cousins and Uncle Murray. We wanted her to know she was loved. We did not explain to her or to them why they were there.

"Look who it is!" we cried, as if their arrival was a complete surprise. Aunt Bernie and Uncle Mel, who hadn't traveled to New York in almost ten years, were inexplicably in for the long holiday weekend. My mother's college roommate showed up ostensibly just to gossip about their friends who had moved to Florida.

The first thing Mom said to everyone who walked in was "Oh, you didn't have to come! You know I have an appointment for Tuesday. I tried to tell them. . . ." She made sure everyone had a comfortable seat. She complimented my cousin Rachel on a new haircut and told Aviva that purple was definitely her color. She asked if anyone wanted a butterscotch candy or bottled water.

Betsy called in one of the Sisterhood ladies from the synagogue, just in case Mom wanted to reveal any private instructions for her funeral. The woman had thick pancake makeup and lips stained a rich crimson. She looked like a clown.

"What are you doing?" I growled at my sister. "Did you ask her to bring balloon animals too?"

"What?!" Betsy spat back. "I thought maybe Mom would feel more comfortable telling her!"

"Telling her what?!"

I was defiant in my denial. It was my only means of absorbing the splotches ripening on Mom's arms, the dark cavities that were swallowing her rouged cheeks. I didn't get upset with G-d. I thanked Him for every moment that I got to swab Mom's fevered forehead. I told my mother she looked great and there was no way Dr. Rossman would let her languish here past Tuesday.

It was also five days of fruitless repetition. I had been training for this blowout all these years and now that it was here I sprang into action. I tried all my rituals—one day starving and pounding, the next scrubbing my hands and counting squares in the hall linoleum. Praying for everyone on the hospital staff and the distracted-looking woman who leaned on the piano in the lounge for support. Adding more emphasis to the word *completely* and then to *soon*. I thought of Dr. M.'s theory that recognizing I was caught in a loop was 99 percent of finding my way out. Only this time I clung to that stubborn last 1 percent, meeting my reflection in the mirror and pounding another one hundred times for good measure.

It was five days or seventy years now roiling inside my mother. Rich bruises were snaking up her limbs, brownpurpleyellowblue. Her face twisted and turned, her wandering eyes caught between this room and some place too far away to see clearly. In her sleep she grasped at her cheekbones as if she were reaching for her eyeglasses or applying more blush. She would wake herself up with a start and remind us again about Dr. Rossman's imminent return. But as the days passed she sounded as if she had marbles in her mouth. Her tongue lolled, and her teeth were uncooperative. Sometimes her lips opened and her breath was stolen by a slow moan that rolled up through her chest.

The next thing she said to us was a direct order. She sat up authoritatively, with her eyes wide open.

"Come on. Let's go! Into the car!" She gripped the bedrail and tried to pull her body straighter, taller.

"Into the car! Move it!" *Damn it.* Nobody was listening to her. She fell back onto her pillow, her soft curls stuck to the back of her sodden neck, her teeth thrusting out through dry, lopsided lips. My brother and sister and I nodded back numbly as she looked wildly around the room. *Why aren't you taking me seriously?* Her commands used to work. She'd led car pools to Hebrew school, soccer practice, sleepover parties, and skating lessons. Surely we knew she meant business when she clapped her hands and said, "C'mon. Move it!"

She pulled so hard on the rail that she started to pitch over the side, and we ran to nudge her gently back down. Her skin felt like hot, wet laundry.

"Please?" She was pleading now. It wasn't fair. It was inhuman. A grown woman begging for something so simple—just a ride home—just a break from the whir of the fluorescent lights, the tubes draped from bags, cinched to her wrists, holding her hostage in her bed. She just wanted to go home and see the faded flowers in her sheets, to smell her towels, to find a patch of sunlight through her shuttered windows before it was all gone.

By the fourth day, I couldn't take it anymore. I told Jay to watch her while I ran out to the hall to find Jackie, my favorite nurse.

"We have to take my mother home. How do we do it? Do we rent a bed? I don't know how to do it! Tell her to stop asking, please!"

"Sometimes it means they want to go home but sometimes they're just saying that because they want it over. They want it—done," Jackie explained tenderly. My mother was already part of a *they.* She was poised on the threshold.

When I got back to her room, Jay was cowering next to her, his eyes wide.

"Get me out of here," she whispered conspiratorially like they were two superheroes planning their great escape. It was as close to loving as she ever was with him.

"I can't, Joan. Abby won't let me," he replied sorrowfully.

She looked up and saw me. Then she broke into an odd grin.

"Don't listen to her." She sniffed in my direction. "She's boring."

The last moment of my mother's life was exquisite. It was dignified. Poetically succinct. A release.

I was next to her in a chair. Her hand was warm underneath mine. Jay stood behind me, holding me up. There were other bodies in the room—my brother, my sister, Uncle Mel. My mother's best friend, Lynn, was stroking Mom's hair, which was freshly combed. Her face was serene, tipped upward, with small puffs of blush coloring her cheeks.

She exhaled. And then without taking in any more air, exhaled again.

It was Wednesday, and July. The middle of a day. When we walked outside it was so ridiculously bright and sweltering that it stung my teeth. Uncle Mel said, "You want to come with us?"

Jay said, "I got her."

He led me into the garage and we walked up the ramp until we found our rusting Honda, named Dwayne. The man at the gate told Jay he had to pay eighteen dollars before we could leave. Jay only had a fifty-dollar bill in his wallet, which somehow made me giggle.

At home it smelled of Aunt Bernie's turkey meatballs, and I told Jay I was going to take a shower. The water moved too fast for me to count the drops. Instead of *AbYn* I wanted to write *Help!* in the top left windowpane. Maybe kiss it a few times. Only it was too humid out and the glass couldn't gather enough of a mist.

While I was drying off, Aunt Bernie called up the stairs, "Terry Jaffey is on the phone asking about coffee urns and Uncle Mel is going to get some pizza! Does that sound good?"

I nodded even though she couldn't see me, and I wondered how I would eat pizza in front of my family. I told Jay to distract my family for a half hour, then opened my closet door and sat with my back against it.

I'd sat here for *quiet time* every day that my mom had been in the hospital. Even when I slept in a chair or rollaway cot, I made sure that I got home for at least a half hour the next day to usher my words up to heaven. The thought occurred to me more than once that she could die while I was tucked behind this door, but that was the chance I had to take. I didn't know that my prayers could heal her. I just knew they were my only way in and out of this day and every other day since I first begged those ambulances to get there in time. My prayers were the only way to absolve me of my mother's death.

I said the Shema. Twice in Hebrew and three times in English.

Then I started listing the top twenty-five things I was grateful for. *That Jay remembered how to drive and that Jackie the nurse let me tell her the names of everyone in our photographs and that Lynn was so good at wetting Mom's lips.*

I prayed for people who were sick. *Miranda, who has MS, and Jay's cousin Alex and Alison's boyfriend, who has a weak heart. May they heal completely painlessly soon.* I prayed for forgiveness. *Fighting with my sister. Snapping at the lady in the lounge. Hating the Sisterhood woman's makeup.*

Then I recited the Kaddish.

Then I paused.

I didn't know how to tell G-d that Mom had died.

Which, I knew, was laughable. Of course He knew that Mom was gone. Maybe He was having her sign on the dotted line and assigning her a locker right now. Or bathing her in lavender and chamomile salts until her skin resurfaced young and new. Leading her across the dance floor to find my father, who had been keeping her glass of white wine cool.

As I sat there I could hear every generation of cicadas hurling themselves at the window screens. I knew there were other repetitions to complete but my brain was vibrating, my lips were unsure.

How could I pray now?

I wanted to ask His forgiveness and Mom's forgiveness for the catheter infection and all the lying I did and most of all for this feeling of relief that it was over. I wanted to tell both of them how empty and bewildered I felt. That I didn't know what I believed anymore. I was out of ideas. Mom didn't do anything bad that would make her deserve to die. He didn't strike her down and in my heart of hearts I knew I didn't kill her either, at least not intentionally. But I didn't know what her death was supposed to mean or how to solve the mystery of her disappearance. I didn't even know what to fear would happen next. I didn't know how I'd stumbled all the way back to this same place I'd been nineteen years ago, tearless and remote as I let go of the person I loved most. Searching for a pattern in the walls that could lead me to the answers.

I heard Aunt Bernie calling for lunch. I still hadn't finished praying. If I went back to the beginning it would be another half hour before I got to the table. I wondered how Jay would lie for me. I could tack on another Kaddish and be done. What else did I have to lose? Who else could die?

It was easier just to start again.

I said the Shema. Twice in Hebrew and three times in English.

Then I started listing the top twenty-five things I was grateful for. *That Jay remembered how to drive . . .*

It is the only way I know to find peace.

And so it goes. *Amen.*

start spreading the news

· ·

Abigail Sher 3/23/84

My favorite person

If I could rate all the people in the world I love, my mommy would be "top choice." She is a tall, slim, beautiful lady with a big smile that she flashes at you all the time. Her hair is black and wavy. Her eyes are sparkling blue, but she wears contact lenses or glasses over them, because she is very nearsighted.

My mommy is very open, and she let's [sic] me be open with her. She listens to me, and tries her hardest to help. She makes all my awful times just memories, and makes my good times stay. My mom is one of the most loving, caring, and understanding people I've ever met.

My father put a down payment on this house on a blustery day in March 1969. He said the winds blew so hard that as he walked through the empty rooms he could feel the local train tracks chatter in his molars.

My mother lived in this house for thirty-five years, keeping its deed and closing papers, the pamphlet welcoming us to our *New! Panasonic Colored Television!,* the prescription medications dating back to 1972 with tablets still rattling on the bottom to arm us against every cold, earache, and flu.

My brother and sister and I had been in this house for the past week. Cleaning, fighting, making piles, and then cleaning or fighting again. The real estate agents were going to show it the next day. Everything had a lime-colored Post-it note attached to it with our initials to indicate who wanted what. When more than one Post-it was on an item that meant we still had to discuss it or flip a coin.

Hat rack—J.

Rug—B.

Grandpa's clock—A. B. J.

There was too much for us ever to be able to sort through. Rows of Charles Dickens novels that said *Lady Lucy Edmonton, 1874* on the first page and smelled like wet dust. In the freezer was a Cool Whip container filled with chicken fat, labeled *Schmaltz, 1989.* In the matchbook collection was a human tooth. Betsy counted seventeen used toothbrushes. I tallied up Mom's writing—three poems, two travel pieces, three children's books, a half-finished novel, and thirty-six short stories, but I knew there were more. My brother held up the surgical hat and mask my father wore in the hospital the day I was born.

There were heavy-duty garbage bags lining the hall, full of letters, pictures, cracked lampshades, outdated warranties, birthday balloons, and humidifier tablets. There were piles of refuse in the filing cabinet, the desk, the game drawer, the bathroom sink, another closet, behind each lamp and in front of every step. Because this was not a house anymore. This was a scrap heap. A landfill of too much for too long. My mother had stowed every toothpick and lint ball from our family's past and we were collapsing under the weight of her hoarding. She kept file boxes filled with condolence cards. She'd lost the love of her life; her sister and sister-in-law, both of whom she adored; her parents and another husband, just months after she began to trust again. She didn't want pity. She refused to be characterized by grief. That's why she carried her own tissues.

Everywhere there were tissues.

In her pockets, her sleeves, her dresser drawers, her pillowcases, her bags. Her coats, sweaters, suitcases, blouses. Flattened between couch cushions, cookie tins, and book pages. She started her day reaching for the tuft under her pillow, then folding it into a fresh one and putting them both into the wrist of her work blouse. There was another stash in each zippered compartment of her purse. A third set in her blazer. With sporty outfits she stuffed them in fanny packs. Rain or shine, arming herself for whatever lay ahead.

There was too much to count. Too much to hide and list, tag and decipher, clean and sort and piece together from all its decomposing parts. From my father's dented saw and barnacled screws in the basement to the headless Raggedy Ann in the attic. It wasn't fair that I was living in a three-story crazy wing and I wasn't allowed to cut or punch myself. Even though it was August, Jon had cranked up the thermostat so we could dry out the freshly shampooed carpets. He also bought orange-flavored air freshener tubs and put them at the bottoms of all our closets so they wouldn't smell like mothballs. Instead it smelled like a giant Creamsicle had detonated.

Jon was supposed to be leading this excavation but the last time I checked he was snoring on the couch with his mouth drooping open like a dead fish's. Betsy was in her room, dismantling bookshelves. I was picking apart the alcove behind the staircase that Mom called her office. The drawers of her desk were splintered and disintegrating. I had a bottle of wine next to me and was trying to reattach a drawer knob but if I found a match to strike first I was ready to light a pyre and carry us all away in its ash. I was so wounded and furious at her for leaving so much unfinished. I felt cheated and gypped and irreversibly interrupted. I was not done with my disease. She had left me in the middle of learning how to eat and learning how to talk and learning how to feel love and anger and not run away. She had abandoned me with incomplete odes, unmailed checks, and a swimming pool permit from my first summer when I was a toothless eight months old.

How could she save all of this junk and not save me?

She had always been here. She had known me and nursed me through each chapter of my illness and listened to all my blue couch confessionals. And I had so much left to say to her, so much to apologize for. What did she want me to do now, go back to where it all began, shredding napkins under the dinner table? I didn't know what He wanted me to do either. I didn't think starving or cutting or jumping or even praying would work to ease my pain. There was nobody keeping track of me. Jay had gotten work at a construction company and Mom was forever gone and I was repeating my rehearsed phrases to G-d in the morning, unable to translate my jumbled thoughts beneath them. I had never felt so alone. How was I supposed to finish this recovery, this life, without her here?

I upended another drawer of file folders and started throwing fistfuls of paper straight into the garbage. But one time when I picked up a pile, a piece of manila construction paper fell out.

I pulled it in to my chest and sniffed its pulpy edges. I was so in love with my father and I didn't want to rip the page but I couldn't help clasping it, begging him to lift me onto his lap again. I remembered the day he packed my lunch bag with two sliced pickles because I insisted that was the only food I liked. By midmorning my whole classroom reeked of brine and the teacher asked if anyone had brought something that might be spoiling in their bags. I raised my lunch slowly into the air, and each soft drip of the soggy bag elicited an *Ewwwww* from the class. I couldn't wait to get home and tell my father the story at the dinner table. We were a salty dilly team.

After that, I pawed through boxes hungrily, almost convinced that I might find him. In a way, searching for my dad felt like a respite. I was familiar with the dull ache of his goneness; the pressure under my ribs and on the back of my tongue. When I saw remnants of his life, I could smell his mouthful of chalky Tums; I could almost lean against his potbelly and smile. I dove nose first into the pickle box, eager for his *ya dada dida doobi da!*

I found his first, last, and only painting, *Watermelon on the Rocks*. It was a seascape, the waves so close that when I peered in, I could feel the tide leaving its silhouette in the wet sand. In the distance, a sailboat glided by listing slightly, its sail cupping a new breeze. In the foreground was a boulder, and perched on top of it a crescent of fresh, pink watermelon. It was not enough, though. I felt him slipping further away as each closet emptied. I groped at his shirts, kissing their musty sleeves. He had grown so large in my memory and I was so desperate for him to pull me out of this wreckage.

I called Jay just as he was getting back home to our place in Brooklyn.

"You want me to come get you?" he asked.

"I can't," I moaned. "There's too much left."

"Promise me you'll eat?" he said gently.

My brother found me in the kitchen, pouring a bowl of cereal. Staring at the picture on the wall. A giant tomato that my mom's friend Barbara had silkscreened.

"You want that?" he asked, pouring himself a bowl of cereal too.

"You can have it." I didn't want to eat in front of him, but I didn't have the energy to come up with an excuse.

"You used to talk to that thing. Remember?" he asked, his mouth dripping milk.

"No I didn't."

"Yeah, you had an imaginary friend."

"I did? Oh, yeah. I did."

"Do you remember his name?"

He waited, chewing noisily and smacking his lips. I had no idea.

"His name was Pretend Daddy."

I don't remember when or why I created Pretend Daddy. Perhaps I adored my father so much that I wanted to take him with me wherever I went, making up jokes and songs with him in the sandbox. Or maybe Pretend Daddy was my surrogate because my real daddy didn't have enough time for me. He worked crazy hours at the law firm and he fell asleep in the chair after dinner and he whistled and paced, which should have meant everything was okay but it wasn't, and then he threw up in the snow and then he was no more.

I could fill in any story because there were no answers, only questions. I hated this. I hated her. I hated him. I hated this night and this house falling on me, the streetlights pouring through the trees in an eerie lace pattern on the scuffmarked floor.

"I don't want any of it," I told my brother desolately.

Jon nodded glumly, opened a newspaper from two weeks ago, and hunched over the sports highlights.

"Abby! Come here!"

Betsy was in my parents' bedroom. Or my mother's bedroom. Or what was now only a room with light blue carpet, a bed, and two matching night tables. Though there were cabinets spilling open and piles everywhere, the room felt empty, shrouded in a veil of loamy stillness.

Betsy was bent over a yellow piece of paper titled *What can I do to help Abby?* It was a list, barely legible:

> Should I go to her?
> What therapy is she using?
> Shouldn't she be on medication?
> Is she vomiting or purging?
> How to control cutting?
> Yellowing teeth, fatigue, fright
> Medical implications—polycystic kidneys
> How can I get her to go back?
> Jay, me

"Where was this?" I demanded.

"Over there." Betsy pointed to the dresser, which was scattered with crossword puzzles, more lists, tissues. Then she came toward me, tentatively. "She loved you so much, Abby. And she just wanted to help in any way."

I gripped the list firmly. My mother's handwriting looked jarring and loud to me, her cursive *J* gaping open at the bottom like it was eating up the paper. It was not written by the hand of someone about to die. I wanted to spit on the paper and mash it together. Unfold it again and see if it would spell out some secret code, some explanation.

My sister asked if she could hold me, and for the first time I can remember, I let her. Jon, Betsy, and I had never been very close. Biologically, we each had different parents. We grew up together, but each night we closed our bedroom doors (mine partway) to process our days separately. Our memories were tinged by different emotions. Even our mourning had been conducted in private. In many ways, my mother helped us stay apart. She always gave us updates on one another—I never called my siblings directly unless there was an emergency or job promotion.

My sister's arms were soft and warm. She was still as beautiful as that porcelain doll in her baby pictures. But I pulled away from her hug. I didn't know how to share my grief with her.

We pored through the rest of the dresser in silence. The light blue pouch filled with our baby teeth. My father's watches. My mother's charm bracelet. I found a list that I had written for her. It was scrawled on the back of an envelope and I could tell by the penmanship (and the fact that I included six) that I was an adult, but I had no idea when I wrote it.

10 things I'd like to do like my mom.....
1. hum a tune every day
2. put fake lipstick on my daughters
3. always stay hopeful
4. calm a child with a hand on the small of the back
5. smell like roses
6. make my kids believe in themselves
7. observe yahrzeits
8. listen with full attention
9. sing New York, New York
10. love unconditionally

"Look." I turned to show Betsy, but she was already lost beneath the first layer of suit skirts in my mother's closet. I put the list in my jeans pocket and moved toward the bathroom. Started trying on each of my mother's thirty-two tubes of nectarine and coral lipsticks, trying to perfect her pucker—halfway between *come hither* and *yes, Mr. Speaker, I'd like to raise an objection.*

"What the hell . . . ? Abby, you have to see this!"

In the back of my mother's closet there was a column of narrow shelves, sagging with deflated pocketbooks, tasseled belts, crushed tennis visors. Betsy emerged with a cracked plastic storage box. The sides were held together with two rubber bands that snapped in a fine pink dust as she tried to pull them off.

In it, a single cassette tape—black with a white label: *Roslyn Grossman Entertainment: Let's Sing and Swing!*

"You know what this is?" my sister asked, and then, without waiting for an answer, she lunged toward the portable radio we'd plugged into the bathroom outlet. And then I did know. It was a karaoke tape Mom recorded at a party in the late eighties. She swore to us multiple times that this tape had been destroyed because it was too embarrassing.

Betsy wiped the karaoke tape with her shirtsleeve, placed it in the portable radio, and shut the plastic door. Pressed Play.

The Casio accompaniment sounded absurdly slow. Mom came in like gangbusters. Her voice was hoarse but strident. Slightly clumsy. Delighted with herself. And though it had been just weeks since she was a person who spoke and sang and breathed, hearing her through these tiny speakers jolted me with a spectacular chill, filled me with a bottomless longing.

Start spreading the neeeews. I'm leaving todaaaay . . .

Betsy and I clung to each other; clung to this voice floating from another dimension. I closed my eyes hoping to see my mother's face, but as she charged through the first verse her image grew dimmer, just as my father's did years before. The more I grasped at the fog of memory for her features, the farther she receded. Her rouged cheeks, her pursed lips, almost gone. Her notes dipped terrifically off-key, the words collided uncertainly at times—she was eager to get to the parts that she knew best, punching them out victoriously.

Make it there! I'll make it an-y-where!

Until she was nothing more than eyes, a broken nose, and bits of sky.

What she used to be scattered in a thousand directions. Her childhood summers on the Connecticut shore; her homemade prom dress; her grocery lists, button collections, recycled tissues, taking flight. Her years editing and writing crumbling into forgettable history. Her Latin prizes slipped through the floorboards and tripped down the basement steps to be carted out with the dried paint cans. Her stolen kisses with a German boy who rode a motorcycle in college dissolved in the evening's humid torpor. And rising above us, wafting, billowing majestically, was my mother's breath, her perfumed shadow, her soul.

I wanted to seal off all of the windows and doors. Stuff each crack and crevice with her pressed linens and knots of hosiery. But there was no way I could stop it all from escaping. And I couldn't hold on to everything like she had, trying to piece together the past. In some ways this was the absolution, or at least a resolution, that she was gone and it was not a question of how or why she died, as with my father's death. It was a question of figuring out how to move on from here.

Wherever here was.

My sister and I were still holding each other when Mom reached for the final *New York, New Yooooork!*

Her voice didn't quite make it, landing flat so the song ended on a doleful minor note. I wanted her to hum through the end, but the tape stopped abruptly.

Betsy clapped gleefully. She began to rewind it so we could hear it again.

"We shouldn't," I said. "She didn't want us to." Still trying to be the good girl. Still trying to please her.

"Oh, come on, Ab."

My mother is somewhere up above, wearing her gray silk scarf with the small red rosebuds. With matching lipstick, of course.

Choose wisely, Joanie. I can only give you one go at this, says G-d.

Got it. She smiles gracefully.

The lamp on the dresser. The one with the blue-and-white china base and the square shade. It has worked reliably for twenty years. It takes a sixty-watt bulb that is changed once a year, and it is always plugged into the outlet by the radiator. There are no other appliances on in the room.

As Betsy's finger lifts from the Play button and the Casio starts up again, the lamp flickers. Slowly at first, then more quickly. The whole room fluttering.

Betsy and I are shrieking with joy and terror.

"But Mom! We have to play it again! You sound great!"

And then, with a dramatic puff, Mom extinguishes the light.

LUCKIEST SONG*

I don't get many things right the first time
In fact, I am told that a lot
Now I know all the wrong turns, the stumbles and falls
Brought me here

And where was I before the day
That I first saw your lovely face?
Now I see it every day
And I know

That I am
I am
I am
The luckiest

*Must be sung at least once a day.
**If unable to sing, sit very still and just listen.

interstate 684

· ·

It was five in the morning, the day hardly yet a dim etching. I woke up twisted and sweaty from the same dreams I'd been having since my mother died six months ago.

In the first I ran into my father at our local fruit market. He has been alive for the past nineteen years, in hiding from us. He's sorry he hasn't gotten in touch sooner, he stammers with a stilted smile; he's just been so *busy*. My dreams of Mom were equally unsettling. We are cleaning up after her funeral when she comes to the door. *Who left the screen door open?* she sings, breezing in. We scramble to hide our half-eaten casseroles and paper cups. *Why are you using a good tablecloth?* It doesn't matter what we do or say. We can't hide Terry's coffee urn. The telltale bowl on the front stoop for rinsing the death off our hands. We can't hide the fact that we've washed Mom away. *But I'm here,* she bleats as we wrap up the coffee cakes, ignoring her existence.

The alarm went off at 5:20 and Jay woke up quickly. The morning was his favorite part of the day.

"You up? You're up! Look at my girl! She's up!"

The first thing he liked to do was ask lots of questions and fart like a trumpet. It was his time to play before he put on four layers of thermal underwear and filled his travel mug with double-strength coffee. In the six months since my mother died, Jay had started his own contracting business, and he'd been driving two hours each way to build a house in Kingston, New York. He was hoping his next job would be in Brooklyn. But one day; one day he would build us a house of our very own. *Won't that be great? It can have an island in the kitchen and space for you to do prayers in the morning and we can make an entire wall out of crushed tile. What do you think, girl? What do you think?*

It was too late to pretend I was asleep. It was also too late to say that I didn't want a house or an island and I would never pick out crushed tile. It was too late to tell Jay to go away.

Jay had propped me up as they lowered my mother's body into the ground. He had carried me back to Brooklyn after the real estate agent and her team took the keys to my childhood home and told me sweetly *You're done here.* He had painted our bathroom a fresh coat of lavender and stood outside the door to make sure I didn't try to hurt myself again. As he drove to and from job sites, he called to sing love songs onto my voice mail. At night he came home dusty and bruised, with concrete caked in his hair. His shoulders had grown broader. But he never tried to lift off my grief. He fed me omelets and pasta and then he draped his whole body around me, his shirt off, his freckled stomach rising and falling smoothly, evenly.

Jay's needs continued to be honest and uncomplicated, just like him. Sometimes he just lay on the couch and said, "You know you're the greatest girl in the world? You're perfect for me." I nodded and buried myself in a pile of old crossword puzzles, too scared to look at him. I felt as if I would shatter from fright and mistrust. My parents had never uttered this kind of devotion. I was confused and irritated by Jay. I couldn't understand why he refused to stick to their simple, eloquent script: "You're okay. You know that?" with two quick squeezes to the knee and a silent assent.

I would never admit it, but I also blamed Jay. It was Jay's fault that my mother was gone. Only months after our first kiss, her blood became overrun with infection. The coincidence was too great. I couldn't stop seeing that night in Spain when she peered up at me in pain from my desertion. It was also Jay's fault that I wasn't performing anymore and that all the stories I tried to write were incomplete and that I was wretchedly adrift and still didn't trust myself with nail clippers. I hated him for not begging me to pursue theater again and for not being a frustrated artist like my father or sick like Ben or at least incomplete in some way.

Some nights we went out with my old friends from grade school and I invented a seventh stage of mourning: gulping too many glasses of pinot grigio and announcing to everyone that I was an orphan with nothing left and that Jay wouldn't have been able to start his company if it wasn't for my parents' estate so why don't I pick up the tab? The weekends were worse. Endless stretches of time together in which Jay wanted to make pancakes and take naps. We lived around the corner from a park where he loved to sit on a bench and gaze at the cloudless sky.

"C'mon, girly. Just for one minute," he urged.

But I couldn't. I needed to move. Pounce. Lunge. Kick the world and strangle its false serenity. Anger was too concrete a word for my impulse. Terror. Heartache. Incensed, incessant mourning. I marked each day by its distance from my mother's last breath. In the six months that Jay had used his hands to build, I had only wanted to rip and shred everything and everyone in my path. I went through three different mindless part-time jobs and four different therapists, regurgitating for each one of them my history of litter piles, death, and dry cereal. I took my Anafranil and followed bits of the food and exercise guidelines from Highland Park, but the effort seemed futile. I'd tossed the inner-child drawings and the lists of harmless evening activities and all the hope that went with them. I was only grow-ing bitter, hardened, and infuriated as I skipped meals and collected trash. I would never be able to look at a slice of pizza or a shopping cart without my whole body seizing. I missed the security of the hos-pital, but I didn't have the stamina or concentration to starve myself again.

My prayers felt stagnant too. Meaningless repetitions that could no longer protect me or anyone I loved from harm. I'd let go of my Cement Mixer song and my ambulance chants. I was too hopeless and enraged. I wanted to be suicidal but I wasn't focused enough to decide whether I would use pills or a blade. I did find some solace in yoga. My first therapist, Dr. S., said I could go a few times a week as long as it wasn't too strenuous and I didn't get obsessed with it. I laughed at her naïveté. Of course it would become obsessive and of course I only went to class to feel lightheaded rather than enlightened.

I also walked. Through side streets, parks, sewage that colored my legs a sludgy moss, and construction sites that burned noxious fumes up my nose. I charged over bridges, under tunnels, along highway shoulders and bike paths, tightroping the yellow lines. I muttered and cried, grating my teeth and growling at amblers who took up too much space in front of me. I had no destination except the steepest hill. No goal except to move fast enough that I could lose my breath or the tornado chasing me. My rule was that I couldn't stop at any traffic lights. If I was absolutely stuck at a crosswalk, I raised and lowered my heels fifty, seventy-five, one hundred times. I had to keep moving always.

"Do you mind telling me why?" asked Dr. S. I did mind. Dr. S. was menacingly straightforward. She specialized in eating issues and unanswerable questions.

"Walking is on my list of approved activities from Highland Park," I defended myself.

"That's good. But that's not what I asked you." She smiled. I refused to smile back. I was using up my parents' estate in order to sit there and hate her.

Because you can't stop me.

Because I like to feel my hamstrings burning. I needed my whole body to burn, to draw together like two dry twigs and erupt into fork-tongued flame.

Because it's been six months, two weeks, three days, and forty-five minutes since my mother left me and she's not coming back and what am I supposed to do, wait around for her, getting lazy and fat?

"I don't know. I guess I thought it would burn more calories? I'm not going to the gym." I was just as disappointed as she was in the lameness of my answer. "You think Kerry's going to be our next president?" I added, just to fill the space.

Every week Dr. S. had a new cognitive behavior assignment for me. Eat a bagel with cream cheese before 1 p.m. Pick one part of my body that was tolerable and write it down. It could be an earlobe if I wanted. Limit my walking to an hour and a half a day and stop at one traffic light without lifting my heels. Spend one full Saturday at home.

Most days I ate my first measly meal at 2:30 just to spite her, wrote down *my ankle* or *my wet hair* on my not-so-bad-about-me list, and did laps around the traffic signs whenever I was stuck waiting for the light to turn green.

The Saturday at home made me the most anxious, though. I avoided it for weeks. After several sessions spent talking about why I was unnerved by Jay's steadiness, Dr. S. let me compromise with a half day at home. I started out with a morning yoga class and a brief walk. I was due home by 12:30 and Jay said he would be in charge of making sure the rest of the day was quiet but full.

When I got home, he asked me to join him on the bed.

"Okay, but I should shower and you said we were going to go for a walk or do something, not just lie here. I really want to *do* something you know," I warned.

"I promise we'll go for a walk," he said. "Just lie down with me for one minute, please." The radiators hissed as we stared up at our ceiling. Our upstairs neighbor climbed clumsily up the scales on his bassoon.

"I know you hate this," Jay said, closer now, kissing up under my chin. "But I'm having an outpouring. I just love you so much and I just want you to be happy and us to be happy and . . ." He sounded weepy.

"I wanted to ask your brother first so I could make it official and maybe you would wear your mom's ring but I just can't wait. So I could get on one knee or I could just say it here. Abby, I love you so *so* much. Will you please spend the rest of your life with me? Forever?"

"What?"

"I'm asking you to marry—"

"No, I know. I mean, really? Okay."

"Are you excited?"

"Yes. I mean, *yes!*" His gaze was patient but intense. I kissed him hurriedly before asking, "Can we still go for that walk?"

I loved Jay. We had been together for only two years, but they were the most awesome and staggering two years of my life. As I lay there and played the time back in my mind, I saw the sprig of hyacinths he'd given me, the sand-caked car we drove back from the dunes, the Highland Park cul-de-sac where he dropped me off in the morning, and his body bent into one of the pink vinyl chairs in the corner of my mom's hospital room. He had stayed with me all night as my mom faded away. I looked at him, at his eyes wide with hope. He was an amazing partner, but there was part of me that bristled as he said the word *forever*. I wanted to ask him how he could be so sure about a future when I still couldn't accept the present.

We trekked across the Brooklyn Bridge in a blizzard that blew us sideways. The ice and wind swept through our nostrils, lips, and lungs so I couldn't find a moment or breath to ask *Why? Where? What?* I didn't know how to tell if he was *the one*. I didn't know how to answer the disapproving glare I imagined on my mother's face. I just kept walking, plowing forward through the swirling storm. Jay took my hand in his. He was firm and stalwart, resolute in his devotion to me. I didn't feel giddy or tingle with enchantment; I felt his stead-fastness. If he wanted to walk too, that was fine, I decided. And if we found the edge of the world, and jumped, that would be even better.

We were married on May 20, 2006—my father's birthday. I tried to set a date in 2005 so we could avoid having a six on our invitations, but Jay's sister was in school overseas and couldn't make it to New York before spring. On the day of the wedding, a sherbet-colored sunset spilled over us as we stood in the chuppah made from my grandmother's tablecloth. We were surrounded by faces flushed with love for us. Our closest friends and cousins had arranged the cut tulips and lit all the candles. Jay's father, who was a minister with azure eyes that matched Jay's, said the traditional seven blessings of marriage in English and my friend Jessica said them in Hebrew. (She left off the extra one for Diet Coke.) Gabra wrote us a song called "We'll be with Abby and Jay." My friend Megan, who helped Jay with my surprise birthday intervention, gave a toast that began *Abby, I like you better when you're with Jay*—there was an unabashed sense of relief in her voice.

I was in a daze. People gave me kisses and glasses of wine, and little cousins wanted to touch the fairy princess in the long white veil. I felt safer on the dance floor. I'd always loved dancing with Jay. I'd made sure there was some Cole Porter on our play list and Louis Armstrong singing the Heaven song. We boogied so hard my ballet slippers split open and my stockings sagged into puddles around my ankles. When we went back to our hotel room at three in the morning, Jay ordered us pancakes and eggs and I ate everything with maple syrup and salt on top, then fell gratefully into sleep.

But the next day, I started sobbing. The ugly heaving kind that usually marked death and destruction. My skin turning the worst kinds of red and purple.

"What is it?" Jay pleaded.

"I'm just so . . . alone!" I gulped.

Jay stared at me, his eyes confused and hurt.

I didn't know how to explain that I *wanted my mommy and daddy.*

We flew to Costa Rica, where Jay had rented us a bungalow at a little beach resort. The ocean crashed fifty yards from our door and the air smelled like pineapples. We made love and lay in hammocks, sidled up to the seaside terrace for fresh-caught shrimp, and drank mojitos until our tongues tickled with rum and sugar and lime.

I found pockets of calm, especially when the howler monkeys made their daily pilgrimage by our window each evening. The first time I heard them bellowing in the trees I was sure they were the most vicious lions. But when I saw them swing from vine to vine just inches away from us, I clapped with glee. Their bodies were no bigger than footballs, their limbs long and dangling, and their masked faces were open and innocent. They looked as delighted and surprised to see us as we were to see them. Their acrobatics mesmerized me as they climbed on top of each other, picking, pawing, and scratching playfully. Most of all I loved watching them because they had been so terrifying to me until I saw them face-to-face. I wanted to think of Jay in the same way—as harmless and playful rather than my newest monster.

Our first year of marriage was steeped in wine and angry tears. I drank until I couldn't hear Jay's hurt. I was anxious and mean. I resented him for eating whatever he wanted and sleeping with his shirt off. For telling me he loved me and that I was beautiful just the way I was and for wanting attainable things like children and a yard and lawn chairs with cup holders. I resented the way he was always unbearably solid and reliable and loving and there.

I continued to see my parents each night in my sleep, then woke up brooding, tears too stubborn to fall down my cheeks stinging the edges of my eyes. I locked myself in the closet to pray, but also to escape mornings with Jay.

Jay didn't believe in G-d. At least not as much as he believed in baseball. Which was another reason I was sure we were doomed. I should have considered his lack of spirituality long before. It had to be a sign. If Jay didn't love Him how could he possibly truly love me? I suspected Jay of trying to keep me from my faith. He asked me why I lit candles on the anniversary of someone's death (*yahr-zeit*) and he pulled me away from the door when I kissed my mezuzah more than thirty times. When he hummed the prayers with me on Shabbat, I suspected he was subtly mocking me. It wasn't that I wanted to share my spiritual practice with Jay. My prayers had always been intensely private and they always would be. But I worried that He would not look kindly on my marrying someone who not only didn't pray but didn't believe in His existence.

Each day, as I grew more anxious and doubtful about my relationship with Jay, I also grew more possessive about my faith. I had added new prayers to my daily routine, including Buddhist chants and meditations I'd learned at yoga. I whispered a short series of *Namaste, thank You, Amen*'s with kisses after every class. I locked the closet door so I could confide in the one Being who truly knew whether Jay and I should be together. I tried to be honest with Him. I asked Him to please help me find peace and love for my husband. And if He didn't approve of Jay, to please help me run away.

I got another part-time job, signed on with a commercial agent, and immersed myself in writing and yoga classes every evening. On Saturdays I did improv at a friend's theater and tried to socialize after shows, but usually I went home, stopping for wine on the way. I continued to walk, prowling for a natural disaster, an end to my hunger, my hangover, my bottomless fury and hurt.

Jay and I began fighting again. Or rather, he got mad and I tried to flee.

"I'm going for a walk."

"No you're not. It's ten o'clock."

"Stop treating me like a baby. I'm not talking to you anymore."

"Stop making me into your parents! You are too talking to me!" His neck turned a prickled pink when he yelled. I told him fighting was wrong. We were wrong. I knew because my parents had never fought like this.

"Never?" Jay spat.

"Never!" It was my history and I could remember it the way I wanted to. Jay couldn't know. My mother was perfect and my father was perfect and they were perfect together, dancing in one long embrace, their love smelling like rose talc and cocktail onions. As I told him about it I could taste my childish desperation. But it wasn't Jay's place to try to rewrite my memories, I reasoned. We went to a couples counselor.

"What about having some date nights or taking salsa lessons together?"

"Abby doesn't like spending time with me anymore," Jay said.

"Is this true?"

"He doesn't read enough."

"He's too opinionated."

"He has red hair."

She laid some ground rules. Jay was not allowed to say we'd be together *forever* and I was not allowed to stiffen myself with silence or compare our relationship to my dead parents'. We had to eat two home-cooked meals together each week. Jay said he would cook.

On Sundays I made sure to be out all day, at yoga and writing in cafés. Jay chopped up plump tomatoes and bell peppers and made thick Italian sauces that simmered on the stove for hours.

"We used to get Chinese food on Sunday nights," I told him.

"Do you like Chinese food? I thought you didn't." He was right. I was still too scared to eat most foods that didn't have the nutritional labels on the back. But I wanted to tell him I would eat Chinese food if he was more like my father. If he would lay out the serving spoons and chop the egg rolls in thirds like my mom did, I would eat anything he put in front of me. Instead I went downstairs to the wine shop below us and bought two bottles of white wine. We sat on the floor and ate and drank until we were both too sated to move. When I woke up hours later on the couch, we were sprawled among the pillows, reeking of garlic and Parmesan cheese. Though my head throbbed and my skin was damp and sour, muddled mornings like this were a reprieve from my usual nervous tension. Jay snored next to me, his limbs limp and warm. It was only in this unclaimed space before dawn that I could admit to loving him.

In private, our counselor asked me if I was afraid of losing Jay, given my history. I shook my head confidently.

"No, I've been in therapy for years. I already thought of that. But thanks."

In fact, I already knew what I would do when I lost Jay. I would make the bed every morning. I would have clearer skin and more time for prayers. I would be sober and unashamed and when people asked me how I was doing without him, I'd say simply, "He was a good guy. It's too bad."

I started seeing a new therapist named Hannah. I was leery about her at first, especially because she was attractive and thin and wanted me to write down what I ate and how each meal made me feel. But then she asked if I wanted to know what she ate and when I said yes she said she'd had three egg sandwiches in one day. She also looked a little bit like my mother. She told me that whenever I felt caught in a tunnel of anxiety I could leave her a voice mail, and soon I was doing so every day. More than once I caught myself just before saying *I love you. P.D.!* at the end of my message.

I confessed to Hannah that I didn't wish Jay harm, but I was terrified I'd made a mistake by marrying him—we were complete opposites and he watched too much television. Instead of blowouts it was visions of his face that now stopped my breath. Our failing marriage was my newest darkest secret obsession. Hannah said she and her husband bickered constantly but loved each other very much. She said she didn't know Jay and maybe he would turn out to be a complete dud, but there would be no conflict if I didn't desire him in some way. She said I had to trust him on some gut level or I wouldn't be struggling. Then she asked me to make a different kind of list. Write five things that were good about Jay. Whatever I might like about him that day.

1. Today Jay made up a song about my dirty breath in the morning.

2. Today we went to the Home Depot and it was okay when we picked out knobs for our kitchen drawers.

3. Today Jay had a wrestling match with our quilt just to make me laugh.

It was the most difficult list I'd ever had to write. Each time I attempted to add to it I felt myself shaking my head, apologizing to my mother, my father, and G-d for marrying the boy who was supposed to be nothing more than a distraction, but instead marked the death of my mother, my career, my childhood.

Until the following summer, when we got on Interstate 684.

Jay loved to drive our pickup truck, which we'd named Snoop. Snoop felt like the one place where we found neutral ground. Sometimes we even sang together to Ben Folds—I had recently allowed myself to sing the words *luckiest* and *got* though I still couldn't speak them. I sometimes heard myself giggle as Jay crooned at the top of his lungs, completely untroubled by lyrics or even syncopation.

Only, this trip was miserable. We were on our way up to Uncle Murray's cabin in Connecticut, and we plummeted into the most gruesome fight yet. I can't remember how it started. It was about him leaving the empty juice container in the refrigerator and about me not eating anything he cooked and about him not respecting me and being critical of me and not really loving me and me not getting what I need and what *do* I need? *Well, I don't know but it's not this!!!* The more durable Jay had proven to be, the more I tested him—and myself—with my rage. For the curtain call I screamed and flailed my arms until we were both stunned into silence.

We spent the weekend with my family in Connecticut. Truce by way of relatives. I was grateful that my uncle and cousins loved Jay. He was handy around the house. He was great with kids. And no one in our family had ever had red hair before. Jay and I orbited each other carefully. I drank too much at dinner, then worried I would leak all my hurt and confusion out during dessert and excused myself from the table to hide under my sleeping bag.

On Sunday afternoon we left for home. We'd agreed to drop off my cousin's desk in Westchester on the way. Jay carefully strapped the desk onto Snoop's bed. Then he sifted through static until he found the Yankees game on the radio. I opened our windows so it would be too loud to talk, hoping the gusts of summer heat could blow away the residual hurt that lingered between us. Then I leaned back and let my eyelids grow heavy. We were on our way.

But Jay kept checking in the rearview mirror.

"What's up?"

"I dunno. The desk looks wobbly. Hold on."

He pulled onto the shoulder of I-684, a winding wooded road that I had traveled often as a kid, with my father navigating through rain, sleet, hail, fog. Dad had made a special tape that we were allowed to listen to instead of Cole Porter if we asked nicely—*Annie* on one side and *The Muppet Movie* on the other. And now *Jorge Posada is . . . to third . . . back for another . . . after this station break* was our soundtrack as Jay stepped out onto the asphalt. The traffic wasn't particularly busy. There were only a handful of cars driving by as we sat on the shoulder. But I saw it clearly, definitively. It made perfect sense. The connection of metal with flesh. Jay's body on the ground, twisted illogically.

The ambulance screaming. The moments, hours, days of unconsciousness and unknowing. I try to measure his belly rising and falling. Everything is uncertain and perilous. I call in to work. *I can't come in today. Or tomorrow. Maybe a month. Maybe ever.* I move into a one-bedroom apartment and stack our wedding presents along the wall. There is nothing in the freezer and the stove is covered in dust. When I call Jay's mom to tell her I miss him she is too sick with sorrow to speak. His aunt gets on the phone and moans, *Why couldn't you love him while he was here?* His father's eyes grow cloudy and listless.

Jay stepped back into the truck.

"Hey!" I yelped. "Don't do that ever again!"

"Do what?"

"Go out into traffic like that where you could get . . . I mean, I watched it all happen. You getting hit and then in the hospital and I get some time off work but it's not a lot and your Aunt Linda was so upset. We were all so upset!"

It took a moment for him to piece together what I was saying. Then he caught on.

"Well, I'm glad you got some time off?" he said hesitantly.

"No, I didn't mean *that*. You were lying there. It was so scary. And you were—it was the first time I'd ever seen you like that. It was the first time . . ."

He waited.

"I guess it was the first time I knew I really loved you."

The two of us sat with my awkward confession between us. Then Jay said softly, "Well, it's about time."

WHAT I BELIEVE NOW THAT I'M
THIRTY-FOUR YEARS OLD LIST

1. I have done a lot of bad things and I will continue to.
2. Lying is bad. Cheating on tests is bad. Stealing is a crime even if it's just candy. I have done all these things.
3. Mom's matzoh ball soup and Dad's Sunday omelets are the best foods on earth. Also Jay's homemade pizza and anything with hot sauce.
4. Anne Frank is a really good role model. So is Dolly Parton.
5. Mom was a beautiful woman who was courageous and flawed. Dad was an amazing artist and father who would do anything for his family.
6. The number six cannot hurt anyone.
7. Aunt Simone continues to visit me through yoga, big sunglasses, and Chopin.
8. G-d is an unknown. He lives inside music—mostly the minor chords, no drums. He is under the deepest parts of the oceans and above the sky's edge. I thank Him for the train. I tell Him my most intimate secrets. I try to make Him responsible for all the universes and everyone inside them, but I'm not sure that He is.

Amen.

someplace to go

· ·

> *Om gaté, gaté, paragaté,*
> *Om gaté, gaté, paragaté,*
> *Parasamgaté Parasamgaté*
> *Parasamgaté Parasamgaté*
> *Bodhi! Svaha! Bodhi! Svaha!*
> > —the Buddhist Heart Sutra,
> > which means . . . Gone, gone,
> > gone over, gone fully over.
> > Awakened! So be it!

The rest of my story begins today.

Today is not going exactly as planned. I have a lot to do. I need to write. I wake up at 8:30, which is an hour after my alarm goes off. I climb down from our bed loft and drink a cup of water by our front door. I sing a small song of thanks to G-d, with one hand on my heart and one on the floor. Then I pick out two things to place on my altar. A Magic 8 Ball that my mother used to keep on her desk next to the stapler. The plastic Charlie Brown figurine that my father gave me on one of our dates. I light a candle and pour a cup of coffee and walk carefully down to our basement.

My prayers continue to change and expand, to evolve. Hopefully they are closer to actual *quiet time.* Today it starts with three minutes of silence. Breathing in the word *Sat* and exhaling the word *Nam,* a mantra I learned in kundalini yoga that means, roughly, *Truth is my identity.* Then I say the Shema, once in Hebrew and twice in English. I say the serenity prayer and *Lord our G-d Thy will be done* five times each. I press my hands on my seven chakras. For each one I name ten hopes, fears, obstacles. I ask Him for healing for Molly's father and Ulla's lungs and I ask for help reconnecting with my sister and looking beyond my own nose and getting rid of my terrible gas. I might as well be honest with Him. I end with the body prayer my therapist Hannah gave me:

Blessed are You, Eternal our G-d, Source of the Universe, who has made our bodies with wisdom, combining veins, arteries, and vital organs into a finely balanced network. Wondrous Fashioner and Sustainer of Life, Source of our health and our strength, we give You thanks and praise.

I kiss the Magic 8 Ball and Charlie Brown, the words You and G-d, and the prayer book in my hands a total of fifty-two times before blowing out the candle. Today *quiet time* takes me a half hour to complete.

I pack a cheese sandwich and fruit. I take a shower and wash my neck twice because my mother once told me it's the most important place to keep clean and if you don't, people could call you Dirty Gerty Neck. I brush my teeth and gums in circular motions as my father taught me—eight tours around my mouth—because my father always wrote perfect number eights and when he had his potbelly he was shaped like one too. I do not put on blush.

Before I leave the apartment, I wake up Jay. He works nights now, teaching at a Jiu-Jitsu school. I've never seen him stand this tall or be this inspired by his work. He even admits that there's a spiritual element to the practice. I kiss our mezuzah thirty times on my way out. As the subway doors close behind me, I mouth the words *thank You* five hundred times, kissing and blinking after each one. When we are stopped for a sick passenger in the train car ahead, I add *I hope all sick passengers heal completely painlessly soon.*

I pull out my journal as we move forward again and make my grateful list. Eighteen things about today that make my life fuller.

1. Time for writing
2. The smell of Jay's hair
3. Digging a new flower bed at Uncle Murray's cabin

Then I write *Dear SiRo* and a page of my thoughts, following wherever they lead me. I end my entry with *Let go and let G-d.* Then I kiss His name one hundred times.

* * *

The rest of my story begins with looking the other way.

My fears about Jay didn't disappear overnight like a switch that turns on and off. None of my obsessions are that easy to resolve. My life is a long, circuitous wandering, on tiptoes and backward, as I sneak away from my fixations—with litter, food, marriage. Sometimes Jay asks me why I don't obsess about him in a good way or want to kiss him one hundred times in a row. I have to remind myself that he needs more affection than the occasional knee squeeze. But I also assure him it's a good thing that I don't idolize or ritualize our love. That I adore him for his constancy and patience.

It took another year of experimenting with new medications until I found a combo that gave me some space to breathe. Each time I came home with a new prescription, I tucked the bottle into the kitchen cabinet among the spices. I hoped my process of healing could become as effortless as sprinkling a pinch of salt. As I walked the streets over and over, I stood still at the traffic lights so I could read the text messages Jay would send:

I am with you now more than ever. We can do this.

It was more of a fading than a switch. I spoke to Hannah's voice mail every day and started sharing my writing with her during our sessions. I described to her and to SiRo the earth-shaking pound of my feet and heart. She challenged me to talk about the aspects of my parents that weren't perfect. She asked me what made me angry, and dared me to scream at her. I only managed a stern tone, but she didn't break, or even frown. I only realized my obsessions had begun softening when my friend Gabra told me Jay and I looked so much happier together.

"Do we?" I asked, surprised and relieved.

Our relationship got easier, eating got easier, walking away from litter got easier because I just had to stop looking at it so much.

My dreams changed too. Jay and I both stopped drinking and I slept more peacefully. One night, I had a headache that rooted in the back of my skull and turned everything a dishwater gray. Jay and I climbed into bed early and he tried to rub my back but I knew he was exhausted. Soon his breath had slowed into the familiar buzz saw. As I lay next to him, I saw my own death for the first time. It was from an aneurysm, like Aunt Simone's. I lay in a vegetative state and Jay was by my hospital bed, standing sentinel. I saw him through my comatose fog but I had no way to verbalize my thoughts. I wanted him to tell both of our families and especially his mom that I loved them and I wasn't afraid to go.

My funeral was brief. It was held at my synagogue and my oak coffin was positioned just like my father's. Stringed instruments played resonant minor chords as at my mother's. A few speeches—Ruthie, Gabra. After the Kaddish the pianist played the four notes from the end of the Nabisco theme song, just like I had asked. *Na-bis-co! Ding!*

It was not tragic. Nobody was crying and nobody needed more time. There were plenty of kugels and tulips at the reception. Terry and the ladies made sure the coffee was properly brewed. And I am calm, meeting my death.

The rest of my story begins with a life. A flicker on a screen.

"That flicker is your baby's heartbeat," the doctor said, pointing to the sonogram screen. Jay and I stared in disbelief, in awe. Our lives were suspended in that flicker, caught in its miraculous, blinking grasp. The world was at once no bigger than a pixel of light and yet infinite in every direction. Jay had been ready for children from the day I met him. I'd agreed to try after a year and a half of marriage. Now I couldn't remember what had come before this moment and I couldn't wait to find out what would happen next. We stepped out into the February afternoon and made our way through Central Park tipsily, leaning on trees too green to be true.

"Can I kiss it?" asked Jay, trembling.

"Yes, please."

I watched as he lifted the edge of my shirt, carefully touching my exposed navel.

The first month with Flicker was breathless and confusing. I was light-headed, exhausted, moody. I tried to rub my stomach delicately and listen for any shifts and flutters. The second month I started crying and couldn't stop. If a love song came on the radio I collapsed into a squall of tears. I cried for all the lost loves of my life and the unbearable thought that Flicker could become another.

It had taken me years to get my medication right, but I asked Hannah if she would help me wean myself off them because I was nervous about their side effects. I promised her and Jay that I would try to communicate my feelings and go back on or look into other drugs if I felt myself spiraling again. The emotional swings were severe, but I didn't try to chant or cut them away. I took long walks and blasted music in my headphones. I made new activity lists for the evenings. I kept on writing.

Month three I had to hold on to street signs to steady my wobbling legs and I broke out in bold rashes of acne. I forgot my keys in the door, forgot my train stop, forgot the word for *soup*. I also dreamt about leaving Flicker in a supermarket unattended, and woke up clammy and inconsolable.

"It's gonna be okay," Jay said.

"How do you know? How does anyone know?! I'm supposed to be pregnant but I'm just bloated and pimply and why don't they use intercoms in stores anymore?!" I wailed.

Month four was blissful. Flicker and I started going on dates together—just the two of us. Gentle yoga and then to a vegetarian restaurant for big bowls of hot and sour soup and spicy noodles with extra garlic sauce on the side. Sometimes I held a magazine or newspaper, but it was just for show. Flicker and I were too busy slurping and daydreaming. I thought of telling the waitress that I was expecting and that's why I ordered for two, but instead I patted my belly softly and smiled into my napkin. Flicker and I licked the plates clean, so pleased with ourselves.

Flicker living in my belly is a beginning to life after anorexia. At least, I hope it is. It has to be. This is something I couldn't learn from a doctor; no matter how many times I replayed my past. Falling in love with Flicker is making me look at myself, accept myself, nurture myself. I've never felt this whole. This big. This uniquely purposeful. And for this I cannot thank Flicker enough. Anorexia is a constricting, self-centered disease, but life now is so much larger than my silhouette or even my ego.

I cannot and will not contain myself in a prescribed shape that I coveted for years. It's simply not about me anymore. There is a soul, and nostrils, arms, legs, and now even fingernails and eyebrows growing, stretching, needing me. I feed Flicker whole-milk cheeses and grilled steak, bright orange ice pops and ripe olives dripping in oil. I no longer suck in my stomach as I pass a plate-glass window or close my eyes in the shower. I can't stop looking at my reflection. And when I do I see a glorious S-shaped vessel. I see hips widening so they can carry us both. I see webbed veins and full breasts and two heartbeats pulsing beneath my skin. I see a radiance that I never knew to wish for.

The scratch marks on my abdomen spread longer and wider but they never touch in the middle. They will never be professional or exquisite like my mother's. I smooth oil on them at night so Flicker can feel my touch and then Jay lies next to me serenading into my wrinkled belly button.

Flicker is also a beginning for Jay and me as lovers. I am just as surprised and enraptured as he is with my new urges and desires as we tumble (under the covers). My back arches and my throat moans without my grasping for it, without my needing it to be the best kind of lovemaking, the right kind of love. Maybe my rekindled passion is the result of hormones and it will ebb and flow, just like us. I know without my mother telling me that Jay is kind and loving, handsome and true. I have no doubt he will be a magnificent father. And even though he fills our apartment with Jonathan Schwartz on Sundays now and makes runny omelets, he will never be my father, nor can I ask him to be.

There are parts of this love affair that I cannot yet see. Today I am halfway through month seven of what I hope is a lifetime. I feed Flicker butter and lullabies, and s/he answers with twirls and hiccups. It's the most profound love I've ever known, and yet almost everything I understand about Flicker is from books. Research suggests that Flicker may know how to dream.

This I know even though there is no scientific proof: Flicker has a soul. I can't say exactly when it formed. Some memories are still too raw to quantify that. But my belief in this new soul is absolute. Flicker could also be my connection to my late parents. Sometimes I imagine them together, bobbing and whirling in a seamless arc of ocean blue. It's late night at the pool and there's an all-swim for new and old souls. Dad pulls through the water deftly, his long arms clearing the air in a nimble sweep. Mom does her lopsided doggy paddle while the ends of her hair spray out like feathers. And Flicker dips and slips around them, drinking in my father's earthy pomade and imitating my mother's thin-lipped pucker.

Flicker is an endless beginning. He or she could be, will be, already is anyone. A patchwork of my mother's aqua eyes and my father's long ribs, Jay's red hair, his mother's soft, cool hands, his father's staccato laughter. Maybe my handwriting. Or my love of pickles. My fear of thunder. Most of all, Flicker is the beginning of a new and completely unpredictable being. Flicker is the starting over that I wanted. Instead of trying to prevent death I am going to give birth. The biggest challenge is reconciling how much control I have over his or her fate. If I can nurture this child that means I can also cause it incredible harm.

"Sure," says Hannah. "But do you think your mother made mistakes?"

"Yessss," I say warily.

"And are you scarred?"

"No," I answer with certainty.

Having Flicker inside me is also full of heartache and unknowns. I stroke my stomach protectively and also possessively. While Flicker is this close s/he can't get lost in the supermarket or hit by a car. And I can't get lost in my self-hatred again. Neither of us has to let go. But soon we'll both be kicking and screaming as we're drawn apart for the first time. A miraculous beginning and end. We'll see this life through two sets of eyes. We'll breathe through separate lungs. And I will have to learn how to accept, nurture, and love each of us as unique and whole beings.

The rest of my story begins with uncertainty. It begins in an unforeseen now.

Today, when I get off the train, I go to my favorite café, order a half-decaf coffee and an apple bran muffin, and sit down to write. I open another notebook. This one unlined. I've told myself that I have to put everything on paper with pen before typing so it is made from scratch.

I'm still learning how my recovery fits together. How I fit together. With a Cement Mixer song that plays on a loop in my brain. When I see the truck go by I sometimes just smile. If its rotating belly full of cement does represent my father, then maybe it's just a reminder that my dad is watching over me, that he is never far away. With a yoga mat and regular therapy. A prescription for Paxil and Wellbutrin that I've put on hiatus until further notice. The comfort and purpose I feel from this new heartbeat and the unlined pages in my notebook have been enough to hold me steady. But I don't know what I'll need once I become a mother. *Progress* feels like an unfair and unquantifiable word. Today I'm somewhere on the list of rituals Dr. F. wrote that summer years ago. Or the one he had two months later, with every other line crossed out.

What I don't fully comprehend yet is how to surrender to life. I've spent thirty-four years trying to outsmart death. Scraping at pink fields and blue polka dots, counting kisses and fistfuls of glass, boxing up secrets and muttering prayers to save people from extinction. Exhorting ambulances forward with my frenzied breath. And still there are wars raging, cancer striking, famine, and bloodshed. The house is flushed in flames. The nail's edge pierces a tire and there is a blowout a heart stopped a face turned up through the cleaved sunroof.

I catch myself picking up stray paper clips and screws on the street. If I try to walk away, the air shimmers and my chest closes up. I sometimes report my possible crimes to Hannah. She says she's been alive for sixty years and she's searched high and low but she's never met anyone who truly has the power to change others' fates through magical thinking.

I try to talk about these sirens with G-d. It is no longer me beseeching Him for forgiveness so much as a conversation. I tell Him I hope no one was hurt because of something I did or didn't do. I ask Him to help me let go of my confusion and fear.

My faith continues to be the greatest uncertainty of all. I believe in a Higher Power who isn't easy to explain, see, or name. I am fully aware that I could be inventing Him out of mere yearning for guidance. Sometimes He is the Creator of all sunsets here and forever. Sometimes He is my Pretend Daddy, who knows the special verse of the Heaven song and the dance that goes with it. Sometimes He is my closest friend, who keeps all of my secrets and private jokes without judgment. I no longer try to exact answers or promises from G-d. I can't cut a deal with Him to save anyone from death. I can't even plead for Him to carry my unborn child safely into my arms. I don't want Him or me to carry that burden of accountability.

Today when I go to yoga class, my teacher has us sing the Heart Sutra in a call-and-response pattern. She says this sutra is liberating because it reminds us of our impermanence and celebrates emptiness. Emptiness is not a void; it is an honor, a release from all attachment and all suffering. Her voice is robust and clear and I chant it out after her, savoring the way the minor notes reverberate inside me and how the whole room feels boundless. I remember a time when I couldn't even say something out loud that began with the *ga* sound. I was too frightened that I would slip and say His name in vain and unknowable and unstoppable bloodshed would ensue. We sing the mantra seven times. The most euphoric part for me is when we stop halfway through the last repetition and linger together in the unspoken end. She tells us the song is left unfinished to represent our infinite potential.

"So we all have someplace to go," she hums.

When I leave the yoga studio, there is a summer storm erupting. Dust and lightning, rain and garbage skidding sideways and upside down. A small tree in the middle of the sidewalk is split in two, its innards a stark white in the suddenly swirling sky.

As I'm waiting for the subway to take me home, a woman in a long flowing yellow dress and canvas sneakers turns to me.

"Did you know about this craziness?" she asks me excitedly. "Did you hear it was coming?" As if it could be holy or apocalyptic or a tsunami that will leave us all flattened.

"No, I didn't," I tell her. "I had no idea."

Even though I prayed this morning. Even though I kissed His name and chanted for peace and have two staples and a sharp piece of paper in my knapsack pocket. Even though I watched Sue Simmons last night. I still have no idea what the rest of today will be.

Lord our G-d, thank You for my heart that beats.
Lord our G-d, thank You for the earth that turns.
And thank You for the sky full of dust and confusion, full of nakedness and flickers, full of whatever comes next.
Thank You for the chance to tell this story without an end.
*Amen**

*To be sung to any tune.

resources

· ·

I AM GRATEFUL FOR . . .

There are so many people who have helped me in this journey and I'd love to offer them as resources for anyone who feels like some of these behaviors are familiar.

THERAPISTS

F. Diane Barth, LCSW
102 W. 85th Street #5H
New York, NY 10024
212-362-7565

Lori Demain
540 S. Taylor Avenue
Oak Park, IL 60304

Ita O'Sullivan, NP Psychiatry/Mental Health
New York, NY, and Westchester
646-234-5502

Suzanne T. Reiffel, Ph.D.
Scarsdale, NY 10583
914-723-5494

RESOURCES

Shaké Topalian, MA, APRN, BC
138 West 25th Street
6th floor, suite 24
New York, NY 10001

INSTITUTIONS

Center for the Study of Anorexia and Bulimia: www.icpnyc.org/
CenterForStudy.nxg
Highland Park Eating Recovery Program: www.enh.org/locations/
highlandpark
Obsessive Compulsive Foundation: www.ocfoundation.org

BOOKS

Chansky, Tamar, PhD. *Freeing Your Child from OCD*
Grayson, Jonathan. *Freedom from OCD*
March, John and Mulle, Karen. *OCD in Children and Adolescents*
Pipher, Mary. *Reviving Ophelia: Saving the Selves of Adolescent Girls*
Shawn, Allen. *Wish I Could Be There: Notes from a Phobic Life*
Siegel, Michele, PhD, Brisman, Judith, PhD, Weinshel, Margot,
MSW. *Surviving an Eating Disorder: Strategies for Family and Friends*
Wever, Chris. *The Secret Problem*

YOGA

golden bridge yoga: www.goldenbridgeyoga.com
lucky lotus yoga: www.luckylotusyoga.com
sonic yoga: www.sonicyoga.com

acknowledgments

· ·

To Samantha Martin at Scribner, I offer my deepest thanks. Her tireless enthusiasm and guidance have been extraordinary. Molly Lyons, my agent, is brilliant and an incredible friend. I've had amazing support from teachers and fellow writers—Paula Derrow, Sue Shapiro, Daniel Jones, the entire Tolchin family, Anna Stone, Gabra Zackman, Jessica Lissy, Sara Moss, Kimmi Auerbach, Sam Karpel, Megan Grano, Joselin Linder, and Anna Marrian, who read and reread my words to find their meaning.

Thank you to the many cafés, synagogues, and yoga studios where I found refuge while writing this book. To Rabbi Sirkman for always making faith something knowable and to Diane and Ita for teaching me how to eat and breathe at the same time.

Thank you, thank you, to my beautiful family for their love and patience: my brother, Jon; and sister, Betsy; my cousins Aviva and Rachel and my Uncle Murray; Gene and Peggy.

And of course Jay, who continues to astound me with his steadfast calm, and our completely happy healthy daughter, Sonya, who is the purest embodiment of joy.

about the author

. . . .

Abby Sher is the author of the young adult novel *Kissing Snowflakes*. Her writing has also appeared in the anthologies *Modern Love* and *Behind the Bedroom Door,* as well as in the *New York Times,* the *Los Angeles Times, Self, Jane, Elle, HeeB,* and *Redbook*. She has written and performed for Second City in Chicago and the Upright Citizen's Brigade and Magnet Theater in New York. She lives in Brooklyn with her husband and their remarkable new daughter.